Legislative Trends
in Insurance Regulation

By Douglas Caddy

Texas A&M University Press
COLLEGE STATION

Library of Congress Cataloging-in-Publication Data

Caddy, Douglas, 1938–
  Legislative trends in insurance regulation.

  Bibliography: p.
  Includes index.
  1. Insurance law—United States.   2. Insurance—United States—State
supervision.   I. Title.
KF1164.C29   1986   346.73'086   84-40562
ISBN 0-89096-222-7   347.30686

Manufactured in the United States of America
FIRST EDITION

Contents

Acknowledgments

THIS book is made possible by a grant from the Moody Foundation of Galveston, Texas, through the sponsorship of Shearn Moody, Jr., a trustee of the foundation. The author wishes also to express his appreciation to the following individuals whose advice and research contributions are incorporated into this work: Allan C. Brownfeld, Darrell Coover, Michael Smith, James McClellan, Nina Sims, and Chris Martin.

Legislative Trends in Insurance Regulation

1

....

The Insurance Industry in an Era of Deregulation and Consumerism

FOR many years, the insurance industry of the United States has operated in a relatively safe and secure regulatory atmosphere in which, on the federal level, it was exempted from antitrust legislation and protected from such potential competition as that from banks and savings and loan associations, which were, in turn, strictly regulated as to what business practices they might and might not engage in. On the state level, the industry was regulated, in many instances, by insurance commissions and commissioners who were prepared to do its bidding. By any standard, this was a comfortable environment.

It is generally recognized that large segments of American business have voiced their support for free enterprise and the free market but, when it came to their own particular industries, sought a far different relationship with government. Murray Weidenbaum, chairman of the President's Council of Economic Advisors, 1980–82, has stated: "I have lost track of how many of my former friends (I use that term advisedly) in the business community and elsewhere in the private sector came to my office . . . to tell me how strongly they supported the president's program to cut the budget, but—I quickly learned that BUT is the most important word in the English language . . . the serious message always followed the BUT . . . every business group enthusiastically supports cuts in welfare programs, BUT maritime or textile or steel subsidies are different. . . . Nor should it shock you that farm groups are always enthusiastic about cutting urban programs. BUT farm price supports are a very different matter. Of course, labor groups are very willing to support cuts in farm-program spending, or what they call business subsidies. BUT only so long as the social programs are spared." [1]

Weidenbaum continued, "All of my business (and labor) visitors explained how much they support free trade, BUT. . . . Of course, everyone wants open markets and free trade overseas. We all know how urgent it is to eliminate 'their' barriers to our exports. BUT our barriers to their exports—well, that is a very different matter which does not seem to generate much interest over here. . . . Virtually every visitor paid the most sincere homage to the essential role of competition in the marketplace, BUT—Yes, far too frequently, the staunch position against 'bailouts' was breached, although always reluctantly, by the plea to acknowledge a special case, which happened to be the one represented by my visitor. Unfortunately, those special cases made up a very long list—the automobile industry, steel producers, timber companies, farmers, savings and loan associations, textile firms, mining industries, energy corporations, exporters, regions affected by imports, defense contractors, airlines and literally, the butcher, the baker and the candlestick maker. Actually, it would have been a much shorter list if I had just enumerated the industries that did not come around for such special help." [2]

Charles Koch, chairman and chief executive officer of Koch Industries, has made similar observations. "Businessmen have always been in front of the crusade for government manipulation of the American economy. Nearly every major piece of interventionist legislation since 1887 has been supported by important segments of the business community. . . . The steel industry is asking for duties because European and Japanese steel sells for less here. This the American producers call 'dumping,' and 'unfair competition.' In fact, it is nothing more or less than effective competition. . . . The industry complains that the competition is unfair because it doesn't operate under the same conditions as American firms. What they don't seem to understand is that the economy is not a game or a race. Its purpose is to satisfy consumers through voluntary exchange. If a Japanese steel firm undersells its American competitor, nothing unfair has occurred. The transactions are voluntary, and that is the only criterion of fairness." [3]

---

[1]Murray Weidenbaum, "All for Free Enterprise, But . . .," *Competition*, January-February, 1983, pp. 1–2.

[2]Ibid.

[3]Charles Koch, quoted in Allan Brownfeld, "Crybaby Capitalists Undermine Free Enterprise," *News World*, May 9, 1981.

Nobel Prize–winning economist F. A. Hayek has noted: "Almost everywhere the groups which pretend to oppose socialism, at the same time support policies which, if the principles on which they are based were generalized, would no less lead to socialism than the avowedly socialist policies. There is some justification at least in the taunt that many of the pretending defenders of 'free enterprise' are in fact defenders of privileges. In principle, the industrial protectionism and government-supported cartels and agricultural policies of the conservative groups are not different from the proposals for a more far-reaching direction of economic life sponsored by the socialists. It is an illusion when the more conservative interventionists believe that they will be able to confine these government controls to the particular kinds which they approve."[4]

Hayek also said that in a democracy, "once the principle is admitted that the government undertakes responsibility for the status and position of particular groups, it is inevitable that this control will be extended to satisfy the aspirations and prejudices of the great masses. There is no hope of a return to a freer system until the leaders of the movement against state control are prepared first to impose upon themselves that discipline of a competitive market that they ask the masses to accept. The hopelessness of the prospect for the near future indeed is due mainly to the fact that no organized political group anywhere is in favor of a truly free system."[5]

Yet, while many industries may have a vested interest in government regulatory agencies that, in effect, protect those already in the market, an increasing body of opinion within American society is urging deregulation as a means of serving the best interests of the consumer and of society as a whole.

The original intent of the various regulatory agencies, of course, was to protect the consumer by encouraging competition. The reality, however, has been far different. The result of having such agencies as the Federal Communications Commission, the Civil Aeronautics Board, and the Interstate Commerce Commission, among others, has been to retard competition. In his book *The Bewildered Society*, George Roche, president of Hillsdale College, argues: "The classic symptoms of monopoly have been (1) an absence of price competition, and (2) an inability for new competitors to enter the marketplace. What would be a more accurate description of a government-regulated industry? The F.C.C. permits the already

---

[4] Ibid.
[5] Ibid.

established giants in the communications field an absolute monopoly of the area by means of government licensure. The Civil Aeronautics Board does precisely the same thing for the airlines industry, and so on throughout American life. Not only are new competitors thus prevented from entering the field, but those noncompetitors privileged to hold government licenses in various areas of the American economy are further privileged by means of government rate-setting policy which removes all price competition." [6]

Prior to its deregulation, the transportation industry was held up as an example of the manner in which government regulatory bodies did serious damage to competition and, as a result, to consumers. Economist Yale Brozen pointed out in the early seventies that "regulatory agencies not only prevent those in the transportation industry from competing with each other—they also protect those in the industry from the entry of additional competitors. You cannot get into the trucking business, the airline business, the bus business as you would enter retailing or manufacturing. You must be certified by the CAB if you wish to enter the airline business. The CAB has not certified an additional scheduled airline in the continental U.S. since it began operating in 1938. The ICC will certify an additional common carrier truck company to operate on a given route only if it can be demonstrated that adequate truck service is not available on the route in question. The only major city in which you can start a taxi business simply by applying for a taxi license and demonstrating that you carry the necessary public liability insurance and have safe equipment and drivers is Washington, D.C. All other major cities stop any additional taxi operators from entering the business. They even prevent taxi operators from increasing the size of their fleets. Transportation regulation very effectively protects transportation companies from new competition and produces the exact opposite of the situation which our antimonopoly laws were designed to produce in other industries." [7]

Despite such insights, the 1970s brought a rapid expansion of federal regulatory activity. Between 1970 and 1979, twenty new regulatory agencies appeared, compared with only eleven during the entire New Deal. Regulatory-agency expenditures in 1984 were six times the 1970 level. Forty-one agencies doubled their budgets in the four years from 1975 to

---

[6] George C. Roche III, *The Bewildered Society* (New Rochelle, N.Y.: Arlington House, 1972).

[7] Yale Brozen, quoted in Roche, *Bewildered Society*, p. 200.

1979. In 1970 the *Federal Register* ran to twenty thousand pages. By 1979 it was up to seventy-seven thousand pages.[8]

Still, even while regulatory agencies were proliferating, a movement toward deregulation continued to grow. It can be argued that many of the new regulatory agencies were simply adding costs to the consumer without serving any public purpose. One area of increasing government involvement in recent years, for example, has been that of job safety. In the past decade, the Occupational Safety and Health Administration (OSHA) has spent approximately $1.6 billion issuing tens of thousands of new regulations. Employers, mostly smaller ones, have spent nearly $25 billion to comply with these regulations.

Has this expenditure of $25 billion during the past decade actually improved working conditions? Many who have studied this question answer that it has not. It is pointed out that between 1973 and 1979—the years of OSHA's most vigorous activity—lost workdays due to injuries and illnesses in the workplace per one hundred workers actually increased by 16 percent. This increase was most pronounced in the areas where OSHA was most vigorous in promulgating and enforcing regulations: manufacturing (26 percent) and construction (18 percent).[9]

In his book *The Economy in Mind*, Warren Brookes concluded that OSHA has clearly been "a huge bust, not merely in its enormous cost and harassment of employers (especially small ones), but in its failure to demonstrate a higher level of safety. Instead, safety has apparently declined since OSHA began meddling in the workplace. This in no way suggests that there are not many cases of highly effective government safety regulation, both on products and in the workplace. The experience with hazardous wastes and chemicals, not to mention mines and oil drilling, indicates that we cannot ignore clear and obvious dangers. The vast majority of OSHA regulations, however, have not dealt with 'clear and present dangers' but with established production and workplace procedures and, more often than not, have generated even more costly and more labor-intensive methods of production, in the name of safety. In the construction industry, for example, whenever some new labor-saving method of construction was being challenged by the unions, OSHA would immediately step in and

---

[8] Warren T. Brookes, *The Economy in Mind* (New York: Universe Books, 1982) p. 146.
[9] Ibid.

raise the safety issue, even where no such issue existed. In this way, OSHA became a tool used by unions to resist legitimate productivity measures." [10]

OSHA, critics charge, is not alone in performing a negative—rather than positive—function with regard to safety. Many charge that environmentalists, who have been using the power of the state to ban a host of pesticides and food additives that they have declared to be harmful, have, in a number of instances, made life more dangerous rather than less so.

Dr. Elizabeth Whelan, an epidemiologist and the author of eleven books on the subject of environmental hazards, has declared that banning a pesticide "may make the environmentalists feel good, make them think they are doing something. . . . But . . . I know that it is not preventing cancer. And as a consumer it makes me angry that even though the banning has no medical benefits, it means that I will pay more for strawberries and corn next year. Such bannings also serve as a disincentive to an industry that could eventually come up with an even better pesticide—which would help us produce more food, for ourselves and the world." [11]

With regard to food additives, Whelan pointed out: "When a food additive is banned, it makes some of the Naderite groups happy, and the government content. But as a scientist I know that, too, will not prevent cancer, but will only serve to remove useful products from the shelves, such as diet soft drinks. What we need, of course, is a new breed of consumer advocate, one who can effectively explode the myth that we have to choose between modern technology and good health. We can have both. Of course we need to keep health-threatening chemicals out of our food, air, and water. However, with today's consumer advocates leading the show, we are heading toward not only zero risk, but zero food, zero jobs, zero energy and zero growth." [12]

Such critics point out that the antigrowth, antitechnology, proregulation forces that exist in America today have mistaken cause and effect. In fact, they point out, rather than being life-threatening, advances in technology have made life more healthy and comfortable. In 1900, the life expectancy of Americans was forty-eight years, and more than 70 percent of the people lived in rural areas, far away from industry, technology, and pollution. Today, the life expectancy of Americans is more than seventy-three years—and farm population constitutes less than 5 percent of

[10] Ibid., pp. 153–56.
[11] Ibid., p. 155.
[12] Ibid.

the nation. The more industrialized we have become, the healthier we seem to have become.[13]

In nonindustrial Third World nations, where there are few food additives, and relatively little pollution or "dangerous" factory work, the average life expectancy is dramatically lower than our own. The average life expectancy in Africa is forty-five years. In South America it is fifty-five, while in the industrialized West it is seventy-three. It is interesting to note that Japan, the most heavily industrialized country, also has the greatest life expectancy and the lowest mortality rate from all causes. The *Wall Street Journal* has pointed out that what the poor of the world need most is not more government protection but more economic growth, "and economic growth means using the world's resources of minerals, fuels, capital, manpower and land. There can be no return to Walden Pond without mass poverty." [14]

Originally created to serve the public, regulatory agencies, more often than not, serve the very groups being regulated. In a thoughtful study, *Instead of Regulation: Alternatives to Federal Regulatory Agencies*, editor Robert W. Poole, Jr., noted: "It began to dawn on people that many of the agencies—particularly the old-line economic regulatory agencies—had become advocates for and protectors of the industries they were intended to regulate. Other agencies, especially some of the newer ones, had become the tools of special interest groups, single-mindedly pursuing the goal of eliminating perceived threats to life and health with little consideration of the costs imposed or of alternative ways of accomplishing their objectives." [15]

In an essay concerning energy, Alan Reynolds showed how government policies—such as price control and fuel allocations—led to serious problems that could have been avoided had the free market been at work. He wrote: "What caused the long lines at gasoline stations in the summer of 1979? The answer is that gasoline waiting lines were the result of deliberate public policy. Consider that this was the only non-Communist country experiencing waiting lines in both 1974 and 1979 and that gasoline was relatively abundant in some areas and acutely scarce only a few miles away. If anything else was in short supply in a few cities and abundant in most

[13] Ibid., p. 148.

[14] *Wall Street Journal*, cited in Brookes, *Economy in Mind*, p. 150.

[15] Robert W. Poole, Jr., ed., *Instead of Regulation: Alternatives to Federal Regulatory Agencies* (Lexington, Mass.: Lexington Books, 1982), p. vii.

suburban or rural areas, it would have been worthwhile for some enterprising middleman to move it from one place to another. With gasoline the allocation systems made this illegal. . . . The U.S. has been trying to offset the effects of bad energy regulations with still more regulations, piling new layers of bureaucracy on top of the old. It is time to unravel the whole mess and let prices work. An unhindered price system would provide the incentives to conserve energy resources and develop both energy saving technology and increased supplies of familiar and novel sources of energy." [16]

David Leo Weimer, writing about drug regulation, related that many new drugs are used in Europe years before they are permitted into the United States. "Under our current system," he reported, "beneficial as well as harmful drugs are precluded from the market. . . . Because any therapeutically active drug cannot be totally safe, the absolute standards of safety and efficacy implied by U.S. law are unrealistic. A more realistic approach . . . is to consider efficacy relative to safety: Greater levels of risk are tolerated for drugs offering greater potential benefits." [17] For example, alprenolol, a drug used in preventing heart attacks and coronary death, has been available in Sweden since 1976—but not in the United States. It could, experts argue, save at least ten thousand lives per year. Still, it has not been approved. The list of similar examples, Weimer stated, is a long one. [18]

Among those who have been criticizing regulations for harming the very public they were meant to benefit are a number of distinguished black economists, among them Professor Walter Williams of George Mason University. In his book *The State against Blacks*, Williams pointed out that a number of the economic handicaps faced by blacks are the result of the "rules of the game"—those federal, state, and local laws that systematically impede the employment and advancement of persons who are outsiders, latecomers, and without resources. He showed how minimum wage laws, occupational and business licensing, the taxicab industry, licensing of plumbers and electricians, racist union policies in the railroad industry, truck regulation by the Interstate Commerce Commission, and other government regulatory policies thwart the right of blacks to work.

When other ethnic groups became urbanized, Williams noted, "markets were freer and less regulated. When blacks became urbanized and re-

[16] Alan Reynolds, ibid., pp. 67–89.
[17] David Leo Weimer, ibid., pp. 239–85.
[18] Ibid., chapter 8.

ceived the franchise, they very often found those avenues of traditional upward mobility closed through forms of business and occupational regulation. For example, an illiterate, uneducated poor person in New York in the 1920s could get a used car and become an owner-operator of a taxi. Today a person seeking a similar route to upward mobility must pay $60,000 just for a license to do so. . . . There are numerous laws, regulations and ordinances that have reduced or eliminated avenues of upward mobility for blacks. The common feature of these barriers is that they prevent people from making transactions that are deemed mutually beneficial to the transactors." [19]

One of the ways government regulates the economy, allegedly in behalf of those who are "disadvantaged," is through the setting of maximum and minimum prices at which transactions can legally occur. In the case of wages, federal and state minimum wage laws intervene in the labor markets—legislating a wage which is higher than would have occurred with free market forces. If a minimum wage of $3.35 is legislated, those workers whose value is less than this will not be hired. Williams declared: "The workers who bear the heaviest burden are those that are the most marginal. These are workers whom employers perceive as being less productive or more costly to employ than other workers. . . . There are at least two segments of the labor force that share the marginal worker characteristics to a greater extent than do other segments. . . . The first group consists of youths in general. They are low-skilled or marginal because of their age, immaturity and lack of work experience. The second group, which contains members of the first group, are racial minorities . . . who, as a result of racial discrimination and a number of other socio-economic factors, are disproportionately represented among low-skilled workers. These workers are not only made unemployable by the minimum wage, but their opportunities to upgrade their skills are also severely limited." [20]

The "intent" of the authors of legislation is, in the end, not nearly as important as the effect of the laws they pass. Williams argued that "truly compassionate policy requires dispassionate analysis. Therefore, debunking of . . . labor market myths is an important ingredient toward that end." [21]

[19] Walter Williams, *The State against Blacks* (New York: New Press, McGraw-Hill, 1982), p. 32.
[20] Ibid., p. 33.
[21] Ibid., p. 49.

In a free society, Williams stated, one would imagine that anyone with the money to purchase a car and the ability to drive should be able to enter the taxi business, or to purchase a truck and haul goods. This, however, is not the case. In many cities, such as New York and Philadelphia, a special "medallion" must be purchased. In New York, 13,566 medallions were issued in 1937. No new ones have ever been issued. If you want to drive a cab in New York, you must purchase a medallion from someone who already owns one. Williams declared: "A poor illiterate Italian . . . arriving in our cities in 1925 or 1930 could, if he had ambition and industry, go out and buy a car and write 'TAXI' on it. Thus, he could provide upward mobility for his family. Today a poor person of any race would find that industry and ambition are not enough." [22]

Wilson cited similar conditions in interstate trucking. "Interstate motor carrier business is an activity that would offer a person with little money and little education a business ownership opportunity, were it not for various forms of government regulation. . . . For many a prospective entrant there are insurmountable entry barriers created by the Interstate Commerce Commission . . . the applicant must show that by his entry he will not take business away from trucking companies already supplying services. . . . The applicant must retain legal services specialized in the administrative law of the ICC. . . . In one recent case, a black-owned trucking company spent over $300,000 in legal fees and other costs seeking authority to haul household goods across all the states." [23]

The examples of government regulations that deny minorities access to the marketplace are many. For many years, organized labor determined who could work as a plumber—or in other skilled crafts. Blacks were not permitted to do so. The fact, declared Williams, is that "black handicaps resulting from centuries of slavery, followed by years of gross denial of constitutional rights, have been reinforced by governmental laws. The government laws that have proven most devastating for many blacks are those that govern economic activity. The laws are not discriminatory in the sense that they are aimed specifically at blacks. But they are discriminatory in the sense that they deny full opportunity for the most disadvantaged Americans, among whom blacks are disproportionately represented. Restrictions of the right to work are not part of America's past value system." [24]

[22] Ibid., p. 75.
[23] Ibid., p. 109.
[24] Ibid., p. 89.

Even as dissatisfaction with government regulation and its effects grows, those who advocate a larger government role in the economy are not only resisting deregulation efforts but are also trying to expand the government's areas of jurisdiction. Early in December, 1982, for example, the House of Representatives voted to exempt professionals—doctors, lawyers, nurses, dentists, accountants, etc.—from regulation by the Federal Trade Commission; James Miller III, chairman of the FTC under the Reagan administration, had advanced the case for increasing the FTC's jurisdiction in the regulation of the professions.

After the House vote, Miller declared that the legislation "would place professionals above the laws which apply to all other Americans, laws which protect consumers from deceptive practices, price-fixing, boycotts and other anticompetitive conduct. . . . This action," he said, "would immunize individuals with graduate degrees from the laws which govern everyone else." [25]

In recent years, the FTC has dramatically expanded its regulatory function. One target area of such regulatory activity has been advertising. If Mr. X says that his bread is tastier than that produced by Mr. Y, the FTC has said, in effect, "Prove it." In one much-discussed case in September, 1981, the Kroger supermarket chain claimed that its prices were as low as or lower than those at other local supermarkets. The FTC said the ads were "deceptive," although it found no evidence that Kroger's prices were higher.[26] Where Kroger erred, in the FTC view, was to base its claim on "price patrols" of comparison shoppers, rather than on a more statistically rigorous survey. In 1977, the FTC found "deception" in claims that Poli-Grip would help denture wearers eat difficult foods. Commissioner Mayo Thompson, in his dissent, declared, "It is inconceivable to me that any denture wearer who applied Poli-Grip or Super Poli-Grip and bit into a red apple and then saw his dentures smiling back at him would ever purchase the Gripper again." [27] The FTC, it seems, rejected the traditional idea that when a product is inexpensive and easy for consumers to evaluate for themselves, the market should be permitted to function without the arbitrary governmental interference.

In another case, a General Motors radio advertising spot cited the

---

[25] James Miller III, quoted in Helen Dewar, "House Votes Doctors Exempt from FTC Regulations," *Washington Post*, December 2, 1982, p. A-2.

[26] Editorial, "Regulatory Mouthwash," *Wall Street Journal*, May 12, 1982, p. 26.

[27] Ibid.

opinion of a *Road and Track* magazine writer that the Vega was "the best-handling passenger car." In 1975, the FTC prevented General Motors from using the quote unless it had scientific evidence to support it. Thus, reputable opinion information from a respected publication concerning the handling qualities of the car could not be used.[28]

Regarding the professions, the FTC in 1975 began an investigation of the American Medical Association (AMA). From then until an April, 1982, deadlock in the U.S. Supreme Court about whether or not the FTC had jurisdiction, the AMA defended itself against a host of charges. Its attorney, Newton Minow, former head of the Federal Communications Commission, charged the FTC with "total staff prejudice" against self-regulation. Later, in congressional testimony, Minow pointed to "the staggering costs and enormous burdens incurred in responding to an FTC complaint. It knows only too well how non-profit associations face an unacceptable choice when confronted by the FTC. They must either divert scarce resources from socially beneficial activities to defend against unfounded FTC charges or simply capitulate because of the overwhelming amount of time and money needed to defend [themselves]. . . ."

Since it entered this area, the FTC has conducted numerous investigative studies. In 1978 it intervened before the Office of Education concerning the AMA's role in the accreditation of medical schools. In 1979 it investigated the American Society of Plastic and Reconstructive Surgeons and its method of certification—but eventually dropped the investigation. In 1982 it issued a consent decree against the Texas Dental Association relating to the use of dental X-rays for insurance purposes. The Food and Drug Administration protested this, arguing that patients would be subjected to unnecessary X-rays. The list, even for this brief period, is a long one.

Critics argue that Congress, which created the FTC, never intended it to have regulatory power over the professions. It simply has assumed such power, they declare, without any legislative mandate. Sen. James McClure (R-Idaho) stated that the FTC "has been consistently rebuffed by Congress whenever they sought jurisdiction over non-profit organizations. Their having proceeded anyway and assumed this power shows further evidence of a prevailing attitude of arrogance and defiance. . . . If the FTC truly had the

[28] *New York Times*, December 14, 1982, p. F-11.

authority it has assumed, then the Supreme Court would have found it and applied it. . . . The Court's inability to arrive at a decision further demonstrates the need for Congress to take action." [29]

In reporting out a bill providing that the FTC would have no authority over state-regulated professions and their nonprofit associations, the Senate Commerce Committee stated that "regulation of professionals by the commission is unnecessary and inappropriate in light of other extensive state and federal oversight authority." The report also asserted that the FTC's consumer protection enforcement authority duplicates the "states' well-developed traditional licensure and regulatory schemes for professionals. . . . Commission intervention is unwise and unwarranted." [30]

The feeling that government regulation serves not the public in whose name it is entered into, but special interest groups, has grown so much in recent years that it has been embraced, more and more, by both Democrats and Republicans, conservatives and liberals. Only those groups that benefit from such regulations seem to speak out in their defense, except in areas such as environmentalism where proponents of an ideology rise in defense of legislative regulations.

During the Nixon administration, Lewis A. Engman, chairman of the FTC, attacked federal regulatory agencies—specifically the Civil Aeronautics Board and the Interstate Commerce Commission—for protecting the industries they regulate, creating an unhealthy relationship that unnecessarily raises costs to the consumer and contributes to inflation. Engman has been quoted as saying: "Most regulated industries have become federal protectorates, living in a cozy world of cost-plus, safely protected from the ugly specters of competition, efficiency and innovation." To correct these problems, he called for reexamination of "every regulation or regulatory policy that contributes to inflation." [31]

It cannot be considered an accident that government regulation of the economy has produced negative results. Liberal reformers in the 1920s learned a lesson that modern liberals—and Republicans who have adopted their policies—are now learning anew. Frederic G. Howe, a progressive member of the Wilson administration, wrote in his 1925 book *Confessions*

[29] *Human Events*, June 12, 1982, p. 8.
[30] Quoted in Dewar, "House Votes Doctors."
[31] Alfred Kahn, quoted in Philip M. Crane, *The Sum of Good Government* (Ottawa, Ill.: Green Hill Publishers, 1976), p. 119.

of a Reformer that he had become distrustful of the government and now "viewed it as the source of exploitation rather than the remedy for it." [32]

Woodrow Wilson also came to recognize the problems of government control of the economy. In 1912 he declared, "If the government is to tell big businessmen how to run their business, then don't you think that big businessmen have got to get closer to government than they are now?" [33]

A prime example for study is the Interstate Commerce Commission. Established in 1887 to protect customers and rail lines from discriminatory pricing and rate wars, the agency, which has more than two thousand employees in seventy-eight offices nationwide, regulates not only railroads but also interstate trucking and barge lines. Its stated goal was to end "cutthroat" competition and serve the public. What it has done is end competition almost entirely and serve the joint interests of the large companies and labor unions. [34]

Looking at the record of the ICC, Sen. William Proxmire (D-Wisconsin) observed: "The ICC has become a captive of the transportation industry itself. Instead of regulating transportation to avoid monopoly and increased prices, it has established monopolies, reduced competition, and ordered high and uneconomic rates to cover the costs of inefficient producers." [35]

The ICC has the power and authority to: (1) dictate which truckers can go into interstate business, (2) determine what a commercial trucker can and cannot carry, (3) decide what areas truckers may serve, and (4) permit the trucking industry to fix its own prices. Each year hundreds of companies apply for operating rights and are turned down by the ICC. Robert Gallagher, a New York attorney specializing in transportation matters, has asserted, "The ICC has a disturbing tendency to be protective of large carriers." [36]

In an article entitled "Highway Robbery—Via the ICC," Mark Frazier reported on the application of the Checker Transportation and Storage Company, a case in point: "Checker has hauled household goods in South Carolina for twenty-seven years, using licenses owned by a number of giant van lines. Each time the company makes an interstate trip, it

[32] Frederic Howe, quoted in ibid., p. 120.
[33] Cited in ibid.
[34] Crane, *Sum of Good Government*, p. 121.
[35] William Proxmire, *The Fleecing of America* (Boston: Houghton Mifflin, 1980), p. 94.
[36] Crane, *Sum of Good Government*, p. 122.

must pay an average of 10 per cent of the revenues to the big van companies that hold the permits it needs. In August, 1972, Checker asked the ICC for a modest interstate license of its own. A half-dozen nationwide van lines and one regional competitor who already held such permits filed immediate protests. Checker had to spend $5,000 in legal fees to present its case. None of these complainants challenged Checker's service or denied the charge that they shunned the short-haul interstate traffic Checker specialized in. Nevertheless, the commission, after a wait of 20 months, rejected Checker's application—thus forcing the line to continue paying virtual kickbacks for the right to haul goods in interstate commerce. . . ." [37]

With regard to the ICC's power to determine what a trucker can and cannot carry, we see a situation in which, according to Frazier, "some truckers are permitted to carry only unexposed film; exposed film must be hauled by somebody else. Other truckers may transport plastic pipe but not metal pipe. Officials at Quaker Oats, starting a new pizza-making plant in Jackson, Tennessee, have had to face problems with certificate-hobbled truckers. Trucks hauling tomato paste to the plant from California are not allowed to carry pizzas back. Trucks bringing pizza crusts from Denver must also return empty." [38]

Mike Parkhurst, a former trucker who later edited the trucking magazine *Overdrive*, has noted, "It's as if American Airlines could only carry people from east to west, while United took passengers from west to east." [39]

Cargo restrictions serve the trucking industry by creating a need for more trucking activity; they harm the consumer by dramatically increasing costs. By limiting what one carrier may carry back to the point of origin, the ICC also increased the demand for truck drivers, something which the Teamsters Union strongly favored. It is estimated that regulated truckers travel empty an estimated 30 percent of their miles, triple the percentage of unregulated carriers. [40]

Equally detrimental to the public is the ICC policy of establishing hundreds of thousands of routes, often specifying to the mile where an individual truck may go. Agency rules, for example, require Cedar Rapids Steel Transportation—hauling sixty truckloads a week to Chicago from

[37] Mark Frazier, "Highway Robbery—with the ICC," *Readers' Digest*.
[38] Ibid.
[39] Crane, *Sum of Good Government*, p. 123.
[40] Ibid., p. 124.

Saint Paul—to go ninety miles out of the way through Clinton, Iowa. Because truckers are often prevented from taking the quickest and most economic route to their destination, the cost to the consumer is increased, as is
the use of energy resources. Conservation groups such as the Sierra Club
estimate that tens of millions of gallons of gasoline are wasted each year as
a result of ICC regulations.[41]

Professor Thomas Gale Moore of Stanford University has shown that
when ICC regulations were removed from frozen vegetables in the 1950s,
shipping rates dropped 20 percent and more. He has forecast savings of
billions of dollars each year if all rates were set by the free market.[42]

The call for regulatory reform has reached a crescendo in recent
years, and many individuals and publications that once supported the concept of government regulation of various aspects of our economy are now
admitting that such regulation has been a failure. In an editorial entitled
"The Need for Regulatory Review," the *Washington Post*, in its issue of
February 10, 1975, commented: "We suspect that much of this regulation
no longer serves the purpose for which it was created and needs to be either
eliminated or drastically changed. The ICC . . . may be a classic example
of an agency that has outlived its useful life by several decades. As far as
we can tell, only it and the industries over which it has jurisdiction defend
the way in which surface transportation is now regulated."

The *Post* editorial continued: "The economic problem of this kind of
regulation is staggering. There is a growing body of data that suggests it
costs far more—not just to the government but in unnecessarily high prices
for consumers—than the value of the benefits the regulation brings. The
President's economic report says one study puts these costs of government
regulation of the surface transportation industry alone at $4 billion to
$9 billion a year."[43]

There has been a growing consensus in recent years that regulatory
agencies as they exist today not only eliminate competition but tend to give
government power over vital sectors of the economy, thus challenging the
very concept of the free market.

In his book *The Social Crisis of Our Time*, economist Wilhelm Roepke
declared that: "An economic system, where each group entrenches itself
more and more in a monopolist stronghold, abusing the power of the state

---

[41] Ibid., p. 123.
[42] Thomas G. More, quoted in ibid., p. 124.
[43] *Washington Post*, February 10, 1975, p. A-20.

for its special purposes, where prices and wages lose their mobility except in an upward direction, where no one wants to adhere to the reliable rules of the market any more, and where consequently nobody knows any longer whether tomorrow a new whim of the legislature will not upset all calculations, an economic system in which everyone wants to live exclusively at the expense of the community and in which the state's budget finally comes to about half of the national income: a system of this kind is not only bound to become unprofitable and thus bound to intensify the scramble for the reduced total profit, but it will moreover in the end suffer a complete breakdown. This is usually called the crisis of capitalism and is used as an occasion for new and revolutionary interventions which complete the ruin and corruption and finally present us with the inexorable choice of either returning to a reasonable and ethical market system or of plunging into the collectivist adventure." [44]

As a result of the growing feeling during the seventies that government regulation has been harmful, many controls over basic industries such as finance, telecommunications, and transportation have been either abandoned or loosened. The results of these deregulation efforts have been widely discussed and commented upon. While there is some disagreement in particular instances, the view of most observers appears to be that the consumer has been served as a result of restoring a freer market to many areas of our economy. [45]

In an essay concerning airline deregulation, Stephen G. Breyer and Leonard R. Stein pointed out that with the Civil Aeronautics Board setting airfares and routes for interstate travel, the consumer paid much more for fewer choices. The fares and routes were set to serve the established airlines—not the consumers in whose name the CAB was originally founded. Thus, the authors point out, "Intrastate travel in Texas and California gave carriers substantial freedom to set fares . . . on routes within these two states, fares were only 50 to 70 per cent as high as those on CAB regulated interstate routes of comparable distance. For example, a traveler would pay $18.75 to fly the 338 miles between San Francisco and Los Angeles on Pacific Southwest Airlines (PSA) but $41.67 to fly the 399 miles between Washington, D.C. and Boston on a CAB regulated carrier." [46]

[44] Wilhelm Roepke, *The Social Crisis of Our Time* (Chicago: University of Chicago Press, 1950).

[45] Crane, *Sum of Good Government*, p. 139.

[46] Stephen C. Breyer and Leonard R. Stein, "Airline Deregulation: The Anatomy of Reform," in Poole, ed., *Instead of Regulation*, p. 17.

Today, with deregulation, there has not been the concentration or monopoly prices some feared. Instead, at least seventy airlines are now fly-
ing—instead of thirty-three before deregulation. In 1970, the volume of
passengers and freight carried per gallon of jet fuel was 33.8 percent higher
than during the years 1970 to 1976. Breyer and Stein concluded: "The first
lesson to be drawn from the airline case is that the application of classic
regulation to a basically competitive industry had inevitable results: Prices
that were too high, excessive service and limited consumer choice." [47]

A nine-page special report in the November 28, 1983, issue of *Business Week* magazine concluded that the economic benefits of deregulation
far outweighed any costs. As deregulation of a number of key industries
took hold, "this $250-billion chunk of the American economy is experi-
encing a burst of competition—a spur that is encouraging innovation, increasing productivity and reducing prices." [48]

The businesses previously protected by government regulation have
been forced to reduce costs and increase productivity. The government's
decision to ease restrictions on entering the trucking industry, for example, have seen the number of interstate carriers increase by 50 percent
since 1979.

"The savings to many shippers have been considerable," the *Business
Week* article reported. "A Harbridge House, Inc. survey of 2,200 manufacturers finds that 65 per cent now get lower rates. . . . Despite a sharp rise
in fuel costs, truckload rates, according to Data Resources, Inc., are 5 per
cent lower than they were in 1980."

In the airline industry, *Business Week* noted, large carriers were "quick
to blame new entrants for all their woes." The reality was really somewhat
more complex, however. "The fuel-price rise in 1970–80, recession, and
flight restrictions after the air traffic controllers' strike explain some of the
airlines' flow of red ink since deregulation," *Business Week* reported, noting that the new freedom to drop unprofitable markets helped carriers control losses.

The magazine cited a study that concluded "that continued regulation,
which would have required airlines to maintain these services would have
cost them $1.2 billion more in 1980 and 1981 than the $358 million operating loss they did incur." Long distance airfares, adjusted for inflation, are
down nearly 50 percent over the past seven years, and productivity is rising.

The 1983 article continued: "United Airlines, Inc., for example,

[47] Ibid., p. 36.
[48] "Deregulating America," *Business Week*, November 28, 1983, p. 80.

operated last year at 96.4 per cent of its 1978 capacity, as measured in available seat-miles, with 21 per cent fewer workers. The entire industry provided 19 per cent more output with fewer than 1 per cent more employees. The drive now, accelerated by the growth of low-cost operators, is for sharp increases in productivity through work-rule changes." [49]

Regarding the finance industry, the magazine pointed out: "Small savers, formerly relegated to passbook accounts with interest rate ceilings, can choose from a variety of money market funds or bank instruments offering competitive returns. Indeed, small money can seek out high-risk, high-return investments or even parts of tax shelter deals once available only to big money."

Still, *Business Week* warned that, despite such successes, a political backlash is developing which might halt the deregulation trend, or even reverse it. Labor unions—especially those representing truck and bus drivers and airline pilots—are reacting to the downward pressures on their wages by demanding re-regulation of their industries.

Some in Washington believed in 1984 that there were growing signs that the Reagan administration was rethinking and moderating its regulatory policies. When he first entered office, President Reagan had a commitment to "get the government off the backs of the people." During his administration, the executive regulatory agencies suspended or rescinded many regulations and stressed voluntary compliance while downgrading litigation.

Writing in the *New York Times* of December 1, 1983, Martin Tolchin noted: "The Administration remains unalterably opposed to what it considers excessive regulation. Still, a number of recent actions indicate it may be softening its stance. . . . Whatever the case, the fact is that the Task Force on Regulatory Relief, headed by Vice President Bush, was quietly disbanded a few months ago. There has been no recent meeting of the Cabinet Council on Natural Resources, which had been engaged in proposing revisions of environmental regulations. Since William D. Ruckelshaus was reappointed Administrator of the Environmental Protection Agency, the agency has abandoned its policy of focusing on voluntary compliance and is taking polluters to court. It also has come out in favor of stronger Federal standards against the use of dangerous pesticides and rescinded an earlier decision not to regulate formaldehyde as a cancer-causing agent." [50]

[49] Ibid.
[50] Martin Tolchin, "Recent Trends Hint Deregulatory Zeal Is Waning," *New York Times*, December 1, 1983, p. B-12.

Other examples of growing regulatory activity include the fact that executive regulatory agencies have begun issuing new regulations. A third brake light on automobiles was ordered by the National Highway Transportation Safety Administration. The Occupational Safety and Health Administration has put out regulations concerning asbestos and other toxic substances, as well as a new regulation that would enable employees to gain greater access to information on chemical hazards in their work environments.

Christopher DeMuth, assistant administrator of the budget office in charge of regulatory affairs, said in December, 1983, "Every Administration matures and mellows a little as the years go by, but I don't think there is any lessening of the desire to get rid of what we consider bad regulations." [51]

Regarding the changes at the environmental agency since Ruckleshaus's appointment, he said, "If you look at the Federal Register, it's not that different." DeMuth also said that at OSHA "there have been a few recent cases where they've been assertive, involving asbestos and E.D.B. standards, but it's a matter of the timing of when the evidence came in." He added that "our workplace asbestos standard is still too high." [52]

Consumer advocate Ralph Nader has said that he believes the Reagan administration is "looking for a way out" of being characterized as anti-regulation. "They read the same polls that we do," he said, noting that public opinion polls consistently indicated great public support for clean air, clean water, consumer protections, and a safe workplace, regardless of cost. [53]

During the early years of the Reagan administration, many believed that the consumer movement had reached its peak and was in a period of decline. Now, this no longer seems to be the case. Many Republicans, and some who call themselves conservative, see merit in certain aspects of consumer awareness. Sen. Warren Rudman (R-New Hampshire), for example, stated, "People are becoming more sensitive to consumer issues because they realize there is a constituency there that is not just the 'consumer activist' groups." [54]

Among the issues which stirred consumer interest in 1983 were the

[51] Christopher DeMuth, quoted in "Onward Consumer Soldiers," *Newsweek*, April 25, 1983, p. 56.
[52] "Onward Consumer Soldiers," p. 56.
[53] Ibid.
[54] Ibid.

deregulation of natural gas prices and the prospect of higher local telephone rates in the wake of the split-up of the American Telephone and Telegraph Company. The crusade for an anti-deregulation bill that would postpone full decontrol of natural gas prices until 1987 and mandate a temporary rollback of some gas prices was led by the Citizen/Labor Energy Coalition, a loose alliance of more than three hundred community, labor, church, farm, and senior-citizen groups. The fight against rising phone bills proceeded on a state-by-state basis, coordinated by the Washington-based Telecommunications Research and Action Center, which succeeded in getting one of its publications, *Reverse the Charges: How to Save Money on Your Phone Bill*, offered as a Book-of-the-Month-Club selection for June, 1983.[55] Senator Rudman noted, "There's more and more of an awareness" that the administration's pledge to keep government out of business "is just a code word to let business do whatever it wants—to the detriment of the consumer."[56]

In February, 1983, pollster Lou Harris issued his study, *Consumerism in the Eighties*, a survey which indicated that consumerism was a growing and vibrant movement, but might be changing somewhat in nature.[57] The poll, commissioned by ARCO in order to get a better idea of consumer concerns, showed that Ralph Nader's positive rating had dropped to 39 percent. A 1976 poll gave Nader a "clear and decisive" 54 percent positive rating. Harris, the *Washington Times* reported, has said, "While [Nader] is still on the positive side, he had undoubtedly suffered a major fall from grace, especially in the light of the continuing depth of feeling about consumer inequities in the marketplace."[58]

Nader came to prominence in the early 1960s with an attack on Chevrolet's Corvair Monza in his book *Unsafe at Any Speed*. It said the cars tended to break in half in automobile wrecks. "He's announced, I should say, he wants to get back to the 'grass roots' and all I can say is that's a good idea, Ralph," Harris said.[59] Harris said that the biggest drops in Nader's ratings occurred among young people under thirty, college-educated people in the suburbs, and those who live in the West, all groups that were once among his staunchest supporters.

Assessing the results, Harris declared: "Certainly there has been no

[55] Ibid.
[56] Warren Rudman, quoted in *Washington Times*, February 17, 1983, p. 5B.
[57] Lou Harris, quoted in *Washington Times*, February 17, 1983, p. 5B.
[58] Ibid.
[59] Ibid.

perceptible surge of activity on the part of the organized consumer movement in the past few years. And, given the sharp mandate of the 1980 election when two-thirds of the voters agreed with Ronald Reagan that the
federal government should get off the back of business, one might have
justifiably wondered if many of the elements underlying the consumer
movement we found in such abundance in 1976 might well have disap-
peared. Well, no such thing is the case. Indeed, if anything, there is every
sign of yet another explosion of consumer concern in the marketplace from
one end of this country to the other. Make no mistake about it, consumer
concerns are still out there and the evidence is that most are rising above
the levels of 1976." [60]

The poll revealed a great deal of concern about sales, service, and
repairs, up from 38 percent to 49 percent; dangerous products, up from 26
percent to 40 percent; and too many products going wrong, from 35 percent to 46 percent. "If consumer demand is going to lead the way back out
of this recession," Harris continued, "then the quality of what they are
going to buy must be viewed as an indispensable ingredient." Harris said
that he was not surprised by the public reaction to the consumer movement.
He said his poll revealed that a majority of persons surveyed felt the consumer movement has done more good than harm, which is roughly the
same as the first poll six years ago. He said that it was obvious to him from
the poll that the consumer movement has kept much of its "luster." [61]

The consumer movement, the continuing efforts to deregulate the
economy, and the accompanying desire by some to slow down that process
form the atmosphere within which any consideration of the insurance industry and the future legislative course affecting it must be considered.

While the insurance industry has not been discussed as widely in this
regard as have others, such as transportation and communication, interest
in it has been growing. Late in 1983, for example, Jake Garn (R-Utah),
chairman of the Senate Banking Committee, introduced major banking deregulation legislation. Among other things, the legislation would have allowed banks and savings and loan associations to perform securities, insurance, and real estate functions through separate subsidiaries. Insurance
companies, as might be expected, vigorously opposed this legislation.

Walter Wriston, chairman of Citicorp, speaking for the bankers, dis-
missed as nonsense insurance industry warnings against bank involvement

[60] Ibid.
[61] Ibid.

in insurance. He noted that insurance companies already were owned by many other types of corporations, ranging from tobacco companies to broadcasting companies, and that insurance companies in turn own 17 percent of the nation's banking assets. Insurance-industry lobbyists have warned that banks would pressure their loan customers to buy insurance from them if allowed to enter that business. Wriston responded, "This is like saying that insurance companies might violate the banking laws since they now own brokers, or they might violate the banking laws since they own banks, or an insurance company might withhold insurance if a customer did not use its brokerage facilities." [62] The debate over Senator Garn's proposed legislation was only beginning, and promising to be lengthy and heated. It is, however, only one of many legal challenges the insurance industry is likely to face in the future.

Before World War II, the regulation of insurance had been ceded to the states by the federal government. Then, in 1944, the Supreme Court held that the sale of property-liability insurance was interstate commerce and subject to the provisions of federal antitrust laws. That decision, *United States* v. *South-Eastern Underwriters Association*, made illegal the private rate-fixing agreements which had determined prices in the property-liability field, and it raised questions about the validity of other types of state regulation of insurance.

In 1945, Congress passed the McCarran-Ferguson Act, which ratified the states' power to regulate insurance, absent specific federal insurance regulation, and provided an antitrust exemption for private concerted price-fixing activities that were subject to state regulation. Now, many are challenging the continuation of the exemption of the business of insurance from the federal antitrust laws. In 1977, the U.S. Department of Justice expressed the view that an alternative scheme of regulation, without McCarran Act antitrust protection, would be in the public interest.

An alternative suggested by the Justice Department was a system of regulation of insurance companies similar to that applicable to other federally chartered financial institutions. Insurance companies, under such an approach, would have the option of either seeking a federal charter and thereby losing McCarran Act protection or retaining the protection under a state charter. A federal agency, such as the Federal Insurance Administration, it was suggested, could develop a uniform system of solvency regula-

[62] Media release, Walter Wriston speech to American Council on Life Insurance Meeting, Washington, D.C., November 16, 1983.

tion that would emphasize the early detection and swift removal of failing companies from the marketplace. It was the Justice Department's view that a large segment of the property-liability insurance industry was favorably structured for competition, with a large number of competitors, relatively moderate concentration, ease of entry, a standardized service, a relatively simple short-term contract, and an increasingly price-sensitive consumer market.

Of growing concern to many observers, in this era of consumerism and deregulation, is the way insurers engage in two principal forms of concerted activities: (1) the exchange of cost information and the formulation of prospective prices through a rating bureau, and (2) the direct or indirect exchange of company rating manuals and rate adjustments. Both are likely to be targets for much legislative reform in the future.

There is a growing feeling, in Washington and elsewhere, that price competition in the insurance industry has been inadequate. In July, 1979, the Federal Trade Commission issued a report that showed how, for example, a company paying a twenty-year rate of return of 2 percent could compete successfully with companies paying 4 to 6 percent. Such a lack of price competition was contrasted with the banking industry, where a quarter of a percent disparity is considered competitively crucial.

The consumer movement has reached the insurance industry. One group active in this connection is the National Insurance Consumer Organization (NICO) based in Alexandria, Virginia. Among the goals of this group, which is affiliated with Ralph Nader's organization, are the following:

1. Accident-free and claim-free drivers should get all the auto insurance they need at standard rates from the companies they choose.
2. Auto insurance rates should depend more on driving records and less on where you live. Age, sex, and marital status should be disallowed as rating variables.
3. Auto insurance rates can be lowered in most states if companies are required to account for the investment returns derived from policyholder premiums.
4. Legislation should be enacted to eliminate those gaps in Medicare that confuse the elderly. An out-patient prescription drug benefit is needed. States should do much more to regulate the sale of Medicare supplements.
5. Life insurance companies should be required to tell policyholders what rates of return they pay on the savings portions of cash value policies. Industrial life insurance should be abolished.
6. Consumers must be represented at insurance department rate hearings and before legislators. Insurers spend tens of millions of dollars to lobby; indeed, they

are allowed to increase premiums to get this money, and the consumer's side is not heard.

The continuing efforts of groups such as the National Insurance Consumer Organization are likely to make the goals it sets forth the issue of debate in the Congress and in state legislatures for years to come.

The application of "truth in lending" and "disclosure" principles, which have been applied to a host of other industries and products, is likely to be a major focus with regard to the insurance industry. In his best-selling book about the insurance industry, *The Invisible Bankers*, author Andrew Tobias made this point: "When you go to buy sugar at the supermarket you are not required to try to guess the weight of the bag. It is printed right on the front. When you buy a car, you don't have to try to guess its fuel efficiency. When you buy processed foods, you are actually told what's in them. Indeed, in most cases you are supplied a breakdown of the nutritional content as well. When you go to borrow money from a bank, or finance a department store purchase, you are told, in bold type, the effective annual rate of interest you will pay. When you purchase newly issued securities, you are issued a detailed prospectus replete with warnings. So why is it that when you go to buy insurance (of any type) you are not advised of the odds? A simple standardized disclosure statement . . . would in many cases be all it would take." [63]

According to Tobias, this one reform, meaningful disclosure, "would go a long way toward 'rationalizing' the insurance industry. If people had an easier time understanding and comparing values, they could shop for insurance more wisely. That, in turn, would force the industry to compete more on the quality of its offers, less on the quality of the parchment they are printed on. By promoting price competition, meaningful disclosure would help to cut out waste. Insurers should be free to offer grossly overpriced protection and customers to buy it. But customers also have a right to know what it is they are getting. Tell us the odds!" [64]

There are a number of other major issues facing the insurance industry. One of these relates to unisex insurance rates and the feminist movement, which demands equality between men and women in all legal areas, including insurance. Another is that of the growing pressure for "no-fault" automobile insurance.

[63] Andrew Tobias, *The Invisible Bankers* (New York: Pocket Books, 1982), p. 59.
[64] Ibid., p. 61.

A report issued in 1970 by the New York State Insurance Department was sharply critical of the traditional auto liability insurance system. The report asked, "What becomes of the personal injury liability insurance dollar?" It replied: "First of all, insurance companies and agents use up 33 cents. Then lawyers and claims investigators take the next 23 cents. Together these items make up the operating expenses, or fractional costs, of the fault insurance system—56 cents out of every premium dollar. What happens to the 44 cents that get through to the accident victim? First, 8 cents of the 44 go to pay for economic losses that have already been reimbursed from another source. Subtracting these redundant benefits as having low priority leaves 36 cents of the premium dollar to pay net losses of victims. . . . of those 36 cents, 21.5 cents go for something other than economic loss. The 21.5 cents are lumped together as 'general damages' or 'pain and suffering' which, in the typical case today, are simply byproducts of the bargaining process of insurance adjustment. Once we look beyond the name which the operators of the fault insurance system have given this noneconomic portion of liability payments and understand what it really is in the usual case, it assumes a low priority by any social or humane standard. That leaves just 14.5 cents out of the premium dollar as compensation for the net economic loss of the accident victim—$100 million out of $686 million which New Yorkers spend each year for automobile bodily injury liability insurance."[65]

Sen. Daniel P. Moynihan (D-New York) has stated that under the current fault system, "the victim has every reason to exaggerate his losses. It is some other person's insurance company that must pay. The company has every reason to resist. Delay, fraud, contentiousness are maximized, and in the process the system becomes grossly inefficient and expensive."[66]

On the other side of the issue, lawyers and others argue that to compensate innocent victims for only their medical costs and lost wages, and not for pain and suffering as well, is unfair. Insurers have also expressed the fear that no-fault auto insurance would lead to the same sort of group coverage as group life and health insurance, and would, as a result, lower income and profits. Those companies which already specialize in group policies have different interests in this debate than do those specializing in individual policies, as well as the seventy thousand insurance agencies that sell individual policies only.

[65] Ibid., pp. 207, 211.
[66] Moynihan, quoted in ibid., p. 11.

The debate over unisex and no-fault insurance is, in many respects, only beginning. It is likely to be with us for some time. What is beyond question is that the many legal issues facing the insurance industry—from the question of state versus federal regulation, to the issues of banking deregulation and the sale of insurance by banks and savings and loan associations, to the issue of no-fault and unisex insurance, to those of public disclosure, rate regulation, rate bureaus, and tax regulations affecting insurance—will be the subjects of increasing discussion and debate in the future. State legislatures, federal administrative agencies, state insurance commissions, the U.S. Congress, and state and federal courts will be the battlegrounds.

How these questions will be resolved will depend, in part, on the political atmosphere in the late 1980s. Will the movement for deregulation and true consumerism grow and flourish, or will there be a reaction to it, and a call for increasing government regulation? Will the feminist movement become more active and vocal, or less so? Has consumerism reached its peak or has it just begun its ascent?

In the mid-1980s the signals appear to be mixed. Assessing the question of deregulation, *U.S. News and World Report*, in its issue of December 12, 1983, noted: "President Reagan's campaign to cut red tape is bogging down and threatens to go into reverse. After three years, the program to get Washington off the people's backs is encountering major legal roadblocks and new calls for more, not fewer controls." [67]

One example cited for this assessment was a federal appeals court's November 29, 1983, decision to overturn a Department of Labor ruling allowing knit-wear makers to hire individuals to work at home. The court called the department's 1981 easing of the forty-year-old ban on such industrial homework "arbitrary and capricious." The court urged the administration to follow congressional dictates, even when the administration disagreed with them.

U.S. News and World Report commented: "Deregulation . . . is becoming something of a victim of its successes, particularly in transportation, banking and communications. Erasing or easing federal rules was designed to stiffen competition and stimulate efficiency. In some industries, such as the airline business, competition has become so fierce that it has triggered a rash of bankruptcies and mergers. Hundreds of thousands of

[67] Clemens Work, "Deregulation Drive Runs into Roadblocks," *U.S. News and World Report*, December 12, 1983, p. 81.

jobs have been lost or downgraded. At the same time, the high-priority push to slash red tape has been slowed by growing skepticism by business and moves by Congress to shore up the government's health and safety protections. . . . In the court of public opinion, most observers believe, overzealous actions by former officials of the Environmental Protection Agency and the Interior Department have given deregulation in health, safety, and environmental areas a bad name. . . . Since the EPA controversy, many agencies have handled deregulation with kid gloves. For instance, Thorne Auchter, chief of the Occupational Safety and Health Administration, who has eagerly endorsed deregulation, has been busy issuing safety standards, most recently for labeling toxic chemicals in the workplace." [68]

In the telephone industry, the breakup of the American Telephone and Telegraph Company has produced a backlash. Increased competition in the long-distance business was expected to lower rates, but proposed monthly "access charges" would have offset the advantage for most users. After consumers and competitors protested, the Federal Communications Commission postponed such fees.

In many instances, it is industry itself that has most persistently resisted deregulation. George Heaton of the Center for Policy Alternatives at the Massachusetts Institute of Technology, quoted in the *New York Times*, argued that industry wants to create or retain rules: "It needs standards in order to plan its investments. You can't arbitrarily change rules in the middle of the game." Milton Freifeld of the Chemical Manufacturers Association has been quoted as saying "Most of our companies ship across state lines. We would prefer to see a reasonable federal regulation that lets us do business, rather than put a different label on a product every time you cross a state line." [69]

Murray Weidenbaum, former chairman of the president's Council of Economic Advisors and a long-time advocate of deregulation, saw 1983 as "not exactly a high-water mark in the movement to reform federal regulation." [70] Weidenbaum pointed to a drop in budget outlays for regulation, after a decade-long rise. Adjusted for inflation, agency budgets would have declined 14 percent for the five year period ending in 1984, and staffing would have been cut by 16 percent, he estimated. Such cuts, he conceded,

---

[68] Ibid.
[69] Heaton and Freifeld, quoted in *New York Times*, November 30, 1983.
[70] Weidenbaum quoted in *Washington Times*, February 2, 1984.

might result in delays in serving the public, "but at least the cuts prevent agencies from expanding their scope."

As 1983 came to an end, federal agencies still produced more than 6,000 regulations a year. The totals, however, were down from the 8,005 rules promulgated in 1980. It is within this atmosphere that we must consider the legal and legislative challenges that lie ahead for the insurance industry.

2

The Effort to Place Insurance under Federal Regulation

DURING the years of the New Deal and beyond, the federal government and its regulatory powers grew dramatically. Major American industries—from banking to transportation to communication—found themselves carefully regulated and monitored by a proliferation of government agencies. Government was, in many respects, a not-so-silent partner in many of these enterprises. In the case of the insurance industry, however, regulation has been exercised at a distance from Washington.

Before World War II, insurance regulation was ceded to the states by the federal government. In the case of *United States* v. *South-Eastern Underwriters Association*, however, the Supreme Court held that the sale of property-liability insurance was interstate commerce and therefore subject to the provisions of federal antitrust laws. That decision made illegal the private rate-fixing agreements that had determined prices in the property-liability field. It also raised questions about the validity of the various types of state regulation of insurance.[1]

In 1945, Congress passed the McCarran-Ferguson Act, which ratified the states' power to regulate insurance except when federal insurance legislation existed. This act provided an antitrust exemption for private concerted price-fixing activities that were subject to state regulation. This provision was justified, it was argued, because competitive pricing in the

[1] 322 U.S. 533 (1944).

insurance field would lead to ruinous competition and the demise of many insurance companies. This, in turn, would deny the public the benefit of a reliable insurance mechanism.]

At this time, all of the states adopted regulatory plans relating to property-liability insurance rates. In some states, the government itself set the rates. Most states moved toward "prior-approval" systems that use private rate bureaus as the major element in the determination of rates] Some states opted for "open-competition" systems that allow cartel rate setting but enable insurers to price independently with little difficulty. In life insurance and most group health insurance, there has been almost no direct state rate regulation. Individual health insurance and Blue Cross/Blue Shield, however, have been subject to varying degrees of state rate regulation.

Early in 1975, President Gerald Ford called for the initiation of a major effort aimed at regulatory reform. He called for the formulation and acceleration of programs to remove anticompetitive restrictions in price and entry regulation, to reduce the paperwork and procedural burdens in the regulatory process, and to revise procedures in health, safety, and other social regulations in order to bring the costs of these controls in line with their social benefits. This set in motion agency and department initiatives, along with a number of studies, reorganization proposals, and legislative proposals. For approximately eighteen months, the Department of Justice, at the request of the Task Force on Antitrust Immunities of the Economic Policy Board, conducted a study of the regulation of insurance. Its final report is titled *Federal-State Regulation of the Pricing and Marketing of Insurance.*

The report's editor, Professor Paul W. MacAvoy of Yale University, has commented: "Focusing primarily on property-liability insurance, the department gathered information on the question of whether existing state regulation and federal antitrust immunity were in the public interest. The complexity of regulation and of the other institutions in the industry made answering the question extremely difficult, and the Department of Justice experts concluded that regulation of insurance entailed diverse and sometimes conflicting economic and social goals/ Furthermore, knowledgeable opinion differed substantially on the weight to be assigned to each such goal and on the best methods for their realization. Nevertheless, the Department of Justice analysts did reach tentative conclusions and did produce a proposal which would allow for greater competition among issuers of in-

surance without interference with the beneficial operations of regulation as
now practiced. In essence, the proposal would allow insurers that wish
to adopt a more entrepreneurial approach to choose a less regulated national system under which they would enjoy no special antitrust immunity.
Other insurers, who continued to opt for state regulation, would continue
to operate under the antitrust immunity embodied in the McCarran-
Ferguson Act." [2]

In his book *The Invisible Bankers*, Andrew Tobias argued that state
regulation of insurance has not served society very well: "State regulation—a $150 million annual enterprise—leaves much to be desired. After
a 1980 hearing on auto insurance in New Mexico, throughout which a consumer advocate kept arguing that insurers' *investment income* should be
taken into account in the setting of rates, New Mexico's insurance commissioner pulled the consumer advocate aside. 'You keep talking about investment income,' he said, slightly embarrassed. 'What's investment income?'
In North Carolina, in 1981, three of the eleven members of the Senate Insurance Committee owned and operated insurance agencies. A fourth was
a director of Columbus Standard Life. In the House, four of seventeen
committee members owned and operated insurance agencies; two more
were lawyers representing insurance companies." [3]

A report issued by the General Accounting Office in October, 1979,
found "serious shortcomings" in the way states were regulating insurance.
It stated, "Insufficient regulation is not characterized by an arms-length
relationship between the regulators and the regulated." [4] The GAO found
that about half the state insurance commissioners had been previously employed in the industry and that approximately the same proportion joined it
after leaving office. According to the GAO report, the National Association of Insurance Commissioners' model laws and regulations, which
many states adopt in full, are drafted "with advisory committees composed
entirely of insurance company representatives."

Tobias stated: "The problem is not one of malicious disregard of the
public good but of common assumptions and comfortable relationships. It
is a club. Most of its members are nice guys. Robert J. Bertrand was a nice

[2] Paul W. MacAvoy, ed., U.S. Department of Justice Study "Federal-State Regulation of
the Pricing and Marketing of Insurance" (Washington, D.C.: American Enterprise Institute,
1977), p. 2.
[3] Andrew Tobias, *The Invisible Bankers* (New York: Pocket Books, 1982), p. 318.
[4] Ibid., p. 319.

guy in 1966, when he was employed by the Wisconsin legislature to help revise that state's insurance laws; he was a nice guy in 1967, when he went to work for State Farm; he was a nice guy in 1969, when he left State Farm to become deputy New York insurance commissioner; and he was a nice guy in 1973, when, still in New York, he switched from regulating to lobbying. Among his clients: State Farm. Thomas A. Harnett, meanwhile—also a very nice guy—quit as New York's chief regulator in 1977 because the pay was too low ($47,800). He went to work for the Travelers Insurance Company ($100,000). In truth, he had taken the regulatory post in the first place only after a lot of urging. It wasn't his fault the governor had decided an attorney who represented insurance company interests, and who would likely represent them again after his stint as a regulator, was the best man for the job." [5]

The "revolving door," Tobias pointed out, is not unique to the insurance industry and its regulators but is "nowhere more pervasive." He reports: "In four out of five states, the insurance commissioner is a political appointee. Politically powerful, the industry can often, in effect, appoint its own regulators. . . . Insurance companies and state regulators both oppose federal regulation. Insurers would rather risk the occasional maverick state regulator, and incur the cost of conforming to fifty different sets of regulations, than chance regulation by a federal agency they could not dominate. And dominate they do. 'I once asked a friend in the game how come the Connecticut Insurance Department only had twenty-nine examiners,' says the former state regulator, 'and he said, "Because the Travelers doesn't want them to have thirty".'" [6]

J. Robert Hunter, former Federal Insurance Administrator and now president of the National Insurance Consumer Organization, has argued: "As things stand now, a fellow gets appointed commissioner of some state and he wants to do a good job. He wants to hear both sides of each issue and then make a fair decision. He feels judicial. So he holds hearings, and first one side comes in to tell its story (the industry)—and that's all that comes in." [7]

The basic question under study by the Department of Justice in 1977 was whether continuation of the present exemption of the insurance busi-

[5] Ibid., p. 320.

[6] Ibid.

[7] Interview with J. Robert Hunter, president, National Insurance Consumer Association, Alexandria, Virginia, January, 1983.

ness from the federal antitrust laws, by virtue of the McCarran Act and state regulation, was in the public interest.[8] Had thirty years of state regulation provided the public with the benefits normally attributed to competition, namely, reasonable prices, efficient services, and innovation, as well as the utilization of new or improved products or services and methods of distribution?

The department found that during the previous decade a number of states had adopted an "open-competition" system of rate regulation. This experimentation with competitive controls as a substitute for concerted rate making, it was felt, was evidence that state rate regulation might be inadequate. In addition, the emergence of independent pricing in segments of the property-liability industry, despite restrictive state laws, was seen as an indication that an industry structure favoring competition existed and that there were inherent weaknesses in traditional forms of state regulation.

The Justice Department considered that rigid state regulation of rates in automobile insurance had fostered greater adherence to bureau rates and had discouraged reduction in rates. It was also seen as establishing forms of cross-subsidization between good and bad drivers and as imposing unnecessary restrictions on the merchandising and the direct writing of insurance. In the commercial lines, the findings of the Justice Department indicated that state regulatory plans were largely illusory and that insurers were generally free to set their own prices as a result of the availability of state-authorized rating plans that permitted insurers to price risks individually based largely on their business judgment and competitive pressures. The fact that such plans were prevalent in the commercial lines raised the question of the purpose and the need for state rate regulation in these lines of insurance.

It was felt that the insurance industry was no different from other industries and should be able to conduct its business without any special exemption from the federal antitrust laws. Precedent in the antitrust field seemed to indicate that insurance companies could pool their loss experience through a statistical bureau in a way that would not conflict with federal antitrust standards. It was also believed that federal antitrust laws would not prohibit any necessary trending of future losses on a composite basis by advisory organizations that operated independent of the com-

[8] MacAvoy, "Federal-State Regulation," p. 5.

panies they were serving. In addition, the antitrust laws would not prevent voluntary risk-sharing arrangements, such as insurance pools and reinsurance agreements.

The Department of Justice concluded that the insurance industry had the ability to function effectively in a fully competitive environment without McCarran Act antitrust protection. It recommended a system of regulation of insurance companies similar to that used for other federally chartered financial institutions. Insurance companies would be given the option of either seeking a federal charter and thereby losing McCarran Act protection or retaining that protection under a state charter. Insurers operating under federal auspices would participate in a federal guaranty system. Those companies meeting minimum financial standards of eligibility could qualify for a federal charter. Some companies that write insurance in a way that generates "reverse competition," that is, competition for the services of the agent rather than the consumer, might have to remain subject to state regulation.

Under the plan set forth by the Department of Justice, federally chartered companies would be exempt from state rate regulation, state restrictions on collective merchandising and direct writing of insurance, state guaranty funds, and state solvency regulation. A federal agency, such as the Federal Insurance Administration, would be able to develop a uniform system of solvency regulation that would emphasize the early detection and rapid removal of failing companies from the marketplace. State regulation, on the other hand, has tended to emphasize "keeping every insurer afloat." A guaranty fund, much like the Federal Deposit Insurance Corporation, could operate to provide reserves in the event that a weak company went undetected.

According to this proposal, federally chartered companies would be required to participate in a federal guaranty fund, and the insurers would be subject to such controls as federal solvency and investment standards; federal laws against invidious discrimination in the selection and classification of risks based on race, age, and sex; and federal standards on disclosure of price information and underwriting experience. Federal antitrust laws, without any special exemptions, would also apply.

State governments would continue to play a role in the regulation of federally chartered companies. States could impose taxes on companies doing business within the state, although the Department of Justice urged further study concerning the competitive effects of retaliatory state taxes.

Companies could also be required by the states to participate in a residual market plan in order to service drivers unable to obtain protection in the voluntary marketplace. In addition, states could regulate the rates charged by the plans, provided they were administered on a self-sustaining basis. In the absence of cross-subsidization between high- and low-risk drivers, the state could furnish a direct "external" subsidy to individuals who could not afford insurance protection.

State governments, under the proposals of the Department of Justice, would continue to play a major role in regulatory matters relating to the insurance contract, such as minimum coverage requirements, cancellation and renewal of policies, financial responsibility laws, compulsory insurance, policy forms, licensing of agents, and systems of liability, as in the case of fault and no-fault auto insurance. Insurance companies electing to remain under state charters would be subject to the full scope of state insurance regulation, as well as to McCarran Act protection.[9]

Assessing the Justice Department's recommendations, MacAvoy argued: "The dual system of regulation, with respect to either federally chartered companies or state-chartered companies participating in the federal guaranty fund, would require the reconciliation of federal and state regulation. In this regard, the experience of the banking laws may provide some guidance, so that all insurance companies would be subject to state law unless they are expressly exempt by federal law or unless the state laws interfere or conflict with the purposes of the federal scheme."[10]

Summarizing the recommendations, MacAvoy wrote that they would produce: "a predominant segment, with a large number of competitors, relatively moderate concentration, ease of entry, a standardized service, a relatively simple and short-term contract, and an increasingly price-sensitive consumer market. The available evidence suggests that unrestricted price competition would be an effective alternative to state rate regulation and would be compatible with regulatory objectives for a reliable insurance mechanism. It is the opinion of this study that all of the major lines of property-liability insurance should have the option of operating in a fully competitive environment under a dual system of regulation. Other lines, including life insurance, are probable candidates, subject only to state regulation designed to limit compensation to intermediaries and

[9] Ibid., pp. 1–6.
[10] Ibid., p. 5.

thus to counter the phenomenon of reverse competition. Further study appears necessary to reach definitive conclusions in health insurance and medical malpractice." [11]

A study issued by the College of Insurance Research Institute, entitled *Insurance Regulation at the Crossroads* (1976), concluded, "This may be the time for the insurance industry to surrender the cloak and face the antitrust elements ungarbed because only then can it be treated equally with other segments of interstate commerce." [12]

The Justice Department, looking at 1975 statistics, found that the insurance industry generated approximately $110 billion in premium volume and administered about $383 billion in assets, comparable to bank trust operations. Yet, unlike bank trust departments, insurance companies are essentially unregulated at the federal level, although there are broad federal regulatory plans which do apply to them. The Federal Trade Commission has the authority to regulate certain interstate trade practices, such as advertising by insurance companies (*FTC* v. *Travelers Health Association* [1960]). Insurance companies are subject to Securities and Exchange Commission regulation with respect to the issuance of publicly held securities and to federal taxation. The McCarran-Ferguson Act expressly provides for the application of certain federal labor laws to the insurance business. A program administered by the Department of Housing and Urban Development through the Federal Insurance Administration involves the federal government, the states, and private insurers in an undertaking to provide property insurance to persons affected by riots, civil disorders, and floods (Titles X and XII of the Housing and Urban Development Act of 1968, P.L. 90-448).

There have, of course, been previous efforts to place the insurance industry under federal antitrust jurisdiction. The U.S. Supreme Court, in 1944, in the case of *United States* v. *South-Eastern Underwriters Association*, held that insurance transactions across state lines were essentially interstate commerce and therefore subject to federal antitrust laws.

In this case, the court rejected the idea that the sales contract was the only relevant portion of the insurance transaction. It held, instead, that there were many transactions in the negotiation, execution, and performance of the contract that were interstate in character. Among these were

---

[11] Ibid.
[12] Cited in ibid.

the collection and investment of premiums and the payment of policy obligations. The case came as a result of an indictment obtained by the government against nearly two hundred private-stock fire insurance companies for allegedly conspiring to fix premium rates and agents' commissions and intimidate insurance companies into the conspiracies. The lower court had sustained the defendants' demurrer to the indictment. The Supreme Court, in reversing that decision, held that a conspiracy to fix and maintain insurance rates and monopolize trade and commerce in insurance would violate sections 1 and 2 of the Sherman Act. The court also rejected the argument that the application of the Sherman Act would invalidate state laws regulating the insurance business.

The government, in its brief, reviewed various state laws regulating concerted rate making by insurance companies, and argued that some state regulatory approaches might be considered "state action" immunizing concerted rate making from antitrust prosecution under the policy established in *Parker* v. *Brown*.[13] Defendants argued that the government's position was equivocal. Citing *Parker*, the court viewed the defendants' argument that applying the antitrust law to their activities was inconsistent with state regulatory policies as "exaggerated" and noted that "few states go so far as to permit private insurance companies, without state supervision, to agree upon and fix uniform insurance rates."[14]

At this time, the insurance industry and its regulators on the state level advocated and promoted federal legislation that would protect certain concerted rate making activities from the federal antitrust laws. The National Association of Insurance Commissioners (NAIC), for example, urged the exemption from the Sherman Act of the pooling of statistical data, as well as the rate-making activities of insurance companies whose rates were approved or "subject to" disapproval by a state official. This provision was designed to "remove any doubt as to the validity of state regulation of insurance rates."[15] Regulation of this kind was considered a substitute for unrestricted competition, which allegedly would result in inadequate rates, unfair discrimination, and the insolvency of insurers.

Observers at the time considered the McCarran-Ferguson Act a compromise between those who wanted to place the insurance business totally

---

[13] 317 U.S. 341 (1943).

[14] MacAvoy, "Federal-State Regulation."

[15] Proceedings of the National Association of Insurance Commissioners, 76th session, 1945, p. 33.

under federal antitrust legislation and those who wished to make it totally immune from such controls. Section 2(b) of the act provided that after a three-year moratorium, the federal antitrust laws would be applicable to the insurance business "to the extent that such business is not regulated by State law." Section 3(b), which appeared to be related to the abuses uncovered in the *South-Eastern Underwriters* case, stated that the Sherman Act would continue to be applicable to all agreements or acts to boycott, coerce, or intimidate.

The legislative history of the McCarran-Ferguson Act shows that many in the Congress were in favor of a competitive rate structure based on the demands of the free market rather than a state-regulated structure of rates. The House Judiciary Committee report declared: "Nothing in this bill is to be construed as indicating it to be the intent or desire of Congress to require or encourage the several States to enact legislation that would make it compulsory for any insurance company to become a member of rating bureaus or charge uniform rates. It is the opinion of Congress that competitive rates on a sound financial basis are in the public interest." [16]

The message issued by President Franklin D. Roosevelt when he signed the McCarran-Ferguson Act included the following: "After the moratorium period, the Anti-Trust Laws and certain related statutes will be applicable in full force and effect to the business of insurance except to the extent that the States have assumed the responsibility, and are effectively performing that responsibility for the regulation of whatever aspect of the insurance business may be involved. It is clear that Congress intended no grant of immunity for monopoly or for boycott, coercion, or intimidation. Congress did not intend to permit private rate fixing, which the Anti-Trust Act forbids; but was willing to permit actual regulation of states by affirmative action of these States." [17]

Section 2(b) provided the industry and the state regulators the opportunity to preempt federal antitrust laws with state regulation. The industry's opposition to price competition is viewed as having been the major force behind the industry-wide effort to adopt uniform legislation giving the states clear control over rates in the property-liability field.

Most states soon adopted the "All Industry" model legislation under which rates prepared by private rate bureaus were submitted to the insur-

[16] H.R. Report No. 79-143, 79th Congress, 1st Session, 1945.
[17] *Automobile Insurance Study*, H.R. Report No. 90-185, 90th Congress, 1st Session, 1967, p. 22.

ance commissioner and deemed to be effective if not disapproved within a specified period of time. Under the uniform law, membership in the rate bureaus was voluntary, and deviations from established bureau rates by members were, in technical terms, permitted as long as regulatory approval was obtained. In practice, however, the delaying tactics of the rating bureaus and their opposition to partial subscribership are said to have effectively curtailed competitive pricing. The insurers, under prior-approval laws, were authorized to act in concert in establishing rates, underwriting rules, and policy forms. In addition, they could enter into agreements requiring the parties to adhere to those rates and rules. They were limited only by the general statutory prohibitions against excessive, inadequate, and unfairly discriminatory rates.

A number of states—Louisiana, Mississippi, North Carolina, Virginia, Texas, and the District of Columbia—retained the system of state-made rates, or the requirement of bureau membership as a condition for writing insurance. Three states—California, Missouri, and Idaho—adopted "open-competition" laws which permitted the implementation of rates without the filing of rate schedules with the state authorities. Such open competition laws resembled the prior-approval legislation in that they prohibited excessive, inadequate, or unfairly discriminatory rates and permitted concerted rate making. What distinguished these laws was the prohibition against agreements to adhere to rates fixed by the rating bureau and the ability of the insurer to price independently without the prior approval of the state commissioner.

These three systems of regulation have been upheld by the courts as satisfying the requirements of the McCarran-Ferguson Act. The prior-approval laws were upheld in *North Little Rock Transportation Co.* v. *Casualty Reciprocal Exchange.*[18] The mandatory rates were upheld in *Allstate* v. *Lanier.*[19] The "open-competition" laws were upheld in *California League of Independent Insurance Producers* v. *Aetna Casualty and Surety Co.*[20] Upon amendment of the complaint in the latter case, the court held that even if the conduct is regulated by the state, the Sherman Act applies where there is coercion, boycott, or intimidation.[21]

The McCarran-Ferguson Act has been held to be satisfied if state stat-

---

[18] 181 F. 2d 174 (8th Circuit, 1950), Certiorari denied, 340 U.S. 823 (1950).
[19] 361 F. 2d 870 (6th Circuit, 966), Certiorari denied, 385 U.S. 930 (1966).
[20] 175 F. Supp. 857 (N.D. Calif. 1959).
[21] 179 F. Supp. 65 (1959).

utes generally authorize or permit the fixing of rates by a private bureau and provide a "comprehensive scheme for the regulation" of such rates.[22] The courts have refused to consider the effectiveness of the particular regulatory plan or the enforcement of such laws in determining whether the requirement for state regulation is met.[23]

While state regulatory plans have normally exempted insurance companies from both state and federal antitrust laws, state regulation does not preempt federal antitrust laws where: (1) the anticompetitive agreement or conduct involves a boycott, coercion, or intimidation;[24] (2) the state does not regulate rates,[25] or the regulation is a "mere pretense," that is, no supervision or enforcement mechanism is provided for;[26] or (3) the activity of the insurer is extraterritorial (Advertising of an insurer dealing directly with residents of another state is subject to the Federal Trade Commission Act,[27] and mergers of national insurance companies are subject to the Clayton Act.[28]) or does not constitute part of the "business of insurance." [29]

A staff study issued by the National Association of Insurance Commissioners on open competition laws concluded the following in 1974: "Today the industry is earnestly advocating the enactment of open competition laws. In doing so, we are witnessing a classic reversal of historical position. An industry which fought for the right to make and maintain rates in concert for over 100 years has abandoned that approach and now maintains that its rates should be subject to the rigors of competition in the open marketplace." [30]

[22] Ohio AFL-CIO v. Insurance Rating Board, 451 F. 2d 1178 (6th Circuit, 1971), Certiorari denied, 409 U.S. 917 (1971).

[23] Federal Trade Commission v. National Casualty Company, 357 U.S. 560, 564 (1958).

[24] U.S. v. Insurance Board of Cleveland, 144 F. Supp. 684 (N.D. Ohio, 1956) and 188 F. Supp. 949 (N.D. Ohio, 1960); United States v. New Orleans Insurance Exchange, 148 F. Supp. 915 (E.D. La., 1957), affirmed per curiam, 355 U.S. 22 (1958).

[25] In re Grand Jury Investigation of the Aviation Insurance Industry, 183 F. Supp. 374 (S.D. N.Y., 1960).

[26] Federal Trade Commission v. National Casualty Company, 357 U.S. 564. Also, Ohio AFL-CIO v. Insurance Rating Board, 451 F. 2d 1178 (6th Circuit, 1971).

[27] FTC v. Travelers Health Association, 362 U.S. 293, 1960.

[28] American General Insurance Company v. Federal Trade Commission, 359 F. Supp. 887 (SD. Tex., 1973), affirmed 496 F. 2d 197 (5th Circuit, 1974); U.S. v. Chicago Title and Trust Company, 242 F. Supp. 56 (N.D. Ill., 1965).

[29] American General Insurance Company v. Federal Trade Commission.

[30] Jon S. Hanson, Robert E. Dineen, and Michael B. Johnson, *Monitoring Competition: A Means of Regulating the Property and Liability Insurance Business*, NAIC staff study, 1974, pp. 37, 655–56.

At present there seems to be a definite change in the regulatory atmosphere in favor of competitively determined rates. Approximately one-third of the states have adopted some form of open competition laws, and the NAIC has expressed its support for price competition as a means of regulating rates. Prior-approval laws have been liberalized to facilitate independent pricing.

The 1977 Department of Justice report expressed the view that the experimentation with competitive controls as a substitute for concerted rate making in certain major insurance states is evidence of the inadequacies of state regulation. In 1983, Congressman James J. Florio (D-New Jersey), chairman of the Subcommittee on Commerce, Transportation and Tourism, requested an in-depth study by the General Accounting Office (GAO) of the costs to the country of inefficient insurance systems that exist under the current exemptions from Federal antitrust laws.

In a letter to Congressman Florio endorsing his request for a GAO study, J. Robert Hunter, president of the National Insurance Consumer Organization, noted: "Insurance is vital to America; it performs a great service. But it costs too much. America spends 12.0 per cent of its disposable income on insurance (excluding Social Security and Unemployment Insurance). In 1982, that was $261 billion—$1,125 for every man, woman and child in the country—$4,300 for the average family. The average American worker worked 31.2 days to pay for insurance. Yet the insurance mechanism as it operates today typically requires overhead costs of 50 cents to $1.00 for every $1.00 benefit delivered. On a cash basis, the property/casualty insurance industry has paid out less than $1 for every $2 of cash flow it received over the past 25 years." Hunter also argued that the underlying problems are the impediments to competition under exemption from the federal antitrust law. "Protected by the McCarran-Ferguson Act's exemptions from anti-trust law application, the insurance industry has been able to engage in activities which we think severely impede the functioning of competition." [31]

Two recent studies of insurance by the federal government similarly indicate that serious problems may exist. A report entitled *Issues and Needed Improvements in State Regulation of the Insurance Business*, issued by the General Accounting Office in 1979, indicated that, for automobile insurance, the industry is "structured to facilitate competition.

[31] Media release of J. Robert Hunter letter to Congressman James Florio, April 15, 1983.

However, there are limits to what competition can achieve due to a lack of consumer information, legal impediments, selective underwriting and other factors." [32] The GAO cited the requirements in twenty-five states to purchase auto liability insurance and of all states to hold insurance for physical damage by lenders as making "the demand for the product somewhat inelastic." [33]

On January 22, 1979, the National Commission for the Review of Anti-Trust Laws and Procedures issued its *Report to the President and the Attorney General*. This report called for repeal of "the current broad antitrust immunity for the business of insurance granted by the McCarran-Ferguson Act" and "study of economic regulation of insurance by the relevant Congressional committees or by a special commission established by the President." The report stated, "The costs of continuing the present system are not insignificant: where members of a competitively structured industry are allowed collectively published industry-wide rates—often without effective state supervision—in a regulatory environment that encourages uniform pricing, insurance premiums are likely to be higher than under a system that relies more heavily on independent pricing decisions."

In addition, the commission said that some "commissioners believe the further study recommended here should aim toward a federal statute prohibiting certain types of anti-competitive state regulation." It urged a study which would "identify and analyze ways in which state regulation of insurance acts to restrict, and acts to strengthen, competition and independent pricing behavior" and which would "suggest the appropriate mix, if any, of state and federal legislation with respect to the business of insurance and determine the appropriateness of limiting the ability of states to achieve their regulatory objectives in an anti-competitive manner."

The National Insurance Consumer Organization points to what it considers major roadblocks to competition in the insurance field:

1. Lack of necessary price information and service information for consumers.
2. Existence of cartel-type rating bureaus. In Workers' Compensation, the cartel still requires adherence. In other lines, the rating bureaus establish rates for many companies and set classes, territories, and policy forms for most companies.
3. State Anti-Rebate laws in all states forbid efficient insurance agents from lowering retail commissions to compete for market share. This sort of retail price maintenance is identical in nature to the discredited Fair Trade–type laws.

[32] GAO report PAD 79-72, October 9, 1979.
[33] Ibid.

4. State Anti-Group laws forbid formation of groups for purchasing of insurance or self-insurance. Federal precedent exists to strike down such barriers to competition. The Product Liability Risk Retention Act does just that for product liability insurance.
5. Closed service systems—which limit claims repairs and other services to insurer-selected companies without competitive bidding or other tests of efficiency or quality of service.
6. Selection competition (also known as "underwriting") is a unique practice that results in fewer sales rather than more. It can be a severe impediment to competition if individuals fear to shop lest they are placed in the assigned risk plan or other high-priced markets.

Most of these alleged impediments were identified in the two major studies of insurance issued by the General Accounting Office and the National Commission for the Review of Anti-Trust Laws and Procedures and in hearings before the Subcommittee on General Oversight of the Committee on Small Business concerning Worker's Compensation Rate-making Reform (February 18, 1982).

In April, 1982, NBC News presented a documentary that argued that the insurance industry is essentially unregulated. NBC reported that not even the largest states are capable of adequately regulating giant multibillion-dollar companies. The states, the program pointed out, have even cut back regulation to allow competition to keep rates low, while the antitrust exemption has remained in full force and effect. The insurers, the program argued, cannot have it both ways because the present situation is costing the consumer too much.

The National Insurance Consumer Organization reported that inquiries and complaints about the insurance business now rank number one with the National Council of Better Business Bureaus.

In his request for a study by the General Accounting Office, Congressman Florio asked that the GAO be authorized to (1) build on its 1979 findings and (2) answer the call for a study made by the National Commission. This study would include the quantification of the costs to American consumers of the currently allowed practices that critics charge are anti-competitive and would address the important social issues of the availability and affordability of insurance.

Robert Hunter wrote to Congressman Florio that: "tens of billions of premium dollars could be saved annually by making insurance competitive. If all that could be saved was 10% (and we think much more could be saved), 26.1 billion in 1982 dollars would be saved. Just think: $430, tax-free, in the pocket of every family to spend to create productive jobs in America; 1.2% of the disposable income saved. At this time of economic distress, the country can ill afford to continue to waste tens of billions of dollars on insurance inefficiency. Congress has the duty to undertake a serious oversight function pertaining to the effectiveness of the insurance regulatory regime which it delegated to the States in 1945, with no standards for performance." [34]

In *The Invisible Bankers*, Tobias claimed: "Roots of the industry's inefficiency are manifold. . . . One might expect the marketplace to impose its own economic discipline—it is competitive based on price that has always been the surest spot to efficiency—but insurance prices, particularly life insurance prices, are notoriously hard to evaluate, leaving consumers unable to spot the best values and insurers under little pressure to provide them. Federal regulation and antitrust statutes largely exempt the insurance industry; state regulators are anxious to keep even inefficient companies profitable, lest policyholders be left stranded and claims go unpaid. . . . There are many ways to improve the system radically. But this is not an industry, by and large, that seeks radical improvement. Inbred and living in comfortable isolation with its state regulators, it has been slow to innovate. A 'cash cow' of the first order, it has resisted change." [35]

Typical of this growing concern is the feeling in New York on the part of many state officials who are concerned about the inefficiencies of life insurance disclosure, regulation, and pricing practices that more—not fewer—laws for the financial services industry may be necessary.

During three days of hearings in November, 1983, by the New York State Temporary Commission on Banking, Insurance and Financial Services, it was pointed out that legislative loopholes are allowing deceptive sales practices by life insurance companies, significant losses of state and city income taxes, and uncompetitive pricing practices at the expense of the consumer. [36]

Testimony about life insurance sales practices and the New York Insurance Department was presented by Joseph M. Beith, a professor of in-

---

[34] Hunter letter to Florio, April 15, 1983.
[35] Tobias, *Invisible Bankers*, p. 18.
[36] C. A. Carpenter, "Critics Blast Practices of N.Y. Life Industry," *Journal of Commerce*, November 23, 1983, p. 7a.

surance at the University of Indiana. The charges elicited a defensive response from New York Superintendent of Insurance James P. Corcoran, an ex-officio member of the temporary commission.

Beith stated: "I have become increasingly concerned as to what appears to be a tendency of the [New York State Insurance] department to serve as a protector rather than as a vigorous regulator of the major mutual life insurance companies domiciled in New York." [37] He also questioned the ability of all "insurance regulators to monitor the activities of life insurance companies adequately when the companies offer a wide variety of financial services" that lean toward short-term gains when their primary business is more long-term in nature. After asking that Beith send him proof of the department's protectionism, Corcoran agreed that the state's monitoring ability is inadequate. He suggested that the state's holding company laws could be improved by requiring a holding company to get prior approval from regulators before any transactions were made between sister subsidiaries. [38]

Beith was critical of the life insurance industry's disclosure practices as well. "Life insurance consumers have been confronted not only by an absence of vital information, but by the presence of deceptive information," he stated. He noted the hidden premium increases that characterize cash-value life insurance as a policyholder grows older. [39]

Banking witnesses have told the commission that consumers would benefit if commercial banks were allowed to sell insurance in the state because banks have a natural distribution outlet. Beith said, however, that the "rigorous disclosure" he called for would not necessarily result if commercial banks entered the field. Concern was expressed that banks might deny credit to applicants simply because they did not want to purchase insurance from the bank. Banking witnesses, on the other hand, said that there is no documented proof in other states that such coercion exists.

The twenty-year history of savings institutions' insurance-selling profile was submitted by Alan Press, general agent for New York–based Guardian Life Insurance Company, as proof that the consumer does not benefit when a bank gets into the insurance business. Comparing costs on a $30,000 whole life insurance policy, New York Savings Bank Life Insurance charged rates that were at least competitive compared with nine mu-

[37] Quoted in ibid.
[38] Cited in ibid.
[39] Ibid.

tual life insurance companies. "All of those nine insurers also projected surrender benefits in excess of net premiums paid, considerably higher than that of Savings Bank Life Insurance," Press said.[40]

New York state senator Franz S. Leichter (D-Manhattan) also testified that commercial banks are avoiding paying millions in state and municipal income taxes by using "enormous loopholes." Those loopholes, he said, cost New York State $62 million and New York City $68 million in income taxes in 1982.

Within the insurance industry itself there has been growing opposition to prior-approval legislation, initially from the direct writers and later from other insurers. The four leading direct writers of auto insurance have acquired approximately one-quarter of the market since World War II. Observers attribute their growth to their ability to charge lower rates based on a more efficient method of distribution and greater underwriting selectivity, which may be described as the process of rejecting those risks thought likely to bring losses larger than the portion of their rates available for losses. For these direct writers, independent pricing was essential. They had to charge lower rates in order to enter markets being served by established insurers. Direct writers thus had the economic incentive as well as the ability to challenge the control of the rate bureaus through price deviation, independent filings, and partial subscribership.[41]

Recently, all insurers, regardless of their method of distribution, have expressed support for a rate structure which is more responsive to changes in actual loss experience and inflationary factors. The Justice Department study declared, "The more efficient insurers have wanted to charge, as a matter of practice, rates lower than those prepared by the bureaus, and all insurers have wanted a more responsive system of rate determination that would permit higher rates where current loss experience and expense factors justify it."[42]

The study went on to say: "A number of state regulators have expressed some dissatisfaction with prior approval laws. They have been 'caught in a squeeze' between insurers who want higher rates and consumers who are outspoken in their opposition to higher rates. Moreover, state regulators have been finding that they cannot fulfill their statutory obligation to prevent inadequate or excessive rates. Under prior approval regu-

[40] Ibid.
[41] MacAvoy, "Federal-State Regulation," pp. 23–40.
[42] Ibid., p. 20.

lations, rates have been inadequate because they failed to keep up with current inflationary trends and loss experience, or the rates have been excessive because in pooling expense experience the inefficient firms have been sheltered from the potential competition of more efficient firms who could not (or would not) reduce their rates to reflect their lower costs of operations. The prior approval laws also have reduced the availability of insurance by forcing insurers to be more selective in their underwriting because of the inadequacy of fixed rates in meeting their expenses or claims." [43]

The experience of a number of states under open-competition regulation—California (since 1947), Illinois (since 1969), and New York (since 1970)—has had a major impact on the debate over the effects upon the public interest of competitively determined property-liability rates. Initially, it dispelled the long-held idea that price competition would result in price wars, mass bankruptcies, or excessive profits—the reasons advanced by the insurance industry for its 1945 antitrust exemption. New York State regulators, for example, concluded in 1975 that there was no significant relationship between competitive rates and insurer insolvencies. Instead, insolvency was due largely to mismanagement and possible wrongdoing. California officials reached the same conclusions in the late 1960s. [44] In addition, the experience of the states that practice open competition in the insurance field shows that price competition, rather than being incompatible with regulation, was a necessary complement to regulation. A study of the California no-file system concluded that open competition: (1) produced a rate structure that was responsive to changes in costs, (2) encouraged innovation in the form of coverage and rating plans, (3) reduced the problems of the residual market (composed of individuals who want insurance protection but are unable to obtain coverage at the prevailing rates or are unwilling to pay the nonstandard rates for liability insurance), (4) enabled new and small companies to enter and succeed in the business, and (5) relieved regulators of the time-consuming task of reviewing rate filings and permitted them to examine actual pricing practices in the field.

Since 1971, Illinois has been without a general rating law. In almost all lines of property-liability insurance, including automobile and homeowners insurance, there have been no statutory standards against excessive, inadequate, or unfairly discriminatory rates.

[43] Cited in ibid.
[44] Ibid.

In 1961, the report on the insurance industry of the U.S. Senate Sub-committee on Antitrust and Monopoly expressed strong opposition to the mandatory rate bureau membership and prior approval laws as inhibiting price competition.[45] The Senate report recommended the adoption of a file-and-use form of open competition law for regulating fire insurance rates in the District of Columbia to serve as a model law for all states. (Under the file-and-use system, proposed rates must be filed with the commissioner, but they become effective immediately upon filing.) The U.S. Department of Justice supported such legislation when it was introduced in the Senate in 1962. Although the legislation was not passed, the National Association of Insurance Commissioners, in the same year, adopted amendments to its model (prior-approval) rating laws designed to remove certain impediments to independent pricing, and in 1968 the National Association of Insurance Commissioners expressed its support for greater reliance on competition as a means of achieving reasonable prices for insurance.

The report issued by the Department of Justice to President Gerald Ford concluded that "rigid state rate regulation has had adverse effects." It declared: "Rigid state rate regulation in insurance—characteristic of a number of state systems—has fostered greater adherence to bureau rates, discouraged rate reductions, contributed to instability in insurance company operations, established various forms of cross-subsidization between good and bad risks, imposed unnecessary restrictions on the collective merchandising and the direct writing of insurance, and aggravated the availability problem in which marginal or high risks have difficulty obtaining coverage in the open market at the prevailing rates." [46]

The authors of the report expressed the view that vigorous competition in the insurance industry is fully consistent with the goal of reasonable prices: "The long-run experience of at least one major insurance state under an open competition system—in which the state has relied on market forces to control prices—suggests that essentially unrestricted price competition can provide an effective substitute for rate regulation as a means of achieving reasonable prices and maximum efficiency in the sale and the distribution of insurance. A comparison of the experience of the same insurers under certain open competition and prior approval systems suggests that competition fosters greater independent pricing, operating

[45] U.S. Senate, "The Insurance Industry." Report No. 87-831, 87th Congress, 1st Session, 1961.
[46] Quoted in MacAvoy, "Federal-State Regulation," p. 89.

stability, and flexibility in the pricing structure. The relatively favorable performance of the insurance companies under the highly competitive system suggests that it provides a more effective mechanism for accomplishing one of the basic insurance goals—generally available coverage at a price reasonably related to cost." [47]

In the commercial lines, the study indicated that "state regulatory schemes are largely illusory and that insurers are generally free to set their own prices. The reason for this is the availability of state-authorized rating plans which permit insurers to price risks individually based on their business judgment and competitive pressures. The prevalence of these plans in the commercial lines raises a fundamental question about the purpose and the need for ostensible state rate regulation in these lines of insurance." [48]

The Department of Justice concluded that the insurance industry could function effectively in a manner consistent with federal antitrust laws. It declared: "The insurance industry should be able to conduct its business within the federal antitrust laws without any special exemption. Antitrust precedent indicates that insurance companies could pool their loss experience consistent with federal antitrust standards. Moreover, the federal antitrust laws would not prohibit the trending of future losses on a composite basis by advisory organizations that were independent of the companies they were serving. Likewise, the antitrust laws would not prohibit those voluntary risk-sharing arrangements, such as insurance pools and reinsurance agreements, that either were necessary to the conduct of business or served some other legitimate business purpose without substantially lessening competition." [49]

In 1969 the New York Insurance Department reported that even in a highly regulated environment, insurers may adopt inadequate prices, may fail to identify marginal or high risks, or may underestimate loss development factors. The New York report discovered that rigid rate regulation, rather than unbridled competition, appears to have had an adverse effect on the stability and solvency of insurers because "it makes rates unresponsive to changing market circumstances" and thereby exacerbates a company's financial difficulties. [50]

A 1974 report from that department, entitled *Regulation of Financial*

[47] Ibid.
[48] Ibid.
[49] Ibid.
[50] Ibid., p. 91.

Condition of Insurance Companies argued that under a fully competitive system on a national scale, inefficient insurers might be forced out of the market. A transition to a highly competitive system, it stated, might require a major shift in regulatory policy, from that of "keeping every insurer afloat" to that of "swift detection and swift removal of a failing company from the insurance marketplace." [51]

The New York Insurance Department recognized the need for a new approach to solvency regulation, concluding: "The legitimate need for improved market performance by insurers also makes it increasingly less appropriate to regard preservation of strong financial condition and prevention of insolvency as absolute goals of insurance regulation. Instead, our objectives with respect to financial condition must increasingly be balanced against the impact on other goals of insurance regulation."

The National Association of Insurance Commissioners, in a report entitled *Audit Ratios for Property and Liability Companies* (1975), recognized the need for a uniform early warning system to monitor the financial condition of property-liability companies. The ability to detect potential solvency problems, however, was shown to depend upon the quality and quantity of the resources of both the state in which the company is incorporated and the state where the company is licensed to do business. In order to perform this function efficiently, the NAIC report indicated, the domiciliary state must periodically examine in depth the insurer's financial condition. The licensing state must monitor the condition of the company, relying in part on the domiciliary state but also on its own early warning system.

The Department of Justice report declared: "Effective solvency regulation in a competitive environment depends on the acceptance of market forces as a mechanism for weeding out weak and inefficient companies and on the willingness to remove, in a timely manner, a company from the marketplace when there is a substantial danger of insolvency. There must also be available an established guaranty fund in the event that the regulatory controls fail to detect a financially unsound company in time." [52]

Concerning the ability of existing state solvency regulation structures to adapt to a competitive environment, the Justice Department concluded that such adaptability was doubtful, stating that the "states vary substan-

---

[51] Ibid.
[52] Ibid.

tially in the amount of resources devoted to regulatory oversight. Very few states administer their solvency regulation in a fully competitive environment. New York, for example, was in the vanguard of regulatory reform, at least in recognizing the benefits of rate deregulation and the need for a drastic change in state solvency regulation under such a system. At the same time, New York has retreated from a truly open competition system in the process of introducing no-fault insurance, and the state has used its pre-assessment security (guaranty) fund to purchase $200 million of state obligations, adversely affecting the liquidity of the fund. We recognize that there are a few exceptional states, like California, whose regulators have approached the solvency issue with minimum interference to the free market mechanism. However, there are also few open competition systems today that are politically secure. The regulators from California, Hawaii, New York, Illinois, and Virginia all inform us that the future of rate deregulation in their states is uncertain." [53]

Competitive forces, the authors of the Justice Department report believed, could generally protect consumers against discriminatory prices, provided that there was adequate disclosure and regulatory effort to make consumers aware of alternative sources and prices of insurance. Within the relatively simple and short-term nature of the contract in the personal lines of property-liability insurance, competition, they argued, would facilitate consumer price shopping. A different situation existed, however, in the life insurance field. In view of the various forms of protection and the long-term nature of the contract, there was, the report declared, a need for improved disclosure of cost information so as to enable the buyer to shop and compare prices.

There is reason to believe that the forces urging an end to the antitrust exemption for the insurance industry will continue to grow. The antitrust status of insurance cannot be considered in a vacuum, but must be reviewed as part of the larger atmosphere within American society concerning regulation and other antitrust immunities that exist—and have existed.

In December, 1983, for example, the U.S. Department of Transportation proposed ending collective rate making in the trucking industry by lifting truckers' immunity from antitrust laws. In papers filed with the Interstate Commerce Commission, the department said that collective rate making in trucking reduces competition and does not have any "significant

[53] Ibid.

countervailing public benefits." At the same time, the Interstate Commerce Commission was considering a petition by two associations of shippers to withdraw antitrust immunity for truck rate making involving small shipments, defined as those weighing up to one thousand pounds. The ICC had asked parties interested in that case whether it should also consider withdrawing antitrust immunity for other kinds of truck rate making.

Trucking companies have been basically exempt from the antitrust laws in setting rates since the late 1940s. In 1980, however, Congress decided to eliminate that immunity for some shipments. The ICC's recommendation would complete the process.

At this writing, trucking companies can negotiate collective rate agreements through various regional rate bureaus. A study commission established by Congress in 1983 voted 6 to 4 to propose eliminating all such collective rate making, but by 1984 Congress had not yet acted upon that recommendation.

Even if insurance companies are placed under the antitrust laws from which they are now immune, the results are difficult to prophesy. Some critics charge that government administration of the antitrust laws has tended to protect the businesses regulated rather than to serve the larger public interest by increasing competition.

Thomas Sowell of the Hoover Institute at Stanford University has pointed out: "Antitrust policy, like utility regulation, exhibits a strong bias towards incumbents—toward protecting competitors rather than competition. This is readily understandable as institutional policy: Competitors bring legal complaints; competition as an abstract process cannot. Competitors supply administrative agencies such as the Federal Trade Commission with a political constituency; competition as an abstraction cannot. It is only when governmental agencies are seen as decision makers controlled by people with their own individual career and institutional goals that many apparently 'irrational' antitrust policies make sense. For example, although antitrust laws are ostensibly aimed at monopolistic practices, the actual administration of such laws—and especially the Robinson-Patman Act—has involved prosecuting primarily *small* businesses, most of whom are not even listed in *Moody's Industrials* and very few of whom are among *Fortune*'s list of giant corporations. The institutional reason is simple: A case against a small firm is more likely to be successful, because small firms do not have the money or the legal departments that large corporations have. A major antitrust case against a giant corporation can go on for a decade or more. A prosecution against a small business can be concluded—probably successfully—within a period that is within the time horizon of both the governmental agencies and their lawyers' career goals."[54]

Sowell continued: "The 'rebuttable presumption' of guilt after a prima facie showing by the government facilitates successful prosecutions, especially on complex matters subject to such different retrospective interpretations that no one can conclusively prove anything. In one well-known case, an employer with only nineteen employees, and who had about seventy competitors in his own city alone, had to prove that his actions did not 'substantially lessen competition'—and he lost the case. It confirms the wisdom of putting the burden of proof on the government in most other kinds of prosecutions. In general, the public image of antitrust laws and policy is of a way of keeping giant monopolies from raising prices, but most major antitrust cases are against businesses that *lower* prices—and most of the businesses involved are small businesses."[55]

Discussing the U.S. government's current antitrust policy, William Baxter, who served for three years as antitrust chief at the Department of Justice and is a professor of law at Stanford University, has stated: "There are two dangers to be guarded against: One is cartels and the other is single-firm monopolies. And there are two corresponding categories of activity that should be watched. One is anything that facilitates or makes cheaper or easier the process of collusion. And the other is destructive or predatory activity by firms with very, very major market shares that throw sand in the gears of their smaller competitors through activities that would not be profitable except that it hurts their competitors. Under very limited circumstances, a long-term contract can be a device for destroying the competitors of a large and dominant firm. And those are the circumstances where tight arrangements among the manufacturer, distributor and wholesaler can continue to be matters of legitimate antitrust concern."[56]

Baxter, asked if he was concerned about the current wave of bank mergers, replied that it all depended on the geographic market. "If there are plenty of competing institutions, there is no problem. And since the thrifts have become effective competitors in many product markets as a result of their deregulation, the numbers of competitors have been increased.

[54] Thomas Sowell, *Knowledge and Decisions* (New York: Basic Books, 1980), pp. 212–13.
[55] Ibid.
[56] William Baxter, quoted in *U.S. News and World Report*, December 13, 1983, pp. 73–74.

But in some markets, usually smaller cities and towns, bank mergers can be anticompetitive."[57]

The antitrust exemption for the insurance industry, in the current atmosphere of growing pressure for deregulation throughout the American economy, and in the face of increasing pressure for banks and savings and loan associations to be permitted to sell insurance, seems increasingly anachronistic.

[57] Ibid.

3

....

Banks and Insurance

In November, 1983, Sen. Jake Garn (R-Utah), chairman of the Senate Banking Committee, introduced major banking deregulation legislation. "We're operating the financial services industry with laws that have been on the books for decades," Senator Garn stated.[1] The proposed legislation would have allowed banks and savings and loan associations to perform securities, insurance, and real estate functions through separate subsidiaries. These provisions had been included in a measure drafted by the Treasury Department and sponsored by Senator Garn earlier in 1983 at the request of the Reagan administration.

The administration plan, which was a major component of the Garn bill, would have permitted banks and savings and loan associations to underwrite municipal revenue bonds, sponsor mutual funds, and engage in insurance and real estate activities through holding company subsidiaries. The bill also included provisions to: (1) require the Federal Reserve to pay interest on the reserves that banks must keep at the central bank; (2) impose consumer protection and disclosure standards on consumer leasing and rental-purchase plans; (3) continue the federal override of state usury ceilings; and (4) permit states to enter into interstate bank branching agreements.[2]

In the period preceding the introduction of Senator Garn's major legislation, banking had undergone a series of deregulation measures. Many

[1] Jake Garn, quoted in *Washington Times*, November 17, 1983.
[2] Cited in ibid.

usury laws had been eliminated and most federal restraints removed on what commercial banks and savings institutions paid on small deposits. Writing in the *New York Times*, Robert A. Bennett reported: "As a result of deregulation of interest rates, individuals and small businesses have received an estimated $40 billion more than they would have earned from ordinary passbook savings accounts, on which banks were not allowed to pay more than 5-1/4 per cent. This has sharply increased the institutions' cost of funds." [3]

Many small bankers have complained that rate deregulation came so fast that adjusting to it has been very difficult. Kenneth Guenther, executive vice-president of the Independent Bankers Association, which represents small banks, has said, "A lot of banks were hurt because, slam-bang, $400 billion moved out of low-yielding accounts in one year." [4]

Most larger banks, however, are seeking much broader powers at the present time. They want to enter the insurance business, and underwrite tax-exempt bonds and, in some cases, corporate securities. Savings banks and savings and loan associations have already been allowed to perform many new services, such as making commercial loans. The services that commercial banks may offer have not been expanded substantially, but they have moved into some fields—such as stock brokerage—that they avoided in the past.

The legal status of banking—both now and in the future—remains unclear and uncertain. For example, federal law restricts interstate banking, but this has not stopped the banks. In December, 1983, Citicorp, the large bank holding company in New York, received permission from the Federal Home Loan Bank Board to buy First Federal Savings and Loan Association of Chicago, which had assets of $3.95 billion. Also in December, Citicorp received permission to buy New Biscayne Federal Savings and Loan of Miami, which had assets of $18 billion.

The *Wall Street Journal* asked: "So what *can't* banks do? . . . Almost nothing, it turns out. They can lend money to just about anybody. Big banks make business loans, credit-card and consumer loans, and mortgage loans through nationwide networks of lending offices. And although banks still can't set up out-of-state branches to accept deposits, they can, as Citicorp shows, take deposits by buying S and Ls." [5] John H. McGillicuddy,

[3] Ibid.
[4] Ibid.
[5] *Wall Street Journal*, December 19, 1983.

chairman of Manufacturers Hanover Corporation, has remarked, "You can call it by a lot of names, but we really think we're in the interstate banking business now."[6]

For many years, none of this could take place. Federal and state laws generally prohibited banks from setting up deposit-taking offices in other states. The McFaddan Act, passed in 1927, gave federally chartered banks only the same rights to set up branches as state banks. Until recently, the law kept federally chartered banks in check. The Douglas Amendment to the Bank Holding Company Act, adopted in 1956, barred a bank holding company from acquiring a bank outside its home state unless the laws of the other state expressly permitted such an action.

In 1970, Congress decided to permit bank holding companies to engage in consumer finance, leasing, commercial finance, and mortgage banking outside the states in which they were based. Major bank holding companies such as Citicorp, Manufacturers Hanover, BankAmerica, and Security Pacific established hundreds of lending offices across the United States. In the case of Citicorp, its Person-to-Person consumer finance subsidiary has 112 offices in 31 states. The holding company has $10.5 billion in housing loans outstanding, only $2.5 billion of which are in New York State, where its Citibank unit is based. Some large banking organizations have also established industrial banks, state-chartered institutions that generally take consumer deposits and make consumer loans. Citicorp has them in three states and is seeking licenses in four other states.

Beyond this, banks have been able to establish offices outside their home states to conduct other activities. These include "loan production" offices for commercial business, offices that handle the banking needs of foreign companies, and discount brokerage offices. Security Pacific, for example, is based in Los Angeles and has discount brokerage offices in New York, Tennessee, Louisiana, Texas, and Florida.

Walter Wriston, chairman of Citicorp, told the *Wall Street Journal* "When the statutes are changed [to allow full interstate banking], we can change the sign and be there with promises already made, computer systems operating and customers being called on."

The *Wall Street Journal* reported: "Banks have learned that they don't even need offices to bank nationwide; a lot of banking business is being done by mail or telephone. Citicorp . . . has seven million credit-card

[6]Ibid.

holders nationwide and offers them certificates of deposit and money-market accounts. Many banks are also linking their automated-teller machines in nationwide networks that let customers get cash but not make deposits. The one thing banks haven't been able to do is take deposits in their out-of-state offices. That rule generally still holds, but banks are finding ways around it. One way they've done that is by acquiring ailing deposit-taking institutions in other states. Citicorp, for example, bought Fidelity Savings and Loan Association of San Francisco in 1982. Now called Citicorp Savings, it has 90 branches in California and assets of $3 billion. Similarly . . . after Seafirst Corp. of Seattle had run into trouble from problem loans, San Francisco–based BankAmerica—with special state and federal approval—took over Seafirst."[7]

The most striking example of the trend came in December, 1983, when Citicorp received permission to move into the Illinois and Florida banking markets, subject to approval by the Federal Reserve Board. Barry F. Sullivan, chairman and chief executive officer of First Chicago Corporation stated, "Citicorp's entry into the local marketplace is further evidence that there are backdoor entries to interstate banking."[8]

In the New England region, Massachusetts, Connecticut, and Rhode Island have a regional banking system that allows cross-border mergers with banks in states that have similar laws. This idea of regional banking systems is now under discussion in other parts of the country. If adopted, such a plan would provide smaller banks with the opportunity to combine and grow stronger. David Kemper, president of Commerce Bancshares of Kansas City, said that with such a regional approach, "you have banks that can compete with any bank in the country."[9]

Such regional arrangements, observers point out, have often been set into motion in order to exclude the large banks. As a result, these larger banks are now seeking other loopholes in state laws. Some states have passed laws allowing out-of-state banks to acquire local banks if their home state has a similar law. Other states permit out-of-state banks to have banks for special purposes, such as issuing credit cards. Citicorp, as a result of such legislation, now has special-purpose banks in South Dakota and Delaware and has applications for full-service banking licenses in South Dakota and Maine and a special-purpose license in Maryland. Citicorp is also ne-

[7] Ibid.
[8] Ibid.
[9] Ibid.

gotiating to purchase a bank in Massachusetts, where it is challenging regional limits on bank mergers. Michael Rosen, a banking attorney, has argued that "the state legislatures are doing piecemeal what Congress is declining to do on a nationwide basis." [10]

On Capitol Hill, it is believed unlikely that Congress will soon move in the direction of promoting full interstate banking. Small-town bankers, who are concerned about the possibility of being overrun by the larger urban banks, have pledged to stop any interstate banking bill. Lester Souba, president of David City Bank in David City, Nebraska, has expressed the view of such bankers, who have widespread influence in the Congress, where rural voters often are able to exert more influence than those from urban areas. Under an interstate banking system, he declared, the big urban banks will end up "taking Nebraska money and investing it in California-condominiums or foreign countries." [11]

Banks and savings and loan associations have changed their views of their own function as the economy has changed and as the forces calling for deregulation have grown, not only with regard to banking, but in the economy as a whole.

Commercial lending is an area into which savings and loan associations are increasingly moving. Some thirty-five savings associations on the Pacific Coast have formed a syndicate to finance real estate development and make other big business loans. Savings and loans are moving into other financial services, too. Many now sell stocks and bonds as well as provide investment counseling. A large number of associations have joined with INVEST, a nationwide brokerage founded by four savings and loan companies. Within a single year INVEST grew to 650 broker-dealers in lobbies and branch offices of eighty savings institutions. Goldome, a Buffalo-based savings bank, is one of many major savings institutions that began offering a full line of consumer insurance, including life insurance, annuities, and homeowner's protection policies.

In December, 1983, a high-level task force in the Reagan administration took the first step toward easing and evening federal regulation of financial institutions, but avoided the issue of bringing all regulation under a single agency. The group of thirteen regulators and government officials, headed by Vice-President George Bush, announced that it had approved

[10] Ibid.
[11] Ibid.

thirty recommendations covering the federal depository insurance system, regulation of banks and thrift institutions that compete directly, and elimination of duplicate federal and state regulations.[12]

Because of opposition from the Federal Reserve Board, the Bush group declined to tackle the most controversial issue: creating a federal banking commission out of existing agencies. Under such an arrangement, the Federal Reserve Board would lose some of its power. Donald T. Regan, serving as secretary of the treasury and the task force's vice-chairman, hoped that a compromise on the issue could be worked out. "The recommendations represent a major step forward toward our goal of simplifying bank regulations and reducing wasteful and unnecessary duplication," said Regan. The changes were to be sent to the Cabinet Council on Economic Affairs and then to the president for review before they went to Congress as legislative proposals.[13]

Under current law, regulation of financial institutions depends not on the type of business they do, but on how they are chartered. The Federal Reserve Board, the Federal Home Loan Bank Board, the Federal Deposit Insurance Corporation, and various state agencies all regulate some financial institutions. This has led to situations in which savings institutions compete with commercial banks while continuing to enjoy the government borrowing privileges accorded to thrifts, while commercial banks making home mortgage loans are barred from the special programs created for other home-loan lenders.

The Bush task force recommended that institutions performing the same functions be regulated and insured by the same agencies regardless of the nature of the charter under which they operate. The recommendations established a minimum percentage of housing loans that must be in an institution's portfolio to qualify for the special advantages of thrift institutions. The measure can be seen as a backlash against the new powers granted to savings and loan associations in 1982 by Congress and an attempt to return them to more traditional residential mortgage lending.

While the three separate federal insurance agencies—for banks, savings and loan associations, and credit unions—would be maintained, the premiums paid by thrifts would be raised gradually to equal those of banks. In addition, the insurers would base their premiums on risk, instead of

---

[12] *Washington Post*, December 24, 1983, p. D-1.
[13] Quoted in ibid.

charging sound and shaky institutions the same rate as they now do. The panel recommended that the government gradually phase out full insurance for large deposits in failed institutions.[14] The regulators approved giving regulation of all securities activities by banks to the Securities and Exchange Commission and leaving all antitrust enforcement to the Justice Department. The regulators agreed to reduce federal oversight in states that have strong regulatory programs.

In the *New York Times*, journalist Kenneth B. Noble wrote: "The Administration has made consolidation of the Government's banking agencies part of its drive to reduce the regulation of business, but like other aspects of the drive it seems to be grinding to a halt. The Bush group had planned to send a bill to Congress this fall [1983]. Now, officials of several agencies say, it seems unlikely that the Administration will resolve its thinking soon." [15]

Noble pointed out: "The Vice President, Mr. Volcker, Mr. Regan and other principal members of the group were supposed to meet at Camp David, the Presidential retreat, on October 31 to settle their recommendations. The meeting was canceled, partly because the Treasury felt Mr. Bush's staff had prepared it inadequately. An adversarial relationship has developed between Mr. Bush's staff, headed by Richard C. Breeden, and the Federal Reserve. The staff has suggested, in memorandums circulated to financial agencies, that Congress limit Fed supervision to the 20 largest banks. Mr. Volcker finds that unacceptable. In private conversations he has argued that the central bank's responsibility for managing the money supply and maintaining the stability of the financial system requires it to keep supervision of state-chartered banks and holding companies."

Another concern was that any proposal to consolidate the federal regulatory agencies would make it impossible to achieve passage in 1984 of the bill introduced by Senator Garn to expand the investment powers of banks. This fear proved to be well founded.

The *New York Times* reported, "In what has become an increasingly bitter turf battle, C. Todd Conover, the Comptroller of the Currency, and William Isaac, the chairman of the Federal Deposit Insurance Corporation, have both signaled that they favor stripping the Fed of some of its bank supervisory powers." [16]

---

[14] *Wall Street Journal*, December 24, 1983.
[15] Kenneth Noble, "Deadlock over Bank Deregulation," *Wall Street Journal*, December 12, 1983.
[16] Ibid.

The other members of Vice-President Bush's task force included the heads of the Council of Economic Advisors, the Office of Management and Budget, the Justice Department, the Treasury Department, the Securities and Exchange Commission, the Commodity Futures Trading Commission, the National Credit Union Administration, and the Federal Home Loan Bank Board.

The proposed Bush plan would consolidate most of the government's regulation of commercial banks in a new, single federal banking agency. The Federal Reserve Bank would retain supervision over the twenty largest banks, but it would lose its regulatory authority over most of the commercial banks that are members of the Federal Reserve System. The bank now examines about eleven hundred state-chartered banks that are members of the Fed and all forty-five hundred bank holding companies.

Under the plan, the staff of the comptroller of the currency would become the nucleus of the new Federal Banking Agency, and it would assume many of the noninsurance functions of the Federal Deposit Insurance Corporation. The proposed plan would also expand the powers of the Federal Home Loan Bank Board to include regulation of some smaller commercial banks in addition to savings and loan associations. This agency would be renamed the Federal Thrift Agency.

Much discussion has been generated by the various proposals for change in the regulation of banking. Speaking before the Conference of State Bank Supervisors, Sen. John Heinz (R-Pennsylvania) noted: "On the one hand, our financial system is the world's most dynamic. On the other, it is also the world's most stable. Nowhere in the world is the depositor and the investor offered greater protection or is there greater competition among institutions. A simple testimonial to our unique dynamism is the existence of less than 150 competing banks in West Germany, France and Great Britain combined, less than the number of banks in my home state of Pennsylvania alone. Yet once again, state bank supervisors, state legislatures and Congress are under intense pressure to abandon this tried and true system, pressure from the very institutions that have prospered under structured competition and from those who seek to root out government regulation as an evil in and of itself." [17]

After the depression, Congress put a legislative wall between the banking and securities and commerce industries. Senator Heinz stated: "Ever since this separation there has been a continuous effort by various

[17] *Congressional Record*, November 17, 1983, p. S16709.

individual institutions and trade associations to recapture the prohibited powers. I would point out that one man's 'deregulation' is another man's 'reconcentration.' Reconcentration would mean abandoning our carefully segmented financial system of the past 50 years for a return to the interwoven pre-crash financial conglomerates that dominated U.S. financial markets until the bank holiday of 1933. Over the years, dozens of arguments for reconcentrating non-banking financial services back into depository institutions have been tried out on Congress: everything from increased capital formation to better financing for small business or local government. Now we are told that there is a competitive imbalance that threatens the depository industry, that the separation of depository and non-depository institutions has irrevocably broken down, and that there is a customer-led revolution that Congress must embrace." [18]

Expressing his own skeptical attitude, and that of some of his colleagues in the Congress, Senator Heinz declared: "Although the term 'deregulation' has become a catch phrase for winning voter approval, Congress is skeptical of arguments that equate reforming the competitive balance between banks and non-banks with the repeal or radical revision of the basic separation of the two. Lingering impressions of bank failures and their role in the Depression remain important political factors. . . . The first reaction Congress will have in its search for a new consensus is 'if it ain't broke don't fix it.' In part, that's because you'll get the blame if it does break. A corollary is that 'if it can be patched up, it ain't broke.' " [19]

Senator Heinz concluded: "The measure of whether the system is broken is neither the number of banks in existence nor their profitability. For Congress, the measure must be the level of the system's safety and soundness, that is, whether our capital markets are orderly and the saving public is protected. Congress strongly believes that it must ensure that when a person places his or her life savings in a bank, he will be 100% sure that his money will be there when he needs it. This is essential if we are to avoid a loss of public confidence that if the nation's pool of savings is to be tapped and converted to the long term credit on which our nation's businesses depend. If Congress does not find the system to be broken, there is only one other standard on which a consensus favoring reconcentration of deposit and non-deposit investment functions can be based. That is if it can be

[18] Ibid.
[19] Ibid.

shown 'beyond a reasonable doubt' that the public can be provided better services with at least the same level of security." [20]

The increasing competition among financial institutions makes it clear that traditionally distinct institutions are moving to provide a complete array of financial services. Insurance companies are introducing brokerage services and even purchasing banks to provide insured depository services. Banks are seeking to test the existing federal and state laws that limit the powers of banks. There has been growing concern over the ability of regulators, especially those at the state level, to cope with the changes that are occurring and to protect depositors and policyholders. This concern by state legislators was discussed by writer Douglas McLeod:

> Financial services conglomerates are growing so quickly that they've outstripped the ability of state regulators to keep watch over them, a new study concludes. In a period of "overnight takeovers" and the blurring of lines among the insurance, banking and securities industries, state insurance departments may not be able to protect the public against insolvencies unless they have better equipment and more manpower, says the study prepared by a task force of the Conference of Insurance Legislators.
>
> The report declares: "In the fast mix and match of their companies and products, America's financial leaders are doing some imaginative things with other people's money. Many of their efforts are very worthwhile. But others are proving a little too inventive, aggressive and perhaps even reckless, and have raised serious questions as to the ability of regulators to keep watch." [21]

The report, entitled *Risk . . . Reality . . . Reason In Financial Services Deregulation*,[22] was prepared by the Conference of Insurance Legislators (COIL) Task Force on Multi-Purpose Financial Products and Regulatory Initiative and presented to the annual meeting of the Society of Chartered Property and Casualty Underwriters in September, 1983, by the task force's chairman, John R. Dunne, a state senator in New York.

"Like it or not, there are some real dangers with the deregulation of financial services," Dunne said. "In this day of quick takeovers and instantaneous fund transfers, a company holding millions of dollars in policyholders' funds can go broke in no time and it could take insurance regulators months to learn about it." [23]

The COIL report pointed to the Baldwin-United Corporation as a cur-

[20] Ibid.
[21] Cited in *Business Insurance*, September 26, 1983.
[22] Reprinted in *Congressional Record*, November 15, 1983, p. E5533.
[23] Quoted in *Business Insurance*, September 26, 1983.

rent and ongoing case in point. The Cincinnati-based Baldwin-United announced in September, 1983, its intention to sell its largest subsidiary, MGIC Investment Corporation, to help pay off the thousands of holders of single-premium deferred annuities issued by six Baldwin life insurance units that were then in rehabilitation.

According to the COIL report, in trying to deal with the Baldwin-United controversy, the insurance regulatory system in Arkansas, "by its own admission, came perilously close to breaking down." [24] The Arkansas Insurance Department's investigation of questionable loans and transactions among various Baldwin-United subsidiaries did not even begin until after the transactions had already been closed out, the report noted. The Arkansas department also encountered long delays in obtaining information about Baldwin and its affiliates from the insurance departments in the other forty-nine states and had to seek outside help when its own staff could not handle the "regulatory overload" imposed by the situation.

Observations that resulted from COIL's six-month review of financial services and the adequacy of current regulatory systems, the thirteen-member task force, composed of state legislators with an interest in insurance matters, included the fact that state insurance departments cannot keep up with the transactions of financial services conglomerates because they don't have the computer capability to rival that of the companies they are regulating. The computers of insurers and their affiliates perform in seconds what would pile up on the desks of regulators, the task force's report observed. While a few states (e.g., Illinois, California, and New York) have "reasonably current" computer facilities, most regulators are at a disadvantage when it comes to monitoring reserve adequacy and other solvency data.

The so-called "early warning system" developed by the National Association of Insurance Commissioners, a basically manual system for identifying potential solvency problems, "may not spot and relay insolvency information until months after the danger should have become clear," COIL observed. The report concluded that "a system that furnishes information once yearly and then five months after the fact limits what regulators can do." [25]

The basis for regulation of insurer solvency is still the triennial examination, a report that takes months to produce. For example, the triennial

[24] *Congressional Record*, November 15, 1983, p. E5533.
[25] Ibid.

examination of the Metropolitan Life Insurance Company by the New York Insurance Department for the period ending December 31, 1978, was still not complete in September, 1983.

The integration of insurance with other financial services requires state insurance departments to monitor information traditionally outside their normal scope, further impeding efforts to keep pace with the action of the marketplace.

Many insurance departments cannot offer attractive enough salaries to draw the brightest people away from private companies. Budget restrictions and compensation parity requirements among departments of state government all contribute to the difficulty many insurance departments have maintaining adequate staffs to handle their growing responsibilities.

Because regulators' preventive steps may not always head off an insolvency, the "patchwork quilt" of guaranty fund laws in the various states needs to be made more uniform and comprehensive, according to the COIL report. Many holes remain, the report said, noting California's failure to create a fund to cover life, accident, and health policies. In addition, the only function of many state guaranty funds is to bail a state out of fiscal crisis, as happened in New York in 1982 when the legislature appropriated $77 million from the Motor Vehicle Liability Security Fund to balance the state's budget. The report argued that states should make similar efforts to revise insurance holding company and investment laws to make it easier for regulators to monitor solvency and protect policyholders in case of insolvency. It declared that the kind of aggressive deregulation pursued by some states to attract business and promote economic development represents "the bad side of deregulation and could lead to a deregulatory free-for-all."

To assist insurance departments in coping with some of the problems noted in its review, the COIL task force made a number of recommendations. First, state insurance departments should have access to state-of-the-art computer equipment that would allow them to monitor insurance company solvency continuously. To start, insurance departments might require only relatively simple microcomputers; the cost of such systems would not be staggering, the task force maintained. The report estimated that the nonrecurring expenses of buying hardware and software and training workers to use a microcomputer might total about $750,000. Recurring expenses of entering yearly and quarterly insurance company financial data and buying supplies might add up to $350,000 per year, the report concluded.

After state departments had their own small computers, a larger mainframe computer could be purchased to handle larger amounts of information, the COIL report suggested. Operated by the National Association of Insurance Commissioners, this central system might cost about $4 million, including hardware, staff, and network charges to individual insurance departments communicating with the system through their own microcomputers.

Next, the report said that legislatures should increase the budgets of state insurance departments to allow for the purchase of modern equipment and the hiring and training of highly qualified staff. State legislatures should strengthen insurance holding company investment and guaranty fund laws to provide more security for policyholders in cases of insolvency.

The report also declared that state officials should start communicating with federal officials who regulate financial services outside the insurance industry so that the state regulators could participate in the formation of a national policy and "avoid being squeezed out of their sphere of influence by federal officials who principally regulate the other financial services." [26]

Many insurance commissioners, state regulators, and insurance industry executives have expressed their opposition to the proposed banking deregulation, which would permit banks to enter the insurance business. Bruce W. Foudree, Iowa commissioner of insurance, has argued that banking and insurance do not belong together because "combining banking and underwriting risks is a very dangerous thing, with very dangerous potential." He criticized the Reagan administration's banking deregulation bill for permitting such a combination of activities, particularly because the bill did not give insurance regulators oversight of "affiliated transactions." Foudree stated, "It's crucial that we have oversight in asset and dividend transfers if banks enter the insurance field." About the financially troubled Baldwin-United Corporation, Foudree said, "That's a good example of what can go wrong and it's been helpful in communicating to the federal government what can happen when transactions of financial affiliates do not have sufficient oversight." [27]

Edward S. Cabot, vice-president and associate general counsel of The Equitable, discussing the Garn-sponsored Financial Institutions Deregula-

---

[26] Ibid.

[27] Media release, "Insurance Commissioner, Attorneys Hit Banking Deregulation," American Council of Life Insurance, November 14, 1983.

tion Act (FIDA), has argued that the life insurance industry might be making an error in one of its principal arguments. "In opposing bank entry into the insurance business, we have argued that there can be no 'level playing field.' In making this argument we make at least this concession: that if there could be a level playing field, bank entry would be all right." That argument, he declared, misses the more fundamental question of whether banks, because of their critical functions as fiscal intermediaries, should be barred from expanding into new fields. "We must assure against excessive risk-taking by banks and insure their stability," Cabot said. Referring to FIDA provisions that would attempt to "wall off" insurance operations in separate bank holding company subsidiaries, he noted: "The bank holding company structure is neither a substitute for prudent management nor a protection against excessive risk. I'm not one of those who believe bank entry into our business is inevitable." [28]

Robert A. Beck, chairman of the American Council of Life Insurance, has expressed the view that Congress must develop a legal framework to deal with issues arising from the rapidly changing world of banking deregulation. Beck, also chairman and chief executive officer of The Prudential, said that serious issues are developing that concern the life insurance industry and that they are not being answered by current "piecemeal" legislative and regulatory responses. Such issues include whether banking deregulation will lead to excessive control of the financial services industry by a small number of institutions, whether federal guaranties should stand behind some financial activities, and whether banks will gain an unfair advantage in insurance sales through tie-ins with other banking services. "As an industry, we have favored a limited moratorium on the changes that are taking place," he declared, "but only if Congress would use this time to come up with a response that is fair to all involved." [29]

Beck said that the insurance industry had endured a great deal of internal struggle over the issues of federal taxes and unisex legislation, but that it had survived these issues and become stronger in the process. "As the issue of deregulation heats up," he stated, "I hope we don't have to fight each other to determine who our enemies are and what the real issues are. This is definitely one issue where our industry must stand together. . . .

[28] Edward Cabot speech to American Council of Life Insurance, Washington, D.C., November 13, 1983.
[29] Robert Beck speech to American Council of Life Insurance, Washington, D.C., November 15, 1983.

We can't take the attitude that politics is beneath us, or we won't survive. We don't need to become partisan, but we do need to be pragmatic and work more effectively in our own best interests." Urging greater support for the Life Insurance Political Action Committee and reminding company leaders that the greatest political clout is the "hometown touch," he concluded, "Our CEOs must get more personally involved in political contact if we want to influence future decisions that affect our business."

Concern about efforts to permit banks to engage in the sale of insurance has produced heated response from insurance agents as well as insurance companies. Frank J. Patterson, chairman of the Independent Insurance Agents of America Federal Affairs Committee, has pointed out: "Less than a year has gone by since Congress enacted legislation limiting bank holding company insurance authority (Title VI of the Garn/St. Germain Act), but already a new effort to eliminate the barriers between banking and insurance is in full swing. "Against a backdrop of a rapidly changing financial services marketplace, and bank regulators prepared to push to the limit, and sometimes beyond, the interpretation of existing law, large bank holding companies and the Treasury Department have combined forces to gain Congressional action on the Financial Institutions Deregulation Act (FIDA). . . .

"FIDA would dramatically expand the powers of bank holding companies and reduce the Federal Reserve Board's supervisory authority over bank holding companies. Among the new bank holding company activities FIDA would explicitly authorize are insurance sales and underwriting. . . ." [30]

The Reagan administration's goal in sponsoring FIDA, which would also permit real estate and securities brokerage and entry into any other financial services the Federal Reserve Board determines to be of a "financial nature," is, stated Patterson, "to put commercial banks and nondepository financial service organizations (like Merrill Lynch) on an equal competitive footing." [31]

The insurance agents, however, have not seen it quite that way. In statements to House and Senate committees and in a letter to the Treasury Department, IIAA criticized the deregulation act as "an attempt to ratify

---

[30] Ibid.
[31] Frank Patterson, *Independent Agent*, October, 1983, p. 13.

current market turmoil rather than construct a framework for banking activities that reflects long-term public policy considerations." [32]

Patterson continued: "Among the public policy considerations IIAA is most concerned about is banks' ability to tie insurance sales to extensions of credit, thus competing unfairly with unaffiliated insurance agents, and depriving consumers of freedom to choose insurance products outside the loan transaction. Given the continuing danger of credit tie-ins, and given Congress's decision less than a year ago to reaffirm the traditional separation between banking and insurance, IIAA sees no reason for a departure from existing public policy recommended by the Treasury bill, and will work for the Treasury bill's defeat in Congress." [33]

The Independent Insurance Agents Association is also concerned, Patterson reported, about what is now taking place on the state level. "At the state level, bank holding companies (BHCs) continue to seek ways around federal limits on their activities through state legislatures. Thus, in South Dakota, Delaware, and several other states, large money-center BHCs have succeeded or tried to get state laws enacted that expand the powers of state chartered banks to permit, among other things, state chartered bank insurance sales and underwriting. By acquiring the state chartered bank as a subsidiary, the BHCs argue they can engage in the new activities otherwise denied them by federal law. IIAA is challenging this argument in Congress and at the Federal Reserve Board." [34]

In a presentation before the Illinois Insurance Law Study Commission, Thomas E. Wilson, a partner in the Washington, D.C., law firm of Charles, Karalekas, McCahill, and Wilson, who serves as Washington counsel for the Independent Insurance Agents of America, set forth the opposition of the insurance industry and insurance agents to permitting banks into the insurance field. Wilson declared: "The essence of our concern has been that the enormous resources of banking organizations, coupled with their control over the decisions of whether to extend or withhold credit, provides them with the capacity to exercise an unusual amount of influence over the choice made by borrowers when nonbanking services are sold in conjunction with extensions of credit." [35]

[32] Ibid.
[33] Ibid.
[34] Ibid.
[35] Thomas Wilson, "Keeping Banks in Banking," p. 43.

With the enactment of the Garn–St. Germain Depository Institutions Act of 1982 (Public Law 97-320), Section 601 contained an express prohibition against most bank holding company insurance activities. Wilson declared: "Before the ink of President Reagan's signature had dried, major bank holding companies were on their way to South Dakota to embark upon what was to be a successful effort to persuade South Dakota officials to authorize South Dakota banks to engage in 'all facets of the insurance business.' The express intention of the South Dakota law was to permit out-of-state bank holding companies to acquire South Dakota banks with the view toward exploiting their new insurance powers, thereby circumventing the insurance restrictions of Garn/St. Germain." [36]

It was Wilson's view that the sale of insurance by bank holding companies was not in the public interest. He noted: "At least since 1864, the nation's banking legislation has required separation between banking and other forms of commerce. Since the establishment of the national bank system, Congress has prohibited national banks from engaging in any activity that was not banking or an incidental power of banks. When Congress enacted the Bank Holding Company Act of 1956 ('BHC ACT') and the 1970 Amendments thereto, it continued and extended that principle. Consequently, the BHC Act generally prohibits companies that own banks from owning the shares of any company that is not a bank." [37]

The limited exceptions to the BHC Act's general nonbanking prohibition appear in Section 4 of the BHC Act, with the principal exception continued in subsection (c)(8). Since 1970, Section 4 (c)(8) has essentially provided that a bank holding company may engage in a nonbanking activity if, and only if, it can make an affirmative showing that (1) the particular activity in which it wishes to participate is "closely related" to banking, and (2) its participation in the activity can reasonably be expected to result in benefits to the public that outweigh possible adverse effects. The insurance industry has expressed the view that, when it comes to actions that are permitted in selling property and casualty insurance, these statutory requirements cannot be met.

It is the view of the insurance industry that bank holding companies have the power to compete unfairly. Wilson has declared: "Banking institutions are the principal source of commercial credit in our economy. As

[36] Ibid.
[37] Ibid.

such, they dominate a very vital element of the economy. Their control over loans provides them with a unique opportunity to influence where borrowers purchase any nonbanking service that might be sold in conjunction with extensions of credit. For these reasons, bank holding companies should be restricted from engaging in nonbanking activities (including the sale of insurance), unless a compelling justification can be provided for departing from the well-established norm." [38]

The principal stated concern of the insurance industry was expressed by the Federal Reserve Board in 1969 in testimony before the Financial Institutions Subcommittee of the Senate Banking Committee. The spokesman for the board stated: "Because of the inferior bargaining position of the debtor, he may be susceptible to the loan officer's suggestions concerning choice of coverage, premium rates, insurer, and agent. As a result, the debtor easily may receive the impression that his loan application may be more favorably considered if he follows such suggestions." [39]

In the conference report issued for the 1970 amendments to the BHC Act, Congress made a similar point: "Tie-ins occur where a customer is forced or induced to accept other products and services along with that product which he seeks. Such tie-ins may result from actual coercion by a seller or from a customer's realization that he stands a better chance of securing a scarce and important commodity (such as credit) by volunteering to accept other products or services rather than seeking them in the competitive market place. In either case, competition is adversely affected, as customers no longer purchase a product or service on its own economic merit." [40]

Wilson argued: "The concerns expressed by both the Board and Congress have in fact proven to be well-founded. Experience since the 1970 Amendments clearly indicates that lending institutions do indeed have the power to compete with retail property and casualty insurance agents in ways that are inconsistent with the public interest.

"Most often, evidence of coercion in the sale of insurance does not manifest itself in borrower complaints. The very thing that provides the lender with the power to coerce (that is, the lender's power to grant or withhold credit) is likely to make an offended borrower reluctant to make a for-

[38] Ibid.
[39] Quoted in ibid., pp. 43, 45.
[40] Ibid., p. 45.

mal complaint. Furthermore, even if such complaint is made, actual coercion would be extremely difficult to prove. . . . Nevertheless, ample evidence does exist that both coercive and voluntary tying do occur."[41]

The following letter is cited, which appeared in testimony before the Senate Banking Committee on S.72 in 1978:

"I regret very much the incident concerning Mr. X. I based my decision regarding this matter on what I thought to be the best interest of Mr. X and the bank. As I indicated to Mr. X, our bank could not accept the loan unless we were allowed to write the credit life insurance. As I discussed by phone, the primary reason for this request to write the insurance was because this action increased the return of income on the loan by a good margin. Had our bank been denied this additional income, we could not have approved the loan. Because of the extremely tight credit situation, I feel Mr. X would not have obtained the loan elsewhere. Therefore, I believe our bank to be doing Mr. X service by granting this type of loan under these circumstances, with credit as tight as it is at the present.

"I can still appreciate and understand your reasoning and regret that Mr. X saw fit to cancel his policy with your company. I am hopeful this situation will not occur again in the future."[42]

In 1976, the agency of a Maryland member of the Independent Insurance Agents of America received the following letter:

Dear Bill: The purpose of this letter is to clear up any misunderstanding that may have arisen as a result of the recent changes in our insurance program. We instructed you to discontinue the automobile dealer's physical damage coverage in the package policies that you have so that we could obtain this coverage through X bank. As you know, X bank does the financing on our new car inventory. This in no way indicates dissatisfaction of your service or that of the company X. As I explained to you, we feel that we have to place the coverage with the bank because we so frequently request special favors of them. Even if their premiums were to prove a little higher, we would still feel obligated in this way. Please also be assured that this in no way implies that the bank has forced us to make this change in our insurance program. . . .[43]

Mr. Wilson advanced this view: "These letters are examples of both coercive and voluntary tying at work. The second letter dramatically illustrates why borrowers are not likely to complain, even if they do feel that they have been coerced. That letter also graphically points out the disincentive that banking institutions have to sell insurance at lower costs. It is clear from the letter that, even if the insurance sold by the bank costs more, con-

[41] Ibid.
[42] Quoted in ibid.
[43] Cited in ibid.

sumers may be willing to pay the additional amount simply to protect their credit relationship."[44]

A 1974 FTC study revealed that significant "tying" between sales of insurance and extension of credit was occurring. The study stated that consumer complaint is "typical of the type of credit insurance complaint the division receives from consumers. The complainant, an unmarried attorney, sought to finance the purchase of a car by obtaining a bank loan. He asserts that when he arrived at the bank to pick up his check he was told that no loan would be made unless he elected credit insurance. Since the consumer had obligated himself to purchase the car the next day, he signed the insurance election in order to obtain the loan and unsuccessfully attempted, at a subsequent time, to obtain a refund of unearned insurance premiums."[45]

The study provided some clue as to why few complaints of explicit tying are brought out: "Once a consumer has signed the credit insurance election, he is without a remedy and has little hope of proving before a court that he did not elect the coverage. Even a complaint to a regulatory agency, including the Federal Trade Commission, will produce action only if the incident is part of an identifiable and deliberate companywide pattern of conduct. In addition, the investigation of such practices is a time-consuming one requiring the regulatory agency to gather and analyze insurance sales data and interview large numbers of consumers. Agency action will normally come so late in time as to have no effect on the consumer's own transaction."[46]

A study conducted by the Federal Reserve Board sought to show that explicit tying between the granting of credit and the sales of the credit-related insurance is "practically nonexistent" and that implicit pressures brought by lenders on borrowers are neither "very strong nor widespread in the industry." The study found, however, that almost two-thirds of the consumers surveyed had purchased insurance to obtain credit, even though such insurance is not generally a condition for obtaining a loan. In addition, more than 25 percent said that when credit was extended to them, they were told that they had to or were strongly urged to purchase credit insurance.

Mercantile Bancorporation, Inc., and Commerce Bancshares, Inc.,

[44] Ibid.
[45] Ibid., p. 47.
[46] Ibid.

sought prior approval from the Federal Reserve Board in 1981 to sell property and casualty insurance. The Independent Insurance Agents of America opposed approval of those applications. The Mercantile and Commerce proposals were before an administrative law judge for formal hearings in 1982. The records show that both bank holding companies had average credit life–loan penetration rates of more than 60 percent. Numerous banking subsidiaries of both bank holding companies had credit life penetration rates above 80 percent. Four of Commerce's thirty-eight banking subsidiaries had credit life penetration rates of 100 percent.

Memoranda from Commerce's insurance subsidiary to the CEOs of Commerce's banks revealed that extraordinary steps were urged to sell credit life and credit disability insurance. The administrative law judge in those proceedings characterized the evidence on the tie-in issue as having been provided by an "impressive array of expert witnesses" whose testimony he found to be "quite persuasive." [47] On the strength of the evidence, the judge concluded that both bank holding companies had been guilty of tying sales of credit life insurance to extensions of credit. Despite the evidence, the Federal Reserve Board approved the Mercantile and Commerce applications. The board's orders went before the United States Court of Appeals for the Eighth Circuit on review.

The Reagan administration has been sharply critical of the insurance industry's opposition to banking deregulation. In fact, speaking to the American Council of Life Insurance in November, 1983, Secretary of the Treasury Regan told his audience that they should end their opposition to the administration's banking deregulation bill, warning that they were "an industry courting chaos. . . . If the insurance industry does nothing but oppose change, it risks being left out of the debate on the direction of change," Regan declared. "It is not sensible to stand by and yell 'Never!' With or without federal legislation, market forces will impel banks and their affiliates to take the steps necessary to enable them to compete. It is a matter of survival and no series of laws can be drawn tightly enough to prevent a determined industry from finding ways to meet the demands of the market." [48] Regan predicted that unless the proposed Financial Institutions Deregulation Act (FIDA) or something like it were passed, the states, particularly those hardest hit by the recession, would be "competing to see who can provide the loosest of [controls on] competition" for banks and other financial institutions.

Responding to the insurance industry's assertions that banks might use their federally insured funds to finance insurance operations, Regan maintained that FIDA addresses that problem by permitting bank holding companies, not banks themselves, to engage in new activities. He also addressed the matter of tie-in sales, when bank customers might feel that getting a loan depends on buying their insurance, even if no actual coercion by the bank occurs. While such activity by banks is currently prohibited, Regan added: "We have gone further. The bill provides for a private right of action by a trade association on behalf of a member in order to obtain an injunction against an institution allegedly violating the 'anti-tying' provision." [49]

Regan stated: "Much of the regulation this Administration would like to see scrapped or altered was born out of economic times or social circumstances which no longer apply. Other regulation has come simply from the government's inevitable propensity to expand and control. Dismantling the outmoded and useless regulation in a careful and organized manner will allow the market to operate as it should. And when the market is allowed to follow its course, the results are efficiency and responsiveness. Financial deregulation is but one aspect of our overall deregulatory program, but it is a very important aspect. The world of finance—personal and corporate— is changing as rapidly and dramatically as any sector of our society." [50]

What is now occurring in the insurance industry, Regan said, is "coming about precisely because of the consumer. The marketplace responds to the consumer. In this particular situation, the market is responding to the radically enhanced financial sophistication of the consumer. The high inflation of the 1970s prompted the first wave of financial sophistication on a large scale. We saw dollars fly from commercial banks and thrifts into money market mutual funds as depositors abandoned low-yielding, fixed-rate accounts. And you [in the insurance field] certainly experienced disintermediation in the form of policy loans in that staple of your industry— the whole life policy. Since then, we've seen a proliferation of new financial instruments targeted at the consumer. As more and more firms enter the financial services marketplace and diversify their activities, consumers

[49] Ibid.
[50] Ibid.

will be offered even wider varieties of financial products at competitive prices, and with greater convenience of selection and service. Life insurance companies should recognize the stake they have in this developing environment and the important role they have to play. . . . Embrace change as the means for strengthening the industry overall." [51]

Walter Wriston, chairman of Citibank/Citicorp, has stated: "Arguments against more banks owning more insurance companies place nearly all their weight on one element: speculation. The speculation runs that if banks were permitted certain freedoms, they *might* use them unfairly; they *might* take over the world, they *might* cause hives. Speculation aside, the *fact* is that the risk of conflict of interest and even dishonesty has always been, and will always be with us. By 'us' I mean all human beings including those who work for the insurance industry, the government, banks, farmers, and blackjack dealers. . . . The protection against this risk is two-fold. One is that most people in all these fields still cling to honesty, ethics, and principles. The other protection lies in our ability to pass laws and hire policemen to control those who are tempted to rise above their principles. Much nonsense has been launched arguing that the banks might break the laws against tie-in sales if they owned insurance companies. This is like saying that insurance companies might violate the securities laws since they now own brokers, or they might violate the banking laws since they own banks, or an insurance company might withhold insurance if a customer did not use its brokerage facilities. There is simply no evidence to support this. The tie-in argument is a non-starter, just as the assertion that brokers owned by insurance companies would violate securities laws is nonsense. The real issue is that protected markets are comfortable—one does not have to have a strategic plan, a pricing policy, or seek out, hire, and train people to compete with world class corporations. The free market is not without pain, particularly to those who cannot adapt." [52]

Wriston concluded: "Since there is no national federal policy on insurance, and, indeed, massive efforts are made to block any national policy, it seems odd to hear the rumor going around that the insurance lobby has joined the cry for a federal 'moratorium' on what states can permit banks to do. As Alice in Wonderland once said: 'It is curiouser and curiouser.' I seem to recall back in the thirties or forties, the Justice Depart-

[51] Ibid.
[52] Ibid.

ment tried to bring insurance companies under the federal anti-trust statutes that apply to most of us, and the Supreme Court agreed with them. Within a matter of days, two gentlemen in the Congress named McCarran and Ferguson got legislation through which overruled the Supreme Court and the Justice Department and left regulation to the state insurance commissioners. There was even a story around that some state commissioners were more than a little helpful to Congress in drafting the legislation. Reasonable people could argue that if the Federal system embodied in our Constitution is good for one set of stockholders, it is good for all. It seems to have worked in Delaware, and no doubt it will work in other states. In the banking world, we call it the dual banking system, and it has been around a long time, with very good results. . . . Today, segregated political and financial markets exist only in the minds of people who do not live in the marketplace. Indeed, the only place you can live and make that judgment is in the past. Sometimes the nonexpert says it best. Gertrude Stein was certainly not an expert in finance, but she understood better than anyone what I have been trying to say. 'The money is always there, but the pockets change; it is not in the same pockets after a change; and that is all there is to say about money.' If the consumer has his or her way, there is going to be a lot of pocket-changing." [53]

In his book *The Invisible Bankers* Andrew Tobias set forth what he believed would be an ideal system of selling and purchasing insurance, one ordained by "the Lord Himself." One element of this ideal system, he argued, would be the following: "Savings banks, commercial banks, *and anyone else* who could satisfy regulators as to the financial soundness and safeguards of their undertaking, would be allowed to sell life insurance. Savings Bank Life Insurance, for one, would not be limited to New York, Massachusetts, and Connecticut, nor to $30,000, $64,000 and $25,000 of coverage. The state legislators who retain these limits are simply bowing to the pressure of an industry that, naturally enough, fears low-priced competition." [54]

Tobias responded to the insurance industry argument that permitting banks into the field would put an end to the traditional agency system: "Allowing the banks and others to compete in the sale of life insurance (in Japan, the post office sells it) would destroy the cherished American

---

[53] Ibid.
[54] Andrew Tobias, *The Invisible Bankers* (New York: Pocket Books, 1982), p. 322.

agency system. Why? Simply because the banks could deliver the product with an efficiency the traditional life insurer cannot. Sophisticated agents would still be required to arrange group sales and to service the complicated, big-dollar cases. And a certain number of insurance agents would doubtless be recruited by the banks to serve as experts at their branches. The difference would be that where many such agents had spent countless hours addressing envelopes (yes, those handwritten envelopes with their offers of a free road atlas in exchange for your birthdate are, as often as not, addressed by the life insurance specialist himself), making cold phone calls and driving from appointment to appointment all week just to make one sale—now they might spend several hours a day actually helping people to buy life insurance. People today buy savings certificates without a salesman having driven out to their homes; so might they buy life insurance." [55]

The debate over banking deregulation—and whether or not banks will be enabled by law to enter the business of selling insurance—is likely to be heated and protracted. The insurance industry will fight this legislation with the resources at its disposal, and these are not insignificant. With Congress adjourning without passing major bank legislation in 1984, the coming years will surely see a full exposition of the various sides of the question of banking regulation and the future of the insurance industry. The *Economist* predicted, ". . . in 1985, unless there is a new round of big bank liquidity tremors, another bill like Senator Garn's is bound to be back." [56]

[55] Ibid., p. 325.
[56] *Economist*, September 29, 1984.

4

·············

Unisex Insurance Rates:
Is "Equality" Really "Inequity"?

ONE of the key elements in the continuing feminist movement is the achievement of "equality" between men and women in all respects. Of particular concern is what are viewed as economic inequities toward women.

Karen Nussbaum, executive director of "9 to 5," the National Association of Working Women, has stressed: "Pay for full-time women clerical workers is extremely low. It averages just over $11,000 a year for women, as compared with male clericals, who earn over $17,000. We feel if we could just get equal pay within our job classification we would be doing well." [1] In the recent past, 9 to 5 has entered into legal action that resulted in more than $3 million in back pay for women in publishing and banking, in addition to major pay raises for female employees in insurance, banking, and engineering, including a $1.34 million settlement from Bechtel, and a multimillion-dollar award against the state of Washington.

Still, inequality in pay between the sexes remains a subject of much concern within the women's movement. In 1980 the median salary for women managers and administrators was $12,936 compared with $23,558 for their male counterparts. A 1981 study by Wellesley researchers showed that once a woman reaches the middle-management level, she is not likely to move much farther up the corporate ladder.

Poverty, critics charge, is a social problem that hits American women particularly hard. Professor Eli Ginzberg of Columbia University has written: "Female heads of households are the disproportionate group of people

[1] Jay Cocks, "How Long Till Equality?" *Time*, July 12, 1982, p. 23.

in poverty."[2] A U.S. Census Bureau report covering 1980 noted: "About one-half of all families below the poverty level in 1980 were maintained by women with no husband present. The poverty rate for such families was 32.7%, compared with 6.2% for married-couple families, and 11% for families with a male house-holder, no wife present."[3] The report indicated that 50.8 percent of the female-headed families with related children under age eighteen were poor. Seventy-five percent of absent fathers contributed no child support at all.

Discussing the impact of the feminist movement, Philip R. Converse, president of the American Political Science Association, said: "The women's movement opened up job opportunities, and a woman is now getting some chances. My wife now has the right to go in and argue with her bosses when she thinks they are wrong. She no longer has to bring her unhappiness home with her."[4]

As the 1984 presidential election approached, there was increasing discussion of an alleged "gender gap." Adam Clymer reported in the *New York Times*: "While other leading political indicators, such as rising approval ratings for the President and squabbling among Democrats, presumably make cheerful reading at the White House, Mr. Reagan's problem with women keeps getting worse. The breadth of the problem is reflected in polls like the November 11–20 [1983] New York Times Poll, which showed that only 38 per cent of women, compared to 53 per cent of men, think President Reagan deserves re-election, and that 49 per cent of women, but just 33 per cent of men, fear he will get the United States into a war."[5]

Clymer noted: "Women who believed that men were superior to women, in qualities such as logic and honesty, were more supportive of Mr. Reagan than were other women, the poll found, but fewer and fewer women believe in those stereotypes. The poll measures how work and freedom now compete with home and hearth as essential concerns of women, who were almost as likely as men to believe that their place was on the job. While some women in the Reagan Administration convey these newer values, the men rarely do."[6]

Dottie Lynch, polltaker for Gary Hart, the Colorado senator who was

[2] Ibid., p. 24.
[3] Ibid.
[4] Quoted in ibid.
[5] Adam Clymer, "If Anything, Gender Gap Is Becoming Even Wider," *New York Times*, December 11, 1983, p. E-5.
[6] Ibid.

an unsuccessful Democratic presidential candidate in 1984, said that recent polls showed that women's issues, especially equality, do carry political weight, but perhaps not in the terms that most politicians think of them. They matter, she said, "in more real life terms than in specific legislative terms."[7] This view is shared by Robert M. Teeter, president of Market Opinion Research in Detroit and a leading Republican polltaker. "Equality is a relatively high issue with women," he said and argued that Republicans could deal with it by adopting as their own such issues as equal pay.[8] Pollster Louis Harris has called the women's vote "a new political force" in America. He has said that "there is now every indication that one of the major developments of the 1980s will be the full-blown emergence" of this force.[9]

As early as August, 1982, Reagan's problem with women voters was apparent, as a survey taken by Louis Harris and Associates showed. Only 34 percent of women rated his job performance "excellent/good," compared with 42% of men. The gap had persisted at least since the 1980 campaign, when President Jimmy Carter's strategist Pat Caddell found "an enormous male-female difference from the outset."[10]

Karlyn Keene, managing editor of *Public Opinion* magazine, published by the American Enterprise Institute, has suggested that "part of the explanation for Mr. Reagan's poorer showing with women may lie in changing currents in men's and women's political attitudes across a broad spectrum of social and political issues."[11]

The editors of *Public Opinion* examined many public opinion polls taken since 1945 and found new patterns in attitudes at the end of the 1970s. Data from the late 1970s, Keene reported, "showed something new. . . . Poll questions on 'risk' and 'compassion' split the sexes with women less willing to take risks and more likely to take the 'compassionate' positions. For example, 58% of men, but only 48% of women favored 'relaxing environmental protection laws if it will help improve the economy' in a May 1981 Time/Yankelovich, Skelly and White sounding. Sixty-one per cent of men and 73% of women agreed that 'the government should work to substantially reduce the income gap between rich and poor'

[7] Ibid.
[8] Ibid.
[9] Ibid.
[10] Ibid.
[11] Karlyn Keene, "Women: Have They Become a New Voting Bloc?" *Wall Street Journal*, September 20, 1982, p. 30.

in a February 1981 ABC News/Washington Post question. The gap on the using force dimension also enlarged. . . . Again and again, women said they were less confident than men about the country's future." [12]

The 1982 elections showed dramatic differences in the voting patterns of men and women. In Virginia, where Republican Paul S. Trible, Jr., defeated Democrat Richard J. Davis in a race for the U.S. Senate, 55 percent of the women voted for Davis, and 44 percent for Trible. Among men, 53 percent voted for Trible, and 46 percent for Davis. In Iowa, where Lt. Gov. Terry Branstad, a Republican, overwhelmingly defeated former U.S. Attorney Roxanne Conlin, a Democrat, men voted for Branstad by 60 to 39 percent. Women, however, voted for Conlin 52 to 48 percent. In New York, where Democrat Mario Cuomo won a narrow victory for the governorship over Republican Lewis E. Lehrman, 53 percent of the men voted for Lehrman and 45 percent for Cuomo. Women, by contrast, voted 52 percent for Cuomo and 46 percent for Lehrman. Carl Ottosen, Lehrman's campaign manager, said: "We showed a gender gap throughout the campaign. Lew was thought of as more conservative, whereas more women think of themselves as moderate to liberal. Lew favored the death penalty, which appeals more to males than females." [13]

Toward the end of his career, Sigmund Freud asked, "What does a woman want?" President Reagan's election strategists grappled with this question as they tried to win back the votes of many women who had moved in a different political direction. In September, 1983, it was announced that the president favored eliminating forty-seven relatively innocuous examples of gender bias in federal statutes: changing "widow" to "spouse," and eliminating references to "able-bodied men." The Reagan administration felt it necessary to make clear its opposition to discrimination based on gender as a result, in part, of the criticism launched against it by former Justice Department aide Barbara Honegger, who issued a detailed denunciation of the administration's effort to eliminate gender bias in federal statutes, calling it a "sham."

As the 1984 presidential campaign got under way, White House officials concluded that the "gender gap" was largely a Republican problem, not President Reagan's personal problem, and that it would damage any Republican running for president. [14] Early 1984 polls indicated that President

[12] Ibid.
[13] Margaret Hornblower, "Dramatic Differences Record in Male-Female Voting Patterns," *New York Times*, November 6, 1982, p. A-9.
[14] *Washington Times*, September 27, 1983.

Reagan's support ran about seventeen percentage points higher among men than among women. One of the political goals of the president's advisors was to narrow this "gender gap" by appealing to women voters on the basis of issues that are of particular concern to them.

It is in this political context that we must consider the crusade on the part of many feminist groups, and some others, for what has been called "unisex insurance." In recent years, much attention has been focused upon the availability and pricing of certain insurance policies for women. Of particular concern have been those health and disability insurance plans and employee pension plans that require women to pay more in premiums or that provide smaller benefits to women than to men.

In response to these concerns, bills have been introduced in both the House and the Senate that would outlaw any use of gender in determining rates for any types of insurance, regardless of the particular justification for it. The legislation that was proposed would outlaw the use of race, color, religion, sex, or national origin as a basis for determining the availability or price of insurance. The provision that concerned the insurance industry was the prohibition of gender as a basis for setting prices. Gender, it is argued, is considered in the pricing of insurance because statistics support its use in risk classification. Women as a group live longer than men. Young women have fewer accidents than young men.

Legislation like that which was proposed, it is generally agreed, would dramatically increase costs to women, men, business, and government. The measure's supporters, however, have indicated a willingness to accept the economic consequences out of a sense of "fairness" to women. Even though the evidence is overwhelming that women will, in the end, have to pay even more for insurance, particularly for the coverages they purchase as individuals, the supporters of the change believed that "equal" treatment of the sexes—not only with regard to insurance but in all legal areas—is the important goal.

The insurance industry argues that this legislation would be an infringement of the McCarran-Ferguson Act, the federal law which specifically gives states the authority to regulate the business of insurance within their own borders. All states now permit the use of gender in the setting of automobile insurance rates. Thus, it is said, the Fair Insurance Act would be a direct interference in the state regulation of insurance.

In the context of automobile insurance, many critics argue, this would be unfair to young women. In that market, gender has proven to be a reasonable, accurate, and fair criterion for setting insurance premiums, its advocates declare. Ignoring gender in this area, it is said, would result in rates for women that are substantially in excess of what is fair.

The American Academy of Actuaries, an independent professional organization which did not take a position on proposed legislation eliminating gender considerations, did assess its economic impact, and among its conclusions was one which stated, "Auto insurance premiums for women would increase by $700 million annually." [15] The academy statement submitted to the Senate Commerce Committee in 1983 said that its assessment should be considered approximate rather than precise since no study could gauge the practical effects of marketplace reactions, judicial interpretation, etc. with complete accuracy. As a result, the academy's analysis did not attempt to prejudge any of those conditions but, rather, took the bill at its face value.

While the actuaries' statement recognized that the actual dollar effect on individual men and women would vary depending on individual circumstances, they concluded that "women as a group will pay more for insurance if this [legislation] is passed." The academy also estimated that implementing the bill would add $1.3 billion to the cost of insurance for everyone.

The American Insurance Association argued that the proposed legislation "violates the fundamental economic principle of pricing in accordance with costs. Risks which present higher costs should pay higher premiums." [16] Several examples are presented:

Houses made of wood will have more fire insurance losses than brick houses—therefore fire insurance costs more for wooden houses than for brick.

The mortality rate for fifty-year-olds is much greater than for thirty-year-olds—therefore life insurance premiums are lower for thirty-year-olds than for fifty-year-olds.

Young drivers (under age twenty-five) are twice as likely to have automobile accidents as older drivers—therefore auto insurance premiums for youthful operators are higher than for adults.

The American Insurance Association (AIA) notes: "The [legislation] would require that insurers ignore very real and statistically significant differences in claim and benefit costs between men and women when determining the premium that may be charged. This means that actuarial con-

---

[15] Media release, H.R. 100 and S. 372, American Insurance Association, 1983.
[16] Ibid.

siderations would have to be totally disregarded with respect to differences between men and women. For example: Female drivers have a lower expectation of losses from auto accidents than do male drivers. Specifically, the three-year accident record for females is slightly more than half the rate of males and young single male drivers have a loss cost in excess of 50 per cent over young single female drivers. Despite this overwhelming statistical evidence young women would be forced to pay the same rate for auto insurance as young men if the bill were enacted." [17]

Available statistics indicate that men drive more miles than women and do more nighttime driving. In addition, men tend to obtain driver's licenses earlier than women, and men are more likely to drive under the influence of alcohol. These characteristics are generally associated with higher rates of accident involvement and severity. As a result of these differences in driving patterns, women have better accident experience rates and generally enjoy lower auto insurance premiums. [18]

It is AIA's view that the proposed legislation, rather than benefiting women in whose name it is being advocated, would actually harm them. "Youthful women drivers have benefited from lower insurance rates than those paid by youthful males for a just cause—their accident experience is better (fewer and less severe accidents). As young drivers mature, the accident rate differential narrows, so that gender is not a rating factor for older drivers. The use of sex as a factor in auto insurance rating has been justified consistently. Both insurance and non-insurance data confirm that males have more frequent and more severe auto accidents than females. Consequently, males and females are classified separately in auto rating. Classification systems allow individuals sharing relatively similar risk exposures to be grouped together for pricing purposes. Classifications are not peculiar to the insurance industry; they are an almost universally accepted pricing measure—from the airline industry to the U.S. postal service. Classifications, though, can be controversial because they involve conflicts in social values." [19]

The statistical data with regard to male and female driving records show that young men have more than twice as many automobile accidents as young women, even when mileage is taken into account. Young men are principally responsible for the most severe accidents.

A U.S. Department of Transportation study entitled *The Effects of Ex-*

[17] Ibid.
[18] Andrew Tobias, *The Invisible Bankers* (New York: Pocket Books, 1982), p. 125.
[19] Media release, H.R. 100 and S. 372.

posure to Risk on Driving Records reported that males driving between 2,500 and 4,999 miles annually had a three-year accident record of .268 accidents per driver, while females within the same mileage category had an accident record of .103—a 62 percent lower rate than males. At the 7,500- to 9,999-mile category, the female accident record of .179 was 22 percent lower than the male accident record of .229. Females, on the average, had an accident record of .163 or 47 percent lower than the male accident record of .305.[20]

Women on the average drive fewer miles than males. Even if females drove the same number of miles as males, using the Department of Transportation accident rates, it has been estimated that the female accident record would remain 23 percent lower than the male accident record. According to a study of California driving performance, the driving records for females under age twenty-five was 35 to 50 percent better than that for males of comparable age, even when adjusted for average annual miles driven.

The American Insurance Association stated: "Insurance premiums are and must be determined prospectively, i.e., before the auto accident occurs, or for life insurers—before the policyholder dies. On an individual driver basis, it cannot be determined in advance who will have an auto accident in any given year any more than it can be determined at what age a specific individual will die. . . . No one, not the insurer, and not even the policyholder, knows in advance, whether he or she will have an accident. What is known with certainty is that the probability of auto accidents is significantly higher for young males than for young females, as a group."[21]

The All-Industry Research Advisory Council (AIRAC), a public policy research council founded by and supported by the property-casualty insurance industry, commissioned a national poll conducted by Yankelovich, Skelly, and White to determine public attitudes on the use of such factors as age, sex, marital status, place of residence, and prior accident experience in setting auto insurance rates. The poll found that 51 percent of respondents said that the groups identified as having higher than average risk exposure should pay higher insurance rates, whereas 31 percent thought they should pay the same rates as other drivers, and 17 percent were unsure. A second question asked specifically about a proposal "that auto in-

[20] Cited in ibid.
[21] Ibid.

surance companies lower the rates charged to drivers who have not had accidents but are in a high risk group," and pointed out that "if this happens, rates for other people will have to be increased." When asked whether they would favor or oppose this proposal, 29 percent were in favor, 48 percent were opposed, and 23 percent were uncertain.[22]

Those in favor were then asked what effect such a change would have on their own auto insurance rates. About three out of four of those who favored reducing rates for the accident-free drivers in high-risk groups were people who thought their own rates would either go down or stay the same if that were done. Only 7 percent of the public favored the idea if they thought their own rates would increase as a result. This 7 percent was then asked how much they would be willing to have their own rates increased in order that rates could be reduced for accident-free members of the high-risk groups. Only 4 percent of the public said they were willing to pay more than five dollars a year extra, and only 2 percent were willing to have their own rates increased by more than ten dollars a year.

T. Lawrence Jones, president of the American Insurance Association, expressed the view of the industry in these terms: "It is a dubious tribute to our society's ingenuity, and gullibility, that we can dress up almost anything with a fancy title and sell it for more than it is worth. A used car becomes a "previously-owned vehicle," while refurbished tenements sell as 'luxury condominiums.' The technique apparently works as well with legislation. Thus, a bill that will force women to pay unfair overcharges for auto insurance is titled the 'Fair Insurance Practices Act' in the Senate and the 'Nondiscrimination in Insurance Act' in the House of Representatives. It is an added irony that sponsors are calling these bills 'women's rights legislation.' "[23]

Jones continued: "What do these bills do? Essentially, they outlaw the use of any gender based statistics in computing prices for any type of insurance. In practice, this would force insurers to charge younger women 25 to 30 per cent more than they presently pay for auto insurance, while undercharging young men, who have far less favorable driving records. . . . The typical American woman—one who buys her life, auto and homeowner's insurance individually and obtains her health and pension coverage through her own or her spouse's employer-provided group insurance plan—

[22] Ibid.
[23] Quoted in ibid.

pays almost $8,500 less for insurance over her lifetime than a typical American man pays. The legislation pending before Congress would force insurers to discard this basic principle and flatten everyone's rates. Thus, women, the better drivers, would be subsidizing the poorer risks heavily. . . . The proponents of this legislation contend that women will pay these extra costs as part of the price of equality. . . . We believe that young women will resent paying unjustifiably higher premiums for their insurance protection. Perhaps they would mind it less if they earned salaries equal to men's. But they do not. What's more, this legislation would impose the extra costs on women at the beginning of their working years, when they are likely to be earning the lowest salaries of their careers." [24]

While women would pay more for automobile and life insurance policies under the proposed "unisex" legislation, in the area of pensions, the advocates of such legislation point out, they would pay less. In the case of *City of Los Angeles* v. *Manhart*, the Supreme Court in 1978 ruled out the practice whereby employers administering their own pension plans require female employees to make larger contributions than similarly situated male employees in order to receive the same periodic payments on retirement. The laws cited were the Equal Pay Act of 1963 and Title VII of the Civil Rights Act of 1964. Women have traditionally paid more for pensions because they live longer than men and collect their pensions for a longer period of time. [25]

Professor George J. Benston, an economist at the University of Rochester, argued in the *University of Chicago Law Review* that certain types of discrimination are necessary to fulfill the aims of the 1963 and 1964 acts. [26] The discrimination in the Manhart case was based on the assumption, which the Supreme Court accepted, that women live longer than men. On the average it will cost a pension plan more to make periodic payments to women than it will cost to make payments of the same size to men because the women will collect over a longer period.

Those who seek to alter the pre-Manhart situation do not ask insurers and pension plan managers to ignore male-female statistical differences. They urge, instead, that pension plans should treat the group as a group. On the average, this would lead to somewhat increased total benefits for women, as well as somewhat reduced total benefits for men. Benston sug-

---

[24] Ibid.
[25] Lindley H. Clarke, Jr., "Speaking of Business," *Wall Street Journal*, May 10, 1983.
[26] Ibid.

gested that one effect of such an approach would be that the relative cost of hiring a woman would increase. Thus, employers would have an incentive to discriminate against women.

Although it is clear that women live longer than men, Benston considered the possibility that insurers were using all of the mortality data simply as a coverup for a basic determination to discriminate against women merely because they are women. "Considering the long and shameful history of discrimination against women, how can we be assured that insurers do not consider an insured's gender to the exclusion of other, more relevant factors because of conscious or unwitting bias against females?"[27]

It can be argued that competition would tend to prevent such action. If one insurer charged higher rates than the rest, it would lose business. Collusion of all major firms to charge higher rates would be difficult in the face of state regulation.

Discussing this question, Lindley H. Clarke, Jr., writing in the *Wall Street Journal*, declared: "History . . . is instructive. Women have not always lived longer than men. Insurance companies for more than 200 years have tried to take into account actual mortality in setting rates. They do so more accurately now than they once did, because statistics have greatly improved. Although women on the average receive smaller total pension payments than men, sex-based rates mean that ordinary life insurance costs them less. The best solution would be to continue the sex-based tables, which in fact do deliver the same product to both men and women, protection against an unknown eventuality. But given the strong pressures for change, why should we stop with life insurance and pensions?"[28]

Clarke concluded: "Women, on the average, have fewer automobile accidents than men. Any parent who has had a young son drop off his family auto policy, only to be replaced by a young daughter, knows the pleasant experience of seeing his premium drop. Is that fair? Many individual men are better, and more accident-free, drivers than the average woman. (Most men *think* they are better drivers than the average woman, but some of them actually are.) But the insurance companies discriminate against the safe-driving man because of the failures of his reckless fellows. If we're going to replace one type of discrimination with another, we might as well go all the way."[29]

[27] Ibid.
[28] Ibid.
[29] Ibid.

A case that has received much attention is that of Nathalie Norris, the Arizona civil servant who sued when she found that her state-purchased retirement annuity paid her $33.95 less per month than her male counterparts would receive. The reason for this: women live longer and, as a result, giving men and women the same monthly payment for the balance of their lives would result in higher total payments to women. Norris's attorney, Amy Jo Gitler, declared, "We must treat individuals as individuals, not as group statistics." Why not, she asked, treat insured motorists or pensioners "as individuals, not as group statistics?" If a particular teen-age boy is a safe driver, refusing to drive after drinking, keeping his car in good repair, why should he pay a higher insurance rate than an equally safe adult or teenage girl?[30]

Discussing these claims, syndicated columnist William Raspberry argued: "There can be no doubt that the insurance company was treating Norris, who has taken her case to the Supreme Court, as a statistic. The tough question is one of fairness. Is it fair for an insurance company to discriminate against women? Of course not. Is it fair for an insurance company to take an actuarially sound look at its risk and set its payments accordingly? Of course it is. . . . Norris, it is safe to guess, never complained when her auto insurance company charged her lower premiums than it charged her male counterparts, on the ground that, statistically, women have fewer and less-serious accidents than men. Grown-ups pay smaller auto-insurance premiums than teen-agers and teen-age girls pay smaller premiums than teen-age boys for the same reason. Is that unfair?"[31]

Raspberry asked rhetorically: "If [Norris] had been a black man, with a statistically shorter life expectancy, would it have been reverse discrimination to make her monthly payments larger? Would she buy a solution that equalized pay-outs for men and women by reducing the size of the payments to men? What is the reasonable way out of the dilemma she has raised?" Raspberry's response to his own question was: "Nathalie Norris says she is a victim of sex bias. It may be more accurate to say she is a victim of common sense."[32]

Those who support legislation in Congress to mandate "unisex" insurance rates include such groups as the American Association of University Women, the Coalition of Labor Union Women, and the National

---

[30] Cited in "It Doesn't Pay to Be a Statistic," *Washington Post*, April 4, 1983.
[31] Ibid.
[32] Ibid.

Women's Political Caucus. Within the Reagan administration, this proposal was advocated by Elizabeth Dole, formerly White House liaison to women's groups and later secretary of transportation.

The Reagan adminstration has, in a sense, also supported this legislation. Solicitor General Rex E. Lee filed a brief attacking "sex-based actuarial tables," thereby lining up the administration with the women's movement and numerous members of the judiciary who are opposed to such tables.

In an article in *Fortune* magazine, Daniel Seligman stated: "It's hard to see why anybody without an ideological slant should view the insurance industry's sex-based distinctions as discriminatory. If young women have fewer automobile accidents than young men—which they do—why shouldn't the women get a better rate? If the industry's experience shows— as it does—that women spend more time in the hospital than men, why shouldn't women pay more for health policies? If female mortality rates are lower than those for males—which they are, at every age from day one to year 100—why shouldn't females pay less for life insurance? And more for pensions and annuities? There is broad agreement that the industry's pricing reflects not bigotry but actual experience. So why should anybody view it as discriminatory?" [33]

Advocates of the "unisex" legislation argue that anti-discrimination laws in insurance are a natural outgrowth of laws that have banned sex discrimination in employment, housing, credit, and other areas. Senate witnesses declared that it was unfair to discriminate on the basis of sex because sex is an immutable human characteristic, like race or color. The principle which seems to have been embraced in recent court cases and in the brief of Solicitor General Lee is that, while it is true that women as a class live longer than men, it is wrong for individual women to be treated as a member of a class when it comes to writing insurance. Treating people as members of a class rather than individuals, such critics declare, is the essence of discrimination—and is what was forbidden by the Civil Rights Act of 1964, at least with respect to classes of race, color, religion, national origin, or sex.

One reason the Reagan administration has supported this approach, some observers point out, is that in the area of affirmative action and other race-conscious preferences, the administration has said that we must move

---

[33] Daniel Seligman, "Insurance and the Price of Sex," *Fortune*, February 21, 1983.

away from group rights and concentrate on individual rights. The Reagan administration's approach can be seen in its position in the case involving the plan of the city of Detroit for promoting racial equality. The plan, adopted in 1974, calls for hiring and promoting equal numbers of blacks and whites on the Detroit police force. The Detroit Police Department has long used a merit selection system in choosing police officers to be promoted. Before 1974, all candidates for promotion were ranked on a single list according to numerical ratings based on various factors, including scores on written examinations.

In 1973, the city elected Coleman Young, a black, as mayor. Black hostility to the police force was cited as one factor in his victory. The next year, an affirmative action plan was adopted for the police department. This plan required the department to keep two separate lists, one for black officers and one for white officers. Rankings on each list are based on the same numerical rating system. Promotions are made alternately from the two lists, so that white and black officers are promoted in equal numbers. This arrangement is designed to remain in effect until half the police lieutenants are black—a goal which is not expected to be met until 1990.

Administration officials said that they favored "affirmative action" in the sense of measures designed to bring in more minority-group applicants for jobs, such as advertising targeted at potential black applicants. They have said, though, that they object to giving preference on the basis of race in actual hiring and promotion decisions, as is the case in Detroit.

The larger question involved in the growing debate over affirmative action—which relates to much of the debate over "unisex" insurance—is whether the traditional civil rights goal of a "color-blind" society is to be replaced with that of a "color-conscious" society that enforces group rights rather than individual rights.

William Bradford Reynolds, assistant attorney general in the Civil Rights Division of the Justice Department, has stated: "There are those who, rather unabashedly, have undertaken to redefine the traditional concept of civil rights. The essential concern for *individual* opportunity . . . has been submerged by this school of thought beneath a rising tide of *group* entitlements. . . . Many of those who over the past decade have sought fervently to propel civil rights enforcement along a group-oriented course are the same men and women who were in the vanguard of the great civil rights movement of the 1950s and 60s—the movement that, for the first time, put individual rights on the pedestal reserved for them by the Founders . . . and framers of the Constitution." [34]

When Supreme Court justice Thurgood Marshall was the attorney for the National Association for the Advancement of Colored People (NAACP), he argued the case of *Brown* v. *Board of Education* (1954), which declared that racial segregation in the public schools was unconstitutional, and he rejected the notion that the Constitution would require the establishment of "non-segregated" schools through race-conscious reassignments. He stated: "The only thing that we ask for is that the state-imposed racial segregation be taken off, and to leave the county school board, the county people, the district people, to work out their own solution to the problem, to assign children on any reasonable basis they want to assign them on." So long as the children were assigned "without regard to race or color, . . . nobody would have any complaint." [35] This is what the Supreme Court held when it declared, "At stake is the personal interest of the plaintiffs in admission to public schools . . . on a racially nondiscriminatory basis." [36]

During the 1964 congressional debate, Sen. Hubert Humphrey, a principal force behind the Civil Rights Act, declared that it "does not provide that any preferential treatment in employment shall be given to Negroes or any other persons or groups." [37]

Discussing the growing demands for "group rights," Alexander Bickel, in his book *The Morality of Consent*, wrote: "The lesson of the great decisions of the Supreme Court and lessons of contemporary history [have] been the same for at least a generation: discrimination on the basis of race is illegal, immoral, unconstitutional, inherently wrong, and destructive of democratic society. Now this is to be unlearned and we are told that this is not a matter of fundamental principle but only a matter of whose ox is gored. . . . Having found support in the Constitution for equality, [proponents of group-oriented racial preferences] now claim support for inequality under the same Constitution." [38]

[34] William Bradford Reynolds speech to Lincoln Institute for Research and Education, published in *Lincoln Review*, Winter, 1984, p. 31.
[35] 347 U.S. 483, 1954.
[36] Ibid.
[37] Paul Seabury, "HEW and the Universities," *Commentary*, February, 1972, p. 38.
[38] Quoted in William J. Bennett and Terry Eastland, *Counting by Race* (New York: Basic Books, 1979), p. 61.

The U.S. Supreme Court, in January, 1984, rejected the plea of the Reagan administration and left intact the racial quota system of the Detroit Police Department. The justices, without explanation or public dissent, allowed the Detroit plan—and lower-court opinions backing affirmative action—to stand.

The outcome of the Detroit case made no new law on affirmative action. In three earlier rulings, the Court had endorsed limited plans that provided preferences for minorities in college admissions, labor-management agreements, and federal government contracts.

It is in this atmosphere that the debate concerning "unisex" insurance is taking place, and will proceed. While the elimination of group rights remains a subject of much debate when it comes to affirmative action, the arguments in behalf of group classification are somewhat different when it comes to insurance.

In his article in *Fortune*, Daniel Seligman expressed his view: "Insurance *requires* group classifications. It needs the law of large numbers to work with. Though nobody knows when a particular person will die, the law of large numbers enables us to predict with considerable accuracy when an average member of a group will die. In agreeing that women as a group live longer, but insisting that it's unfair to apply this fact to individual cases, the courts and the Administration have stepped into a huge intellectual bog. Presumably, we are all agreed that the insurance industry is entitled to classify people by age. But the argument that we must view people as individuals, and not as members of a class, could also be applied to age classifications. After all, some young people die early and some old people just get a lot older." [39]

Insurance executives themselves are divided on the effect unisex pricing would have on the terms and availability of future policies. While some have suggested that a public policy of unisex rates would be acceptable, others believe that, overall, insurance premiums would rise, and that pension plans for companies with predominantly female employees might become difficult to obtain.

Some in the insurance industry fear, in particular, a law or a court decision that would require existing as well as future policies to conform to unisex pricing standards. By some industry estimates, such an approach

[39] Seligman, "Insurance and the Price of Sex."

would cost several billion dollars for pensions alone to bring benefits for women up to male levels.

Interestingly, the nation's leading liberal newspapers, which are usually supportive of the feminist movement and its goals, have taken a somewhat different position with regard to the unisex insurance controversy. The *Washington Post*, after presenting the arguments both for and against the proposed unisex legislation, declared: "Most important to the average taxpayer is the situation of public employee plans. New York state officials have estimated that complying with such a law would cost the taxpayers of their state between $1.9 and $2.1 billion a year. None of this is insured by private carriers; it would simply be passed on to the taxpayer. Congress can avoid these staggering unfunded liabilities by making any such law truly prospective, i.e., pensions earned—as distinguished from pensions paid—after the date of enactment will have to be sex-neutral. If they choose not to make this distinction, lawmakers must face squarely the fact that in righting what they consider to be a social injustice, they are passing on tremendous costs to private industry and to state and local taxpayers."[40]

A *New York Times* editorial noted: "The pressure grows to have Congress prohibit discrimination by sex in insurance and pension calculations. The courts have already ruled such discrimination illegal in certain cases. And Senator Packwood and Representative Dingell are, against industry opposition, pushing broader legislation. Wise social policy should prefer identical insurance premiums and pension benefits for men and women. The fewer sexual distinctions in the market-place the better. But to move from here to there raises troubling practical problems. Congress cannot safely finesse them by declaring for virtue and then leaving the explosive details to administrators."[41]

The *Times* continued: "Women who reach age 65, on average, live four years longer than men. Logically enough, therefore, some employers and insurance plans that charge equal premiums for men and women then give females a smaller monthly retirement check than males. The women's accumulated kitty has to last longer. According to the courts, this disparity amounts to sex discrimination in employment. . . . No one contends, however, that Federal law prohibits sexually distinctive premiums or benefit

[40]Editorial, "Pensions and Probabilities," *Washington Post*, February 19, 1983, p. A-22.
[41]"Be Careful about Unisex Insurance," *New York Times*, April 20, 1983.

payments where the insurance and annuities are sold directly to individuals. The argument so far turns only on pensions that come in employers' benefit packages. Hence the importance of the Dingell-Packwood proposal, which would strike down differences in *all* policies and prescribe remedies for persons holding discrimination-based policies." [42]

Critics of the unisex proposal, the *Times* suggested, were correct in one sense: "Sex discrimination in insurance and pensions should not be confused with discrimination rooted in prejudice. But benign intent cannot be the only test of social policy. Where practical, society would be better off reducing distinctions that leave even an impression of sex discrimination in work and commerce." [43]

It was the view of the *Times* that the Dingell-Packwood bill slipped "too easily past . . . two problems." These problems are: (1) "Insurance for young drivers. In most insurance, the differences in risk between the sexes are relatively small. But not in auto insurance for those under 25: men now cost and pay two or three times as much as women. If insurers were required to switch to unisex tables they would have a strong incentive to beat the system by not insuring young men. A common-sense solution would be to retain sex distinctions in insurance for young drivers"; and (2) "Payment for past discrimination. The Packwood-Dingell bill would require pension plans to 'top up' payments to the disadvantaged sex. That is, if women now get $270 a month and men $300, all would have to get $300. That may be good politics but it is arbitrary economics, raising pension liabilities by about $1 billion a year. The annual bill for New York City alone would amount to $82 million."

The *Times* concluded: "One obvious alternative would allow paying both sexes the average between the current male and female rates. The good reasons to eliminate sex discrimination in insurance do not justify reckless damage to the insurance industry, existing pension systems or present policyholders. Congress should pass an anti-discrimination law— but only after addressing all the consequences."

An editorial in *USA Today* declared: "The dilemma before the court, and ultimately before Congress, is whether sex-based actuarial tables used by the insurance industry should be outlawed simply because they reflect what appears to be a biological truth. And if sex is ruled unconstitutional,

[42] Ibid.
[43] Ibid.

won't other criteria such as age soon follow? If so, then an 80 year old might demand the same monthly price for life insurance that a 25 year old pays. The insurance industry as we know it could not weather such imbalance. Neither would it be fair. Women pay less for life insurance because they live longer. They pay less for auto insurance because they are safer drivers. Low-risk persons should not foot the bill for the high." [44]

USA Today concluded: "Only about 15 per cent of the nation's pension plans will be affected if sex-based statistics are outlawed, but the impact of such a decision would spread like wildfire through many other areas of insurance coverage. A better solution would be to retain the sex-based actuarial tables because they are fair, and for the court and Congress to encourage all employers to set up pension plans that pay equal monthly payments to men and women. The alternative is to spark a revolution in the insurance industry which would leave it in turmoil. That would be a reason to make everybody cry." [45]

The *San Francisco Chronicle* described the idea of unisex insurance rates as a form of equality which "isn't so good." It ventured: "Most enlightened people, we are sure, are all for eliminating sex differences in the pricing of goods and services, in setting job qualifications and in paying retirement pensions. Who could defend such differences? Yet if you are a woman, you don't want to be too sure of where you stand on this question of equality, the insurance industry suggests." [46]

The *Chronicle* quoted a statement from the Alliance of American Insurers that declared that proposed anti-gender legislation is "anything but fair" to women because "women drivers, who have fewer accidents than their male counterparts, would be forced to pay significantly higher automobile insurance premiums under this bill." In addition, "Although women as a group live longer than men, and thus pay lower insurance premiums, this bill would require insurers to ignore reality and charge women the same premiums as men." [47]

The *Chronicle* concluded: "The California State Teachers' Retirement System has estimated that passage of this legislation could create $2.6 billion in unfunded accrued obligations. For its part, the California Public Employees' Retirement System estimates that unfunded liabilities could

[44] "Sex-based Factors Should Be Retained," *USA Today*, March 31, 1983.
[45] Ibid.
[46] *San Francisco Chronicle*, April 25, 1983.
[47] Ibid.

reach $625 million. So in all this we're learning something unexpected about the pitfalls of trying to legislate equality. Down the street from the pension funds' headquarters in Sacramento the California Legislature is urging Congress to submit anew the Equal Rights Amendment that . . . went down in flames. We are wholly for the equality principle of ERA and have given it our faithful support. At least we thought we were for equality. But do we want to extend it to insurance rates, to women's disadvantage? Well. . . ."[48]

Advocates of the unisex approach argue that women's rights demand equality in the insurance field. They state that it is a violation of an individual's civil rights to be classified by sex in the setting of insurance rates. Phyllis Schlafly, the leading opponent of the Equal Rights Amendment, has responded by noting, "An even better civil rights argument can be made if you are thrown into a category that is so large it does not reflect your own personal characteristics that most accurately determine predictable risk."[49]

What occurred in Michigan when the Michigan Essential Insurance Act took effect on January 1, 1981, may be considered instructive. This legislation was passed after a debate which concerned primarily the bill's prohibition against insurance "redlining" in some urban areas, particularly the inner-city portions of Detroit and other large Michigan cities. There was little consideration by the state legislature of the words inserted into the bill to eliminate sex and marital status as factors in the setting of home and auto insurance rates. Before long, women drivers received rate increases of hundreds of dollars. Auto insurance rates for some classes of young women, it is reported, were increased by as much as 195 percent. The state Insurance Bureau's advice to female consumers was to "shop around" for the best rates, but, in fact, the new law had raised the rates of all companies.

The Michigan Insurance Bureau published a report entitled *A Year of Change—The Essential Insurance Act in 1981.* Phyllis Schlafly charged that this report tended to downplay the real impact of the legislation. She wrote: "The Insurance Bureau's tables show the rate changes only in terms of 'relativity'. . . . Thus, a 127 per cent increase in the insurance rate charged to 16-year-old female drivers (which amounts to hundreds of dollars per year) appears in the table only as a change on the relativity ratio

[48] Ibid.
[49] Phyllis Schlafly, "Unisex Insurance Has Hidden Costs," *Chicago Calumet,* May 10, 1983.

from 1.88 to 4.27. But the most interesting thing about the Insurance Bureau's report is that it omits the table for young married females and that is
the very table which would have shown the steepest increases caused by the
sex-neutralization law. . . . insurance rates for young married women were
raised by as much as 32 per cent. Instead of being treated as individuals in
a low-risk group, these young married women in Michigan were thrown
into a larger unisex category and forced to subsidize the claims of high-risk
male drivers." [50]

Elaine Donnelly of Detroit, who testified against the unisex legislation in Michigan, declared that "this new system constitutes a new form of
arbitrary sex discrimination, which does not allow the insurance companies to treat women as female individuals. . . . How can this possibly be
considered fair or equitable. . . . young women in Michigan . . . are being
forced to pay higher rates than they rightfully should pay." [51]

As a result of much criticism, certain changes have been made in the
unisex legislation before the Congress. Revisions would remove some of
the pension plan problems presented by the original bill. Benefits for the
currently retired, for example, could be continued unchanged. Employers
could recover the costs of providing additional benefits to some future retirees by reducing benefits for other future retirees.

The amended bill, however, would still require changes to be made in
existing life insurance contracts. The American Council of Life Insurance
has stated: "This would raise the legally unacceptable prospect of abrogat-
ing policyholders' contracts by changing premium payments for both
sexes. Moreover, this business continues to have deep misgivings about
charging the same price for different risk values. It is unfair and the practical effect will be more costly to women than the existing cost-based
systems." [52]

In testimony before the Senate Committee on Commerce, Science
and Transportation in May, 1983, Robert N. Houser, chairman of the
Bankers Life of Des Moines, Iowa, and John H. Filer, chairman of Aetna
Life Insurance Company of Hartford, Connecticut, represented the 572-
member American Council of Life Insurance, which accounts for 95 percent of the life insurance in force in the United States. "Sex has been and
continues to be one of the most relevant characteristics used by life insur-

[50] Ibid.
[51] Quoted in ibid.
[52] Media release, H.R. 100 and S. 372.

ance companies to develop premium rates that accurately reflect the expected costs of insuring people," said Houser. Data tabulated for about twenty large companies, he said, show "mortality rates for the women have been consistently about 60 per cent of the men's in each of the last 15 years. That means that only about 60 per cent as many women died each year as would have died if they had experienced the same mortality rates, age by age, as did men." He said that because men have higher mortality rates, they are charged more for life insurance, and "the opposite result obtains for annuities."

Filer said that the proposed legislation would have a "quite different" impact on employer/employee benefit plans and on individually purchased contracts. He explained: "In the situation of an employment relationship, it can be argued persuasively that the employer should provide a benefit indistinguishable in its result for all employees regardless of gender. It will cost more or less to provide a particular insurance or pension benefit to men and women but it is seen as inequitable to have any one benefit last longer, pay less or cover less for one sex or the other. As a condition of employment, equality of result can well be expected. The ACLI fully supports the prospective application of such a concept." [53]

He concluded: "With respect to individual contracts undertaken outside of the employer/employee relationship the situation is quite different. Gender based pricing is essential in life insurance to avoid unfair discrimination against women. There is no third entity, the employer, to even out the costs from inaccurate pricing. Prohibition of gender based pricing in life insurance may appear to some to be consistent with civil rights notions of fairness and equality. The trouble with it is that it produces an unfair, inequitable result—in effect it forces an unfair discrimination against members of one sex or the other—and in life insurance the unfairness will be directed against the female population." [54]

Houser argued that both life insurance companies and their policyholders would be damaged if such legislation were approved: "Life insurance companies would be forced to equalize both the premium rates and all future benefits paid under existing contracts. The bill, as drafted, would require very substantial additional insurance benefits for which no premiums have been paid. If retirement plans are required to equalize benefits

[53] Ibid.
[54] Ibid.

for men and women by 'topping-up' for the less favored sex, we estimate the additional cost would be about $1 to $2 billion per year, most borne by plan sponsors, who might then modify or terminate their plans. In the case of existing life insurance policies, premium-rates would have to be made the same for men and women. The life insurance company could do this by collecting more premiums from women than the contract permits or by increasing the death benefits for men to the amount that would have been provided at the lower female rates. The first option may not be legally viable. The second option significantly increases the liabilities of our companies." [55]

Houser reported that a survey of 153 ACLI member companies found that the total immediate increase in their liabilities, if the Senate bill under consideration were applied to their existing policies and contracts, would be $14.5 billion or about 51 percent of the aggregate net worth of the 153 companies. It was found that 24 companies would have liability increases in excess of 100 percent of their net worth, making them insolvent under state insurance laws.

Some women's groups that advocate unisex insurance legislation have argued that as women enter the work force and are subjected to the same stresses as men, the gender gap in life expectancy will disappear. Thus far, available evidence does not seem to support this conclusion. According to U.S. population statistics, the gap is widening. In 1900, the difference in life expectancy at birth was only two years. In 1980, the difference was eight years.

Proponents of unisex legislation also advance the view that whites outlive blacks, and that certain religious groups outlive others, and yet these differences are not taken into account by the insurance industry. The industry responds by saying that race and religion, in fact, are proxies. Blacks do not have shorter life expectancies, it is said, because they are black. Shorter life expectancy is associated with poverty, and proportionately more blacks than whites are poor. In the same manner, certain religious denominations and sects tend to live longer because their members practice moderate lifestyles, but anyone who does the same, regardless of religious affiliation, enhances longevity and pays lower insurance premiums. Nonsmokers and people who maintain normal weight are examples.

Future prospects for unisex legislation may, in the end, have far more

[55] Ibid.

to do with the political imperatives of the coming period than the merits of the debate.

In an atmosphere in which the political impact of the women's movement is being increasingly felt and Republicans seek to alter their image while Democrats seek to maintain the support of women, it is difficult to predict how the Congress will act with regard to the proposed unisex insurance legislation. This issue is one about which a great deal is likely to be heard in the future.

5

No-Fault Insurance

IN recent years the subject of no-fault automobile insurance has produced controversy and discussion. It has been one of the much-publicized issues of the consumer movement, and as a result of the pressure brought to bear by its advocates, twenty-six states and the District of Columbia have passed one form or another of no-fault legislation designed to lower insurance premiums, speed up claims, and ease the burden on overcrowded courts.

In *The Invisible Bankers*, Andrew Tobias insisted: "The reform that fairly screams to be made is the institution of true no-fault automobile insurance. No-fault would be of great benefit to everyone but the lawyers." He pointed out: "Traditional auto liability insurance has been characterized as 'the worst system imaginable: A system that not only fails to spread most of [the] loss but is cruel, corrupt, self-righteous, dilatory, expensive, and wasteful.' It *over*compensates petty and groundless claims, because they are too expensive to fight, and grossly *under*compensates the seriously injured, and then only after much delay. Each time a $100 case is settled for $400, to get rid of it, insurers are in effect paying a 'toll' to lawyers for letting them pass without a lawsuit. Even when no attorney is involved, it is protection money, paid under threat that the client *could* retain an attorney. Settling petty or groundless claims for several times their economic value (medical expenses and lost wages) leaves too little of the insurance dollar for the people who really need it. With no-fault, the idea is to get an accident victim reimbursed promptly and as fully as possible for medical expenses and lost wages. In return for sure, swift compensation, the policyholder gives up his right to sue for pain and suffering." [1]

In his book *Ending Insult to Injury*, Jeffrey O'Connell of the law school at the University of Illinois, has described the traditional tort liability system this way: "After an accident, A claims against B, basing his claim on the fact that he was free from fault and B was at fault. Because A is an 'innocent' party claiming against a 'wrong-doer', A is allowed to claim not only for his out-of-pocket loss but for the monetary value of his pain and suffering as well. But because of the difficulty of establishing not only who was at fault but the pecuniary value of pain (what *is* an aching arm worth?), payment is either nonexistent or, if at long last it does come through, often falls far short of the amount claimed. We all wind up short-changed because expensive experts must be hired to haggle over who and how much is to be paid, and the wages of these experts drain the so-called insurance pool. In short, the tort insurance system is not a system for paying accident victims from accident insurance (as sensible as that idea would seem to be) but a system for *fighting* accident victims about whether to pay them from accident insurance." [2]

The no-fault system would work in a far different way, as O'Connell described it. "After an accident between A and B, each is paid regardless of who may be at fault, by his own insurance company, for his own out-of-pocket loss (relatively easy to total up from, say, his medical bills and lost wages). As a corollary, each is required to waive his tort claim based on fault against the other. As a result of the savings from eliminating legal fees (no-fault insurance has been called 'no-lawyer' insurance) and restricting payment to tangible losses, most people are eligible for payment from the insurance pool, into which fewer—or at least no more—dollars need be paid. This is, in essence, the 'miracle' being wrought by no-fault auto insurance." [3]

A report issued in 1970 by the New York State Insurance Department criticized the efficiency of the traditional auto liability insurance system. To its question "What becomes of the personal injury liability insurance dollar?" it replied: "First of all, insurance companies and agents use to 33 cents. Then lawyers and claims investigators take the next 23 cents. To-

[1] Andrew Tobias, *The Invisible Bankers* (New York: Pocket Books, 1982), pp. 205–206.
[2] Jeffrey O'Connell, "Extending the No-Fault Idea," *Public Interest*, Summer, 1974, p. 112.
[3] Ibid.

gether these items make up the operating expenses, or frictional costs, of the fault insurance system—56 cents out of every premium dollar."[4]

What happens to the forty-four cents that get through to the accident victim? The study reported: "First, 8 cents of the 44 go to pay for economic losses that have already been reimbursed from another source. Subtracting these redundant benefits as having low priority leaves 36 cents of the premium dollar to pay net losses of victims. But of those 36 cents, 21.5 cents go for something other than economic loss. The 21.5 cents are lumped together as 'general damages' or 'pain and suffering' which, in the typical case today, are simply by-products of the bargaining process of insurance adjustment. Once we look beyond the name which the operators of the fault insurance system have given this non-economic portion of liability payments and understand what it really is in the usual case, it assumes a low priority by any social or humane standard. That leaves just 14.5 cents out of the premium dollar as compensation for the net economic loss of the accident victim—$100 million out of $686 million which New Yorkers spend each year for automobile bodily injury liability insurance."[5]

Sen. Daniel P. Moynihan (D-New York) has criticized the fault system of automobile insurance for its effects on the larger order. "The courts are overwhelmed, swamped, inundated, choked. In a futile quest to carry out a mundane mission—deciding who hit whom on the highway when every day there will be thousands and thousands of such events . . . we are sacrificing the most precious of our institutions: the independent judiciary, which dispenses justice and maintains the presumption and perception of a just social order that is fundamental to a democratic political system. . . . the victim has every reason to exaggerate his losses. It is some other person's insurance company that must pay. The company has every reason to resist. It is somebody else's customer who is making the claim. Delay, fraud, contentiousness are maximized, and in the process the system becomes grossly inefficient and expensive."[6]

The idea of no-fault automobile insurance is described by authors Paul Gillespie and Miriam Klipper in their book *No-Fault: What You Save, Gain and Lose With The New Auto Insurance*:

[4] "Automobile Insurance . . . For Whose Benefit?" New York Insurance Department report, 1970, p. 207.
[5] Ibid.
[6] Quoted in Tobias, *Invisible Bankers*, p. 206.

In theory no-fault automobile insurance would replace the traditional method of compensating automobile accident injuries—in which the victim makes a claim directly against an individual wrongdoer or, in reality, the wrongdoer's insurance company—with a more direct relationship. The victim now makes a claim for damages to his own company, instead of turning to his opponent's. The question of who is negligent or at fault is dropped from the legal dialogue.

According to insurance industry spokesmen, the relationship between policy-holder and company under no-fault would be identical to that which exists under a home-owner's or life insurance policy, known in industry parlance as first-party coverage. The adversary system emphasizing negligence would be replaced by a contractual relationship. Two parties, the insurance company and the car owner, enter into a written contract to fix the payment of damages in advance. This protection is extended to the car owner, members of his family, the driver, and occupants of the car, as well as pedestrians struck by that car.[7]

On January 1, 1971, the nation's first no-fault automobile insurance bill went into effect. The heated debate which preceded its passage lasted several years, starting when Massachusetts state representative Michael Dukakis in 1967 proposed a no-fault bill which had been developed by legal experts Robert Keeton of the Harvard Law School and Jeffrey O'Connell of the University of Illinois law school. Although the Massachusetts legislature rejected that plan, it has been the basis upon which much of the later debate has proceeded.

The Keeton-O'Connell plan first appeared in 1965. It is a combination of no-fault coverage and traditional negligence liability, designed by its authors to compensate all traffic accident victims for economic losses up to a limit of $10,000 regardless of fault. In exchange for $10,000 worth of protection, the victim loses the right to sue the wrongdoer for damages that exceed his economic loss, except in catastrophic cases.

Gillespie and Klipper described the Keeton-O'Connell plan: "Suppose that a driver, while stopped at a red light, is struck violently from behind by another driver. The wrong-doer admits the accident is his fault and apologizes. Both are injured to the same extent. The driver who was blameless in the accident suffers a financial loss, through a combination of medical bills and salary loss, of $1,000. The second driver's losses are the same. The Keeton-O'Connell plan would pay both $1,000. It would pay nothing to the first for any pain and suffering or any other general damages that he would have received under a fault system; these damages might

---

[7]Paul Gillespie and Miriam Klipper, *No-Fault—What You Save, Gain, and Lose with the New Auto Insurance* (New York: Praeger, 1972).

have been worth several hundred dollars. The negligent driver, who would receive nothing under a fault system, obtains the same amount as the first, despite the fact that he caused the accident. In effect, the good driver has lost benefits he would have received under a fault system in order to pay economic damages to the bad driver."[8]

Keeton and O'Connell have argued that the effort to determine who is at fault is a luxury that the automobile compensation system cannot afford. Instead of allocating money to fault-finding, they prefer to see this saving go directly to all victims, even those who cause injury to themselves and to others.

The Keeton-O'Connell bill imposes a limit to damages that can be recovered. Without such a ceiling, the cost of premiums would be considerably higher. Gillespie and Klipper have argued that although Keeton and O'Connell recognize equity in theory, they "ignore it in practice, because their threshold of $10,000 prevents innumerable victims from being fully compensated for serious injuries. The no-fault method, useful for dealing with small claims—those claims for which there is no severe or permanent injury and for which the economic loss is the greatest part of the claim— becomes less desirable as the amount of pain and suffering increases. For example, in the case of a man who has lost a limb in a traffic accident, to compensate him solely for wages and medical fees is grossly unfair. The same would be true of a victim who lost his eyesight or who had a permanent and disfiguring scar or a woman who suffered a miscarriage."[9]

In April, 1966, a special insurance commission was established in Massachusetts to study the entire automobile insurance question to arrive at recommendations for change. It was composed of thirteen members. Three were members of the commonwealth senate, five were members of the house of representatives, and five at-large members were appointed by the governor. After holding twenty public hearings, the commission issued its recommendations for insurance reform in January, 1970. The majority urged a plan that was identified as the "safe-driver plan." It was a set of six proposals for insurance revision and highway safety. Of the six proposals, only two were significant insurance reforms. One called for the enactment of no-fault property damage. Drivers would be given the choice of insuring their cars with their own insurance company by purchasing a collision pol-

[8] Ibid.
[9] Ibid.

icy or relinquishing their right to sue for property damage based on proving fault. The purpose was to reduce total insurance costs by eliminating the need to purchase property damage insurance. The second proposal was the offer of an optional $250 deductible to help the costs of compulsory personal injury coverage.

The legislation that was finally approved by the Massachusetts General Court (Legislature) was a modified "no-fault" approach. It contained some of the traditional possibilities for recovery and retained the concept of fault for a limited number of cases. Pain and suffering—or general damage claims—were still permitted with certain exceptions, limited to situations in which the victim, after first proving fault, could show that his injury falls within one of six categories. A general-damage claim, in addition to economic loss, could be compensated in these situations: (1) where the medical bill exceeded $500, (2) where a permanent and serious disfigurement resulted, (3) where there was a loss, totally or partially, of vision or hearing as defined by the Massachusetts Workmen's Compensation Act, (4) where there was a total or partial loss of a bodily member, (5) where the injury resulted in fracture, and (6) where the injury resulted in death. Inclusion within any one of these categories permitted an accident victim to retain his common-law right to a suit for general damages.

O'Connell expressed disappointment that the thresholds for fault claim and the possibility of a claim for pain and suffering were left so low. He felt that maintaining five-hundred dollars as the threshold for allowing a general damage claim made it tempting to make false medical claims. Still, the effect of the statute was to bar all but a small percentage of accident victims from filing suit, since 95 percent of all negligence claims in Massachusetts for personal injuries fell below that amount.[10]

The Massachusetts no-fault law guaranteed a payment of up to two thousand dollars to satisfy all economic losses caused by personal injuries arising from automobile accidents regardless of fault. The two thousand dollar no-fault maximum had a threefold benefit: reasonable medical expenses would be paid in full, 75 percent of actual wages lost would be paid, and expenses incurred for hiring substitute help would be paid in full.

Under the Massachusetts plan, no-fault coverage was given to the following: the insured, the owner of the automobile, members of the insured's household, authorized persons who were operating the insured's automo-

[10] O'Connell, "Extending the No-Fault Idea," p. 112.

bile, the insured's guests and guests of the authorized operator, and pedestrians who were struck by the insured or while an authorized individual was driving the car. This last feature has been considered somewhat revolutionary: pedestrians who are struck by an automobile are treated as having contractual rights with the automobile owner's insurance company.

Several persons were excluded from coverage: a person who was eligible for workmen's compensation insurance at the time of his injury, a person who was injured as a result of his own intentional act, anyone driving under the influence of drugs or liquor, anyone committing a felony at the time of the injury, and a driver who was deliberately trying to injure others at the time he himself was injured. The exclusions adopted by the Massachusetts General Court were missing from the original Keeton-O'Connell bill and have been generally followed in other no-fault plans.

Another new feature of the Massachusetts no-fault plan was that of periodic payments. Under the fault system, claims were settled or won in court on a one-payment, lump-sum basis—often some time after the accident occurred. Payments were frequently delayed for several years, and resources were not available to the victim at the time of his greatest need, immediately after the accident. The no-fault system called for making periodic payments available when the victim was in greatest financial need. Critics pointed out, however, that the two thousand–dollar limit could be quickly exhausted and would do little to assist those undergoing long periods of convalescence. In view of the low minimum Michael Dukakis, the leading proponent of no-fault in the Massachusetts General Court, complained that the legislature had "labored a year and brought forth a mouse." [11]

Assessing the Massachusetts legislation, Gillespie and Klipper concluded: "Notwithstanding all the efforts to restructure automobile insurance embodied in the Massachusetts bill, the greatest single failure was the retention of minimum liability limits at $5,000 per person, per accident. Despite the platitudes about the inadequacy of benefits going to those who are severely injured, nothing was changed to guarantee better coverage. The same inadequate job. Its usefulness ends there. By pouring its resources into small claims, it leaves dangerously little for the seriously injured. Because it is difficult to define what is 'serious,' the Massachusetts statute has opted for as many objective standards as it could find, but these

[11] Gillespie and Klipper, *No-Fault*, p. 64.

thresholds have been chosen on superficial and arbitrary lines, related to costs rather than human suffering. With the passage of time, cost must, as a matter of right, give way to what is equitable. In the meantime, it is an open question whether the motoring public is better off." [12]

The Massachusetts no-fault law took effect on January 1, 1971. On January 3, 1971, an accident occurred which led to a test case before the Massachusetts Supreme Judicial Court. The facts of the case were not in dispute. The rear-end collision was caused solely by the negligence of the defendant. The plaintiff, Irving Pinnick, would have been entitled to collect $1,565 under the previous law: $115 as reasonable medical expense for treatment of his injuries, $650 for temporary loss of his earning capacity, and $800 for general damages, including pain and suffering.

Under the no-fault statute, Pinnick could no longer receive any payment for pain and suffering, because the case did not qualify as one of the six exceptions that allowed recovery for general damages. Pinnick did not have medical bills in excess of $500 and did not have a fracture or serious disfigurement; he did not lose his sight or hearing as defined by the Massachusetts Workmen's Compensation Act and did not wholly or partially lose the function of a bodily member. Since he did not qualify on any of these counts, he could not recover the $800 allocated for pain and suffering. A total of $288.50 was offered to Pinnick under the no-fault system, compared with the $1,565 he would have received from the company insuring the party responsible for the accident under the adversary system.

Mr. Pinnick's attorneys argued that the right of a victim to be fully compensated for pain and suffering and all other incidental and general damages resulting from someone's negligence amounted to a vested property right that could not be taken away from a citizen without a constitutional amendment. The court rejected this position, citing the workmen's compensation case of *New York Central Railroad* v. *White*, which upheld the New York Compensation Law and announced the principle that no citizen owned a vested interest in any rule of law that entitled him to insist that it should forever remain unchanged for his benefit. The court noted that a citizen could indeed find his relationships altered by a new statute and had no grounds for complaint because he found the law had changed to his disadvantage.

The Massachusetts court held that the no-fault legislation did not vio-

[12] Ibid.

late due process because it had not abolished any fundamental rights. Only one right was abolished—the right to collect damages from a wrongdoer for pain and suffering in those cases that did not fall within the exceptions allowed under the statute. The court declared that any other rights in effect prior to the no-fault legislation still remained but were enforced in a different manner. In fact, the court stated, only one portion of the old system was altered by the new legislation. The court concluded that the no-fault plan amounted to "a reasonable and adequate substitute" for existing rights and, on that basis, was constitutional.

The author of the court opinion, Justice Paul Cashman, discussed the fact that the old system had itself become unreasonable. He declared, "The problems of society to which the courts have been called no longer permit the luxury of using them as a forum for resolving the ever increasing numbers of automobile accident claims to the extent that has obtained hitherto." [13] The court, through the majority opinion, held that the no-fault automobile insurance bill was constitutional. The defendant was not liable to the plaintiff in an action of tort for negligence arising out of this accident. The court called motor vehicle negligence cases a "cancer" to be routed not only from Massachusetts but also from the entire American court system. It expressed the view that the no-fault approach was an appropriate step toward alleviating a problem that had "defied more conservative solutions."

A minority concurring opinion by Chief Justice Joseph Tauro argued that while Pinnick had failed to offer sufficient evidence to prove that he should have been compensated for the damages he sought, this would have been an impossible task under the circumstances. Judge Tauro felt that to go from this point to a declaration that the Massachusetts General Court had acted wisely in passing no-fault legislation was premature. He agreed that less expensive automobile insurance was a worthy goal but said that he did not wish to see "a burning down of the barn to get rid of the mice." [14] He indicated that few observers would agree that $288.50 rather than $1,565.00 was a reasonable substitute in the Pinnick case. Judge Tauro also expressed dissatisfaction with the legislature's limitation of recovery for pain and suffering to the six exceptions listed in the statute. He offered a list of several serious injuries that were not exempted from the no-fault

[13] Ibid., p. 79.
[14] Ibid., p. 88.

plan unless one of the six standard exceptions also applied, among them: injuries such as torn muscles, tendons, and ligaments, sprained and dislocated joints, loss and diminution of the sense of taste, loss of the sense of touch, loss of the sense of smell, rupture of the cervical disc, contusions of the brain, and other injuries to vital tissues and internal organs.

Thus, Judge Tauro concluded, because these injuries could not be characterized as nuisance claims and because they were excluded from compensation for pain and suffering unless a listed exception applied, the plaintiff's case was legally the stronger. He declared that the plaintiff's equal-protection argument that the categories allowing exceptions from the restraints of no-fault limitations of compensation were arbitrary and unreasonable was basically sound but would yet have to be adequately documented in court.

Following its adoption in Massachusetts, no-fault legislation with varying features was adopted in Florida, Delaware, Oregon, and Illinois. In Oregon, the law retained claims based upon fault and used no-fault as a supplement. In Florida, claims for damages based upon fault were retained in theory but such high thresholds were imposed as to exclude most possibilities of lawsuits from traffic accidents. At the same time, the law eliminated pain and suffering as a significant compensation factor in automobile insurance. The pattern which has evolved is one of a dual system, which seeks to achieve a degree of balance between fault and no-fault principles.

The "total" no-fault plan was advocated by the American Insurance Association and the State Insurance Department of New York. Under this approach, the idea of fault in automobile accidents would have been eliminated, except in the case of death, when the insurance companies would subrogate or redistribute claim payments. Critics have charged that, with a drop in benefits, the seriously injured would be cut off without compensation and that this system would be efficient only in providing for very small claims. This total no-fault approach has never been adopted, although New York State seriously considered it, with the support of Gov. Nelson Rockefeller.

The Keeton-O'Connell approach maintained the victim's ability to make a claim based on negligence and, in a limited way, retained the concept of fault in extremely serious cases. The plan permitted claims for pain and suffering and other general damages based on fault if losses exceeded a threshold of ten thousand dollars. The authors of this plan have made a number of alterations since it was first proposed, such as providing a choice of purchasing no-fault insurance or remaining subject to the law of negligence.

The Massachusetts and Florida plans both contained elements of the Keeton-O'Connell approach, although there were a number of differences between the plans of these two states. For example, the Florida plan was more generous than that in Massachusetts, carrying a limit of five thousand dollars rather than the Massachusetts two thousand dollar limit. In Florida, the victim was reimbursed for 85 percent of actual lost wages, compared with 75 percent in Massachusetts. To assist the victim during the time of greatest financial need, Florida, unlike Massachusetts, required that the company pay the benefits due at intervals not greater than every two weeks. In Massachusetts, the threshold used to allow tort recovery was five hundred dollars, while Florida doubled this to one thousand dollars.

The no-fault bill adopted by Illinois and endorsed by the American Mutual Insurance Alliance, allowed two separate systems to operate side by side. Minimum no-fault benefits were guaranteed while the fault system was kept alive by imposing restrictions on compensation for pain and suffering. The Illinois plan provided that no-fault medical benefits be offered to a limit of $2,000 per person per accident. It offered 85 percent of lost earning capacity to a limit of $7,800, payable in maximum installments of $150 per week. The wage provision included the right to claim the loss of profits, when the victim was forced to close or restrict business activities because of his injury. Illinois carried a substitute-help provision to pay individuals who performed services for the injured during the time of convalescence and offered $12 per day for up to one year for this help. The insurer was required to offer to each policyholder the chance to buy an excess no-fault policy of $50,000 per person per accident, and $100,000 per total injuries per accident. The option was given to buy unlimited medical coverage, income continuation to $39,000, substitute-help benefits of $12 per day for five years, and $2,000 for funeral expenses, all on a no-fault basis.

Another approach to no-fault was taken by Oregon, Delaware, and South Dakota. As did Illinois, these states embraced a dual fault–no-fault system, but with significant differences. The Illinois system used no-fault reform to alter and restrict the law of damages. The Oregon–Delaware–South Dakota no-fault approach left the fault system of compensation for damages intact and supplemented it with partial no-fault. The method left every policyholder in as good a financial position as in the past.

The Oregon plan, for example, provided for a medical payment of three thousand dollars per person per accident. The victim was guaranteed 70 percent of gross earnings, limited to five hundred dollars per month, with a six thousand dollar limit payable without regard to fault. No-fault protection was extended to the insured, his family, guest passengers, and pedestrians, though not to persons eligible for workmen's compensation. Guest passengers and pedestrians could apply the no-fault coverage only as excess coverage to pay expenses not covered by their own collateral resources.

In the past decade, twenty-six states and the District of Columbia have passed no-fault insurance laws with the goals of lowering premiums, speeding up claims, and unclogging the courts. Reviewing the success of these laws, the *Wall Street Journal* noted that "disenchantment with the laws is spreading. A drive to scrap no-fault is afoot in Pennsylvania; another was recently fought back in the District of Columbia. Bills to change the law have become almost an annual rite in Massachusetts, Kansas and Colorado. New Jersey did amend its law this year. Nevada tried to in 1979—and wound up throwing out the whole system." [15]

The *Journal* observed that of the ten states with the most expensive average auto premiums, six had no-fault laws: "No-fault can't bear unequivocal blame, though, since factors like population density and the generosity of coverage in each state affect cost." [16] The article cited claims by Claude C. Lilly III, director of Florida State University's Center for Insurance Research, that no-fault coverage cost more and that its cost rose faster than traditional auto-insurance premiums. They rose, he pointed out, even more quickly than the overall consumer price index.

Most state no-fault laws have been established in a way that encourages lavish medical treatments for minor injuries, which adds to the cost of the premiums, according to the *Journal*, which also mentioned that no-fault laws have not lessened the number of lawsuits, as they were intended to do. According to the Association of American Trial Lawyers, more litigation goes on at the present in many of the states with no-fault laws than went on before those laws were passed.

The *Journal* article reported that eighteen states compelled people to purchase no-fault medical coverage even if they already had extensive health insurance. Others encouraged such a purchase, but stopped short of

---

[15] Mary Williams, "No-Fault Auto Policies Are Widely Attacked as Costly, Ineffective," *Wall Street Journal*, November 16, 1983, p. 1.

[16] Ibid.

requiring it. This meant that, in many cases, people were buying insurance which they did not need. It also meant that people involved in automobile accidents could, in some cases, be reimbursed twice. The result of this was that everyone's premiums had gone up.

A report by the Pennsylvania Trial Lawyers Association, a group which supports repeal of the no-fault legislation in Pennsylvania, has stated, "No-fault was foisted upon an unsuspecting public primarily as a means of reducing the cost of insurance. . . . The claimed advantages of no-fault have simply not materialized." [17]

Advocates of no-fault have argued that true no-fault insurance has not been adopted in any state and that it is therefore impossible to determine whether or not it would work successfully. The *Wall Street Journal* agreed, pointing out that "many measures have been put on the books under the name of 'no-fault,' and it is their spotty performance that has been giving no-fault insurance its shaky reputation." J. Robert Hunter, president of the National Insurance Consumers Organization, has declared, "The fault with no-fault isn't no-fault. The fault with no-fault is faulty no-fault." [18]

The *Wall Street Journal* described the criticisms of pure no-fault: "There were simply too many problems with taking away a person's right to sue. Opponents argued that the hypothetical Sunday-school teacher shouldn't be denied the chance to clobber the hooligan who knocked her down. They said the fear of lawsuits made the hooligans—and everybody else—drive more safely. Besides, they said, if crash victims weren't allowed to recover the cost of their pain and suffering along with their medical bills, they would be getting cheated." [19]

William A. K. Titelman, a lobbyist for the Pennsylvania Trial Lawyers Association, has argued: "Medical benefits are only a small fraction of the need. What about the young pianist who has a promising future on the stage whose hands are injured? You'd look up the medical benefits for her: Hand—$500. This is fundamentally offensive to the Western concept of justice." [20]

Lawyers were, in turn, criticized by proponents of no-fault as simply defending their own interests. No-fault, after all, took away their right to collect fees for handling lawsuits relating to auto accidents.

The states responded to all of this by enacting compromise legisla-

[17] Cited in ibid.
[18] Quoted in ibid.
[19] Ibid.
[20] Quoted in ibid.

tion. Nine states established no-fault systems that provided first-party coverage but did not take away the driver's right to sue for pain and suffering. Other states permitted pain-and-suffering suits, but sharply restricted them. They did not limit the amount that crash victims could seek through lawsuits, but they imposed a system of thresholds that victims must meet before they could file suit. In some states, the thresholds were difficult, in others easy. It is these easier thresholds which are the subject of increasing debate at present.

The reason for this debate is that these less stringent thresholds do not prevent enough lawsuits, and prevention is one of the key reasons for embracing the no-fault system, according to its advocates. In Colorado, Kansas, Massachusetts, Utah, and Georgia, people are able to file suits for pain and suffering as soon as their expenses exceed five hundred dollars. In Connecticut, they can sue after spending four hundred dollars. As health care costs rise—as they have been steadily doing for many years—it is increasingly easy to reach the threshold amount and begin litigation. Insurance companies argue that many people receive unnecessary treatments precisely to reach the threshold so that they can sue. James A. Stahly, a spokesman for State Farm Mutual Automobile Insurance Company, commented, "You don't have to stretch your morals very far to get past the thresholds, if you know what I mean." [21]

What has happened in a number of states is that because of low thresholds and padding of medical expenses, insurance companies have discovered that they have not saved enough money on pain-and-suffering suits to pay for first-party benefits under no-fault insurance plans. When such systems are unable to finance themselves, premiums must be increased.

This is what happened in Pennsylvania, which had established what many observers called one of the most generous no-fault laws in the country. In that state, an automobile accident victim is guaranteed unlimited medical coverage. Pennsylvania also has a $750 threshold. It has, in addition, the eighth highest average auto insurance premiums in the United States, because the system has not been paying for itself.

Initially, Pennsylvania attempted to enact a pure no-fault law but found this impossible. The chief drafter of this legislation and the legislature's director of Republican research, Otis W. Littleton, has explained, "The trial bar was so adamantly opposed that it was impossible." [22] The leg-

[21] Ibid., p. 22.
[22] Ibid.

islature then considered the kind of legislation it finally adopted, with thresholds that maintained the right of citizens to sue in the courts for pain and suffering. Finally, a plan calling for a $750 threshold and $25,000 in coverage for every driver was adopted. Thinking that $25,000 was not sufficient, the legislature raised the coverage to infinity, but did not make the corresponding restriction on lawsuits to pay for it.

In Colorado, the legislature approved a plan with a $500 threshold and $25,000 in compulsory medical coverage. J. Richard Barnes, Colorado insurance commissioner, has said that inflation in health-care costs requires a threshold of $3,500, which the legislature has been reluctant to adopt.

New Jersey adopted a system in which it attempted to pay unlimited benefits by permitting anyone to sue who had medical expenses of more than two hundred dollars. As a result, premiums have been the highest in the country, and a number of insurance companies refused to write auto insurance in that state. In October, 1983, New Jersey made certain changes. Now drivers can choose less expensive insurance with a fifteen-hundred-dollar threshold, but the two-hundred-dollar threshold is still available.

The system adopted by Michigan is somewhat more balanced. In that state, unlimited first-party benefits are paid. To reduce lawsuits, however, it has retained a list of the injuries a driver must suffer before suing. Thomas H. Hay, chairman of the Michigan Trial Lawyers Association, complained, "You darn near have to have an amputation. . . . A broken bone, no matter how bad the fracture, isn't going to make it." [23]

Hay noted, however, that while lawyers in Michigan do not like that state's no-fault law, it does seem to work well. When it was adopted in 1973, 9.9 percent of Michigan lawsuits involved auto negligence. By the 1980–81 court year, the figure had fallen to 5.4 percent. "We recognize that some citizens are better off," Hay admitted; "they get prompt payment, and they have the right, in the serious cases, to continue with a lawsuit." Jean Carlson, Michigan's deputy insurance commissioner, declared, "We have a real no-fault law and it works great." The insurance industry in Michigan, however, has been attempting to increase the threshold. [24]

The *Wall Street Journal* reported: "One person who thinks that no-fault has worked well is James R. Guernsey, a 33 year old Pennsylvanian who was riding in a van that hit a hole in the road and crashed in 1971. Mr. Guernsey was paralyzed; he has lost the use of his legs, arms and hands.

[23] Quoted in ibid.
[24] Ibid.

But today he is still working, running two delicatessens in the Philadelphia suburbs. He attributes his comeback to Pennsylvania's unlimited medical coverage. For him, even costly, trouble-ridden, watered-down no-fault insurance has proven a boon." [25]

The *Journal* continued: "Mr. Guernsey can recite his medical bills from memory: hospital, $100,000; rehabilitation center, $65,000; two wheelchairs, $11,500; a special van, $15,000; a 24-hour attendant, $50,000 a year for the rest of his life; medication, $4,000 a year. Prudential Insurance Co. of America paid the whole thing—'no qualms, no nothing,' says Mr. Guernsey. 'Anything that happens to me because of my accident that wouldn't have happened to me before is covered under the no-fault,' he says. 'There's no way I would have been able to afford it myself.' Yet Mr. Guernsey is doing what any other accident victim might be tempted to do in a pseudo-no-fault state. He has filed three lawsuits." [26]

Much of the discussion that has taken place about no-fault insurance in the United States had its beginning in the mid-1960s when Congress directed the Department of Transportation to undertake a study of the entire automobile insurance system. In March, 1971, the Department of Transportation issued a final report urging the states to adopt a system of first-party or no-fault insurance. The department expressed its support for a state-regulated no-fault system to provide compensation for economic losses of all descriptions. Cost reduction for the consumer was to be achieved by the emphasis on coordination of benefits, the use of deductibles to make the victim a self-insurer, and the termination of the adversary system as the primary method of determining who would receive automobile insurance compensation. The right to sue would be retained for only the most severe cases.

One of the most discussed questions in the entire debate over no-fault insurance is whether there is a moral obligation for society to extend benefits to all traffic victims, regardless of their conduct in contributing to their own situation. The Department of Transportation report argued that all motorists' economic losses should be covered regardless of fault, including medical expenses, wage loss, and property damage, although it would not make such benefits unlimited. It suggested that the insurance industry offer motorists optional coverage against the most catastrophic losses. It would

[25] Ibid.
[26] Ibid.

permit the individual to absorb his own smaller losses by liberal use of deductibles.

Another guideline set forth by the Department of Transportation was greater coordination of benefits from automobile insurance with other available resources. It recommended that all government insurance coverage be primary, used even before automobile insurance. In the absence of some applicable social insurance plan—Social Security, Medicare, Medicaid, welfare—automobile coverage would be used prior to all other private collateral health insurance sources. Duplicate medical coverages should be allowed, the report stated, only with the prior knowledge and consent of the insurer.

With regard to the desirability of private versus public insurance, the Department of Transportation study expressed a preference for private insurance plans up to the point where they demonstrated beyond doubt that they could no longer function efficiently. It suggested that small amounts of compulsory insurance be used to induce the consumer to purchase more than the minimum needed to ensure his own protection. The study discussed the need to make available additional supplementary coverage, but on a voluntary basis.

The study supported the use of the adversary system as the method for awarding general and intangible damages, including pain and suffering. The Department of Transportation argued that if a compulsory low-level, no-fault program were maintained, there would be more room in the system for general-damage awards. It acknowledged—because more individuals could become successful claimants and benefits in some circumstances would be improved—that the transition to no-fault coverage from a tort system might, in fact, increase the price of insurance.

Where the use of fault was retained, the study urged a high, though unspecified, medical threshold before a victim could make a fault claim for pain and suffering. No objective standards, however, were presented as a basis upon which such a determination should be made. The study also suggested that intangible losses be recoverable in cases of permanent loss of function or disfigurement. This appears to be an acknowledgment that compensation for economic losses only is inequitable, especially in cases of severe injury. Thus, the report said that a permanent injury to a vital function, a significant and embarrassing disfigurement, or serious emotional upset should not be overlooked.

According to polling data, the Trasnportation Department study reported, the public is willing to forgo general damages in smaller cases in exchange for a reduction of insurance premium cost. It was unclear exactly what definition should be given to "small case," and it is this debate over appropriate thresholds that has created much division and controversy in many state legislatures and within the insurance, legal, and medical communities.

With regard to loss of income, the Department of Transportation called for a payment ceiling of $1,000 per person per month to be included as part of a compulsory package, accompanied by an option to purchase higher limits for those who believed that their earning capacity required greater protection. Loss of income protection was expected to accompany the chance for rehabilitation, even if an accident involved an injury that in no way interfered with an individual's employment. Wage continuation was given a three-year limit with benefits having a ceiling of $1,000 per month, or a maximum of $36,000. As did other no-fault bills, that of the Transportation Department called for a provision for hiring substitute services at $75 per week.

The Department of Transportation also advocated compulsory no-fault property damage insurance. Ideally, the accident victim would turn to his own insurance company to receive payment for personal injuries and property damage with the exception of claims for pain and suffering, which would remain part of the adversary system. The use of deductibles and self-insurance for a major portion of the damage to one's own automobile could significantly reduce the cost of insurance.

The Department of Transportation suggested that group marketing of no-fault insurance coverage would provide major savings. It noted that employee associations, unions, and fraternal and religious groups could jointly purchase no-fault insurance as a block, lowering costs for the participants. The study recognized the fact that while some would save from such an approach, it could add to the cost of automobile insurance for those who were not included in a group.

Some observers predict that there will be growing pressure for some form of federal rule concerning automobile insurance. Gillespie and Klipper have written: "The McCarran-Ferguson Act . . . has left the regulation of the insurance companies exclusively to the states. The industry has prospered under the shield of laissez-faire. With increased recognition that automobile insurance is an interstate problem, the outcry for federal regulation is going to become louder. And with greater reliance on compulsory insurance, the private insurance companies are sure to face a future of tighter regulation by state or federal government. The private insurance companies will have to be more closely watched as to the amount of profits they should be allowed to retain from compulsory insurance. Where excess profits above a statutory maximum are achieved, any compulsory insurance plan, be it first-party no-fault or third-party fault, must provide a statutory rebate to the consumer. Investment profits and losses under a compulsory system should be considered as part of the rate as well. To reduce price, rate-setting by prior approval must give way to open competition among the companies." [27]

Gillespie and Klipper continued: "Whether or not the federal government has the constitutional right to impose its guidelines over automobile insurance, which the states regard as their domain, remains to be decided. When the Massachusetts Supreme Court considered the constitutionality of its no-fault insurance reform, it relied upon the constitutional grant of power of a state to control automobile insurance through its police power. The Department of Transportation saw the power over automobile insurance as resting with the national government, based upon federal control over interstate commerce. If that power does exist—and it is likely that it does, because automobile insurance has an undeniable impact on interstate commerce—the case of Pinnick vs. Cleary, decided on the premise that the state has the right to control automobile insurance, may be open to further inquiry." [28]

Shortly after the Department of Transportation issued its report, senators Philip Hart (D-Michigan) and Warren Magnuson (D-Washington) introduced legislation outlining a complete national no-fault insurance program. The Hart-Magnuson proposal included restructuring of both personal injury and property damage protection. First-party no-fault insurance, under this legislation, would become compulsory nationwide, for all owners and drivers of automobiles.

Under this plan, every company authorized to write automobile insurance would be required to offer a noncancellable policy binding the insurer to the insured, except in cases of nonpayment of premiums or revocation of the insured's driver's license, which Senator Hart believed were the only two legitimate excuses for refusing to sell automobile insurance. What first

[27] Gillespie and Klipper, *No-Fault*.
[28] Ibid.

led Hart to his interest in automobile insurance reform was his concern about what he viewed as discriminatory classifications—higher rates for people in some lines of work, such as waitresses or bartenders, and lower rates for some others. The failure of insurance companies to provide certain segments of society with needed protection spurred Senator Hart and some of his colleagues to advocate change.

The Hart-Magnuson bill called for payment of all medical and rehabilitation costs which would be open-ended and not subject to any restriction other than that they be appropriate and reasonable. The plan called for the guaranteed payment of net lost wages and reimbursement for impairment of earning capacity less deductions for taxes, until there was complete physical recovery. A limitation of $1,000 per month was placed on the wage provision, with a mandatory option to purchase more protection if the policyholder so desired.

Property damage in the Hart-Magnuson bill would be covered, regardless of fault, by the insured's insurance company. If a parked car were struck, the claim would be made against the company of the driver striking it. If a moving car were struck, each driver would make claim for property damage to his own insurance policy.

To replace benefits eliminated by no-fault, the Hart-Magnuson bill offered two options. The first paid for economic losses above the no-fault limits. The second paid for general damages, including pain and suffering. In order to collect under either option, the victim would have to prove fault by the driver causing the injury. The availability of these options would allow free competition between the choice of fault or no-fault compensation.

The Hart-Magnuson optional personal injury coverages did not call for a minimum threshold before a claim for pain and suffering could be pursued. There were no projections of what this kind of coverage would cost, leading some critics to point out that it represented a change in the no-fault advocates' tactics. Thus, rather than eliminate general damages claims outright, it was argued, the advocates of no-fault would simply seek to price them out of existence.

The Hart-Magnuson plan clearly called for federal no-fault insurance and rejected the Department of Transportation's suggestion that each state develop its own system of no-fault insurance. This legislation was never approved, however. It faced the combined opposition of the insurance industry, the American Trial Lawyers Association, the advocates of other versions of reform, and conservatives who feared the growth of power and authority in Washington and the diminution of states' rights.

One of the most vigorous advocates of no-fault insurance is Herbert Denenberg, former Pennsylvania insurance commissioner. In congressional testimony, Denenberg declared: "The automobile insurance and reparations system operates like a legalized racket of colossal and cruel proportions and everyone knows it. The automobile insurance and reparations system is barbaric in its slowness to compensate, its inadequacy and uncertainty of compensation—and everyone knows it. The automobile insurance and reparations system is the most wasteful, the most inefficient, the most extravagant of our methods of paying accident victims—and everyone knows it. . . . The automobile insurance and reparations system now has only a single class of beneficiaries—trial lawyers—who have made a billion dollar business of claims and lawsuits, in a grand legal war in which they are the only real victors—and everyone knows it." [29]

Denenberg further argued, "No-fault automobile insurance gives the consumer what he wants—payment right after an accident rather than a slow and uncertain gamble, with chances of success less than fifty-fifty for the seriously injured who need compensation the most." [30]

Shortly after this, a group called the Lawyers Committee for Public Education began a campaign in Pennsylvania to counter Denenberg's efforts to promote no-fault insurance in that state. They produced a radio commercial that claimed, "No-fault auto insurance is a hoax!" This advertisement listed various drawbacks of no-fault and stated that the no-fault approach "relieves the reckless driver of responsibility for his own negligence" and that "a careless driver has exactly the same right to compensation as you, his innocent victim." The commercial ended, "If Pennsylvania gets no-fault, it will be your fault." [31]

To the argument that no-fault limits the victim's right to go to court, Denenberg responded: "That is just not a fact. You always have a right to sue. You just may not have a right to sue for pain and suffering unless you fit into a certain category (depending on the no-fault plan). But you can always sue for medical losses, wage losses, and pain and suffering if you exceed the threshold (the minimum specified amount of hospital bills that

[29] Howard Shapiro, *How to Keep Them Honest* (Emmaus, Pa.: Rodale Press, 1974), p. 92.
[30] Ibid.
[31] Ibid., p. 93.

must be acquired before the no-fault plan allows you to go to court). Here's the real point of no-fault and why we need it: You can get a service to people when they really need it. By that I mean you can pay people very quickly, because you do not have to judge fault. And along with that, you've eliminated pain and suffering claims in all the small cases where they're likely to be phony or exaggerated anyway. In the process, we save the insurance company money and waiting, and that's passed on to the policyholder." [32]

Some critics of no-fault argue that because automobile insurance costs tend to be much lower in rural areas, no-fault's statewide impact—in any state—would have little effect on reducing costs for policyholders in rural areas. Denenberg, on the other hand, reasoned: "O.K., they say that in the suburbs, for instance, the costs are already low. But what they mean, specifically, is that the costs of insurance are already low. That doesn't help the guy who gets his brains bashed out in the suburbs, in an automobile accident. How is the cost of his insurance relevant to his serious injuries or huge medical bills? Even if you're giving the insurance away, even if it costs zero, that would not be an argument against no-fault. You're still not paying the guy's medical bills when he gets them, his lost wages when he needs them. Under the present system, he's flat on his back in the hospital and you give him a goddam lottery ticket, a chance of a lifetime to spend three years playing games in court before he gets his money. If you sat down a bunch of people and you told them to design the worst auto reparations and insurance system they could, what they would do is come up with exactly what we've got now—incredibly expensive, incredibly slow, incredibly uncertain, incredibly inadequate, incredibly discriminatory." [33]

In *The Invisible Bankers*, Andrew Tobias declared: "Even under no-fault, drivers have enormous incentive not to cause accidents. They risk personal injury, death, criminal penalty or, at the very least, property damage, license suspension and hiked insurance rates. True no-fault auto insurance allows a much larger proportion of each premium dollar to reach the accident victim. Fair, fast and efficient, it was recommended to the nation by a team from Columbia University as long ago as 1932. But the fight for no-fault only got under way in earnest in the late 1960s." [34]

Although the casual observer may think that the fight for no-fault au-

[32] Ibid., pp. 101, 102.
[33] Ibid., p. 102.
[34] Tobias, *Invisible Bankers*, p. 207.

tomobile insurance has been won, Tobias disagreed. "Many states today have one or another form of no-fault insurance. In fact, however, no state had a true no-fault auto insurance system. . . . In all but a few 'no-fault' states, the threshold of damages beyond which the fault system took over was so low—$500 or less in many cases—that it merely encouraged victims and their lawyers to incur unnecessary medical expenses in order to 'build up the claim,' exceed the threshold, and thus qualify to sue for pain and suffering. . . . Lawyers object that to compensate innocent victims only for their medical costs and lost wages, and not also for their pain and suffering, is unfair. Which is true. But life is unfair, and it is only a relative few serious accident victims who have the good fortune to have been injured by someone rich, or richly insured. The drivers with the least insurance cause the most accidents. And even if the offending party is well insured, there is the small matter of proving that he was at fault. Years may pass. And then in all but a few cases it is questionable whether the injured party, after giving up a third or a half of his award in legal fees and expenses, retains more than would have been paid, promptly, under no-fault." [35]

The debate over no-fault insurance is likely to continue into the future. On one side, consumer groups and other citizen organizations, including labor unions, have been advocating such laws. On the other side, lawyers and many insurance companies have been fighting them. And many who believe that true no-fault legislation would be inequitable—in that those who were most seriously injured would find it difficult, if not impossible, to be adequately compensated for the true extent of their injuries, including pain and suffering—have been vigorously opposed to such laws.

Some insurance companies have also been concerned that no-fault would lead to the same kinds of group coverage as life and health insurance have in the past. Employers, it is believed, would provide no-fault automobile insurance as a fringe benefit. Those insurance companies that specialize in group policies are far more inclined to support the no-fault concept. Insurance agencies that exist to sell individual policies, however, see little benefit to themselves in this approach.

In addition, a no-fault system that would shorten the length of time between an accident and the reimbursement to the injured party of his award would give insurance companies a much shorter length of time to invest premiums.

Advocates of no-fault blame the legal profession for the fact that, thus far, true no-fault laws have not been adopted in any state. Thus, Tobias charged: "Our failure to adopt true no-fault auto insurance is a nuts-and-bolts example of the country at its most obese; arteries hardened and clogged by special interests, its heart having to pump $1 in liability premiums to get 14.5 cents where it is most needed—the economic losses of the accident victim. But what special interest group is better able to strangle the system than the lawyers? They write the laws." [36]

Similarly, CBS News reporter Fred Graham concluded an hour-long television report: "If you've wondered about such reforms as arbitration or small-claims courts or no-fault laws, what we found is that very little reform is really going on, apparently because the lawyers control the system and they lack the will to reform it." [37]

The debate over no-fault, of course, is not quite that simple. There are legitimate arguments on both sides of the question, and they are likely to be debated in state legislatures, in the Congress, and in the press for some time to come.

[35] Ibid., p. 207, 213.
[36] Ibid., p. 216.
[37] "See You in Court," CBS Special Report, transcript, July, 1980.

6

Disclosure and Insurance

WE live in an era in which "truth in lending," "truth in packaging," and "truth in advertising" have become, more and more, legal mandates. In September, 1982, for example, the Federal Trade Commission considered a case concerning the Kroger supermarket chain. Advertisements claiming that Kroger prices were as low as or lower than other local supermarkets were found to be deceptive, even though the FTC found no evidence that Kroger's prices were higher. Kroger's mistake, the FTC declared, was to base its claim on "price patrols" of comparison shoppers rather than on a more statistically based and verifiable source. In dissent, Commissioner Patricia Bailey argued that Kroger emphasized the informality of the surveys and said she feared that "the majority opinion will chill the development of useful comparative price advertising." [1]

James C. Miller III, as chairman of the FTC in the Reagan administration, believed that the commission had been going too far.

Miller defined deception in advertising this way: "There are two aspects. One is to show that reasonable consumers to whom the ad is directed would be deceived to their detriment. Secondly, we have to consider that there may be vulnerable groups, such as children, and the best way to protect them is to have a standard that says that an advertiser is guilty of deception if he knew or should have known that the advertisement would de-

[1] Quoted in "Regulatory Mouthwash," *Wall Street Journal* editorial, May 12, 1982.

ceive such a person. Suppose, for example, that someone claimed to have a miracle cure for cancer. A terminally ill person would be very vulnerable to that type of message."[2]

Shortly after he assumed his FTC post, Miller was asked if advertisers should continue to be required to substantiate their claims. He responded: "Our goal is to determine if the advertising claim is accurate. When a firm can come up with evidence to substantiate the claim, that should be sufficient. In other words, I want to focus more on whether the claim is accurate or inaccurate, and less on whether advertisers did lots of paper work before making the claim. Moreover, we need to ask ourselves whether the volume and type of information we require from firms are excessive, since the associated costs are passed along to consumers. Finally, if we have an impossibly high, inflexible standard for factual claims, advertisers will engage far more in puffery and imagery and less in factual information that benefits consumers."[3]

In March, 1983, the FTC launched a major, yearlong effort to seek industry and public help in clearing up its rules governing substantiation of advertising claims. The five commissioners voted unanimously to request comments over the following six months on how its ad substantiation program could be improved and then to take at least six months to examine comments before making final changes.

This was the first effort at a major overhaul of the enforcement program since the 1970s, when the FTC began requiring advertisers to produce evidence backing up factual claims and any claims that could be reasonably inferred from the facts stated.

"The issue is a complicated one. It also proved to be a much more controversial subject than I ever imagined," said Chairman Miller.[4] He stated that there would be no change in the commission's requirement that advertisers have "a reasonable basis" for factual claims made. But the commission, he said, "has a duty to examine [its] implementation of the substantiation requirement, and to determine if any improvements are possible."[5]

At that time, FTC staff members said that rules and procedures for

[2]Quoted in "A Curious Push to Weaken FTC Advertising Rules," *New York Times*, November 14, 1982, p. F-11.
[3]Ibid.
[4]Quoted in *Washington Times*, March 4, 1983, p. 5B.
[5]Ibid.

implementing and enforcing this requirement had often been vague and contradictory. FTC commissioner David Clanton said that existing rules and procedures were "sufficiently amorphous and ambiguous so that advertisers will be deterred from making claims because of the fears that whatever specific kinds of evidence they have, or some kind of implied claim . . . the evidence will be found to be inadequate."[6]

Michael Pertschuk, holdover Democratic commissioner, who had been commission chairman in the Carter administration, charged that there had been "a marked slowdown" in the enforcement of the ad substantiation policy. He said: "I can continue to have reservations about the actual operation of the ad substantiation program in the commission, and the perception of relaxed FTC enforcement that it may be creating among advertisers. . . . My suspicion is fueled by the emergence of a new 'de-enforcement' trend."[7]

Pertschuk's contention was disputed by Tim Muris, director of the commission's Bureau of Consumer Protection, which runs the ad substantiation program. Muris said that over a period of several months the bureau had forwarded sixteen ad complaints and sixteen consent agreements to the commission for action.

Miller said the commission should offer as much guidance as possible to advertisers "about what the program requires and what it does not." He listed the following areas as needing clarification: (1) Which types of advertising claims require substantiation, i.e., "Can we clarify the line between objective performance claims requiring substantiation and subjective claims that do not?"; (2) How to make advertisers prove a "reasonable basis" for "implied claims that are not reasonably apparent on the face of the ad and whose very existence is in dispute"; (3) Should the commission evaluate substantiating evidence that a company did not develop until after a particular claim was made in an ad? And if so, how and when?; (4) Can the commission offer advertisers more guidance on how much evidence is necessary to constitute a reasonable basis of substantiation?[8] The chairman commented that all three major advertising trade associations were endorsing the FTC's effort and had promised full cooperation.

Muris noted that, although the FTC's rule forbade accepting substantiation evidence developed after an advertiser's claim had appeared in an

[6] Ibid.
[7] Ibid.
[8] Ibid.

ad, the accepted practice was to look at it only after a complaint. He indicated that this apparent discrepancy should be clarified.

It is in the context of these discussions and events that we must consider the controversies that have arisen in the insurance industry concerning the questions of full disclosure and the ability of customers to make intelligent and informed decisions with regard to which policies they should purchase.

An FTC staff report issued in July, 1979, said: "Price competition is so ineffective in the life insurance industry that companies paying 20-year rates of return of 2 percent or less compete successfully against companies paying 4 to 6 percent. This disparity should be contrasted with the banking industry, where differences of a quarter of a percent are considered to be competitively crucial." [9]

Andrew Tobias has noted: "In many instances purchasers have no idea what insurance should cost—and so cannot shop for it intelligently. Unlike a simple coin toss, where both parties to the bet know the odds, in an insurance bet it is generally only the insurance company that knows the odds. State regulators have shown little interest in requiring them to pass this exceptionally useful information on to their customers. As a result, some lines of insurance—life insurance prime among them—have tended to compete not so much on price as on elaborate (and inefficient) selling methods." [10]

It is Tobias's view that a simple, standardized disclosure statement along the following lines would resolve much of the problem faced by purchasers of insurance: "Based on past loss experience, it is expected that less than 15 per cent of your premium dollar will be used to pay claims. The remainder is used to cover expenses, overhead and profit." [11]

"This one reform," Tobias claimed, "simple, meaningful disclosure—would go a long way toward 'rationalizing' the insurance industry. If people had an easier time understanding and comparing values, they could shop for insurance more wisely. That, in turn, would force the industry to compete more on the quality it offers, less on the quality of the parchment they are printed on. By promoting price competition, meaningful disclosure would help to cut out waste. Insurers should be free to

---

[9] Andrew Tobias, *The Invisible Bankers* (New York: Pocket Books, 1982), p. 53.
[10] Ibid.
[11] Ibid., p. 59.

offer grossly overpriced protection and customers, to buy it. But customers also have a right to know what it is they are getting. Tell us the odds!" [12]

Herbert Denenberg, Pennsylvania insurance commissioner, wrote: "You can't escape death, taxation, or life insurance salesmen. So you better get some life insurance to take care of your wife, children, and other dependents. And you better know enough about life insurance to be able to buy the product intelligently—or it will be rammed down your throat." [13]

During his first years in office, Denenberg tried to stop what he felt were unfair sales practices in the insurance industry. He published *A Shopper's Guide To Life Insurance* so that consumers could see cost comparisons and evaluate the merits of competing policies. He also criticized those insurance companies he believed were conducting their business in a less than fair manner. [14]

During the Pennsylvania Insurance Department's studies of policies for *A Shopper's Guide To Life Insurance* and subsequent supplements, Denenberg noticed that Canadian-based companies often offered similar, and sometimes the same, coverage for lower prices. He said the companies in Canada could afford the lower prices because, generally, they did not have expensive home offices and because their system of agents was completely different and less expensive than the American insurance system. "Americans buy radios and televisions from Japan, cameras from Germany and watches from Switzerland," Denenberg declared. "Maybe they should start buying their life insurance from Canada." [15]

Concerning what he called "the failure of the life insurance companies to make proper disclosure of prices," Denenberg's guide pointed out that "the same coverage at the same age may show as much as a 324 percent cost difference between the highest and lowest companies on the ratings. Because the public doesn't understand the true cost of coverage, the insurance industry has been free to operate on what I call 'competition by confusion.' The whole emphasis in the industry demonstrates that my charge is true. The emphasis is on paying big commissions, having sales drives, playing around with the policies to make them look slightly differ-

---

[12] Ibid.

[13] Herbert Denenberg, *The Insurance Trap: Unfair at Any Rate* (New York: Western Publishing, 1972).

[14] Quoted in Howard Shapiro, *How to Keep Them Honest* (Emmaus, Pa.: Rodale Press, 1974), p. 59.

[15] Ibid.

ent, and manipulating the cash values. So in order to figure the right costs, you have to look closely at the premiums, when they're paid, the cash values, the curbs at which they accumulate and the dividends—if paid and if any—and when they come in. That's what we do in our guides when we publish the listing, and that's why they've been dynamite." [16]

Denenberg charged: "Insurance companies have tried to discourage devices for selling life insurance, such as savings bank life insurance and group life insurance, which are more economical. The heavy emphasis is on selling through the agents, and there's an unbelievable turnover in agents. And they may be trained in a day or a few days, then turned out on the public. There's never been a suitability requirement to prevent a company from selling you a needless policy for instance, like there is for securities, so what happens is that people who have no need or use for endowments are sold endowments by an agent, when they should get term life insurance, for example." [17]

He noted: "The whole picture is totally confusing—even the simple choice between term insurance and whole life—there's very little information that says, 'This is term life and this is whole life and you ought to make your choice based on what you're getting out of the coverage.' Do you know I've talked to agents who sell millions of dollars worth of this stuff and *they're* often confused? They use fallacious sales pitches to the public. You know, 'buy it early and you'll save money,' which is just nothing more than a phony pitch. There's a lot of misrepresentation of coverage, too, and that's not hard to do when you're talking about life insurance. It's very easy to confuse the public. Nobody's sure of the product, and then they see fancy graphs and projections and schedules and get totally confused about what the hell's coming off. Add to that the problem of phony and weak companies. To summarize it, you've got an incredible problem. Companies that are not always strong are pushing life insurance through agents who tend to be incompetent, selling policies the public can't understand at a price structure so confusing that it's hard to tell which is the best deal and which is the worst." [18]

Before becoming Pennsylvania insurance commissioner, Denenberg had written an article in which he noted: "Consumerism is emerging as an overriding factor in politics and in insurance legislation. We hear in gener-

---

[16] Quoted in ibid., p. 63.
[17] Ibid.
[18] Ibid., p. 64.

alities that it will affect the insurance business, but few have appreciated the full scope of its likely impact. . . . Ironically enough, the one product the insurance industry seems to be able and willing to sell profitably and vigorously is life insurance, and particularly cash-value life insurance, which in many of its forms has become obsolete. Inflation is making cash value life insurance more obsolete every day, whatever your view of its suitability in more tranquil times; and the desire to share in the economic growth of the country is likely to make investment life insurance as we know it more obsolete and is likely to spell continuing decline in the demand for cash-value insurance. The only 'guarantee' by cash-value life insurance is continual erosion of its investment component." [19]

Denenberg continued: "There are other factors which indicate insurance is going to be hit with special force by consumerism. It has been an industry slow to innovate. . . . It has an unhappy public image, looked at askance by many groups and especially despised by the black population of our cities. It is an industry viewed with suspicion by our legislators. It is an industry ripe for muckraking, ripe for consumerism, ripe for legislative reform. The changes in the future are likely to be continuous and dramatic, eclipsing by far the velocity and magnitude of . . . social legislation such as Social Security and workmen's compensation. Existing norms in the insurance business are likely to be replaced by radical new departures." [20]

Denenberg expanded upon these views in a speech in Columbus, Ohio, to a group of insurance underwriters: "The life insurance industry has had over 200 years to make insurance agents and the public understand cash-value life insurance, and it hasn't been able to do so. . . . Unless the life insurance industry can find better ways to make its most profitable product understood, consumerism may find ways to make this understanding unnecessary. It may simply abolish cash-value life insurance. The life insurance industry needs a massive attack on the problem of public misunderstanding. It has ignored its critics for too long, apparently on the theory that the subject is so complex the public won't be able to understand it anyhow. This stance will no longer do, and it in fact involves a damaging and unacceptable admission. . . . There is no escape from ideas except by better ideas, and the cash-value life insurance industry had best be prepared to prove its case more persuasively . . . and to educate the public

---

[19] Herbert Denenberg, "Insurance in the Age of the Consumer," *Best's Review*, April, 1970.
[20] Ibid.

more effectively than it has in the past. In the long run, forthright attention to these problems of consumer education and market clarity will pay off, for the public and for the life [insurance] industry." [21]

One of the earlier criticisms of the insurance industry for misrepresenting its product and failing to disclose information consumers need to make an informed judgment was the book *The Grim Truth about Life Insurance*, written by Ralph Hendershot, the former financial editor of the *New York World Telegram and Sun*. Hendershot wrote: "Of course, life insurance is important; it is, indeed, vitally needed to provide against the financial vacuum created by untimely and unexpected death; it is a cornerstone in any long-range program designed for family financial security. But just because we accept and recognize life insurance as functional in family finance, does not immunize this smug and sanctimonious institution from provable charges that it has overglamourized, oversold and overcharged for its product. Life insurance is, in fact, far more costly than it should be; and most persons acquire it without the faintest knowledge of comparative values in policies. They shop well for motor cars, appliances or houses, but buy their life insurance blindly. They meekly purchase whatever some agent or broker, with one eye on the fat, prospective sales commission, decides they should have. . . . The need for life insurance is, of course, genuine; but it does not follow that because you need it, companies should trade on your necessity by mercilessly overcharging for it. It's not the size of the premium you pay that counts. It's how much net insurance do your dollars buy? In a great, great majority of cases—not enough." [22]

While other forms of insurance are straightforward, life insurance is presented as something far different from automobile insurance or fire insurance. Hendershot declared: "When it comes to life insurance, you are asked to forget such straight-line reasoning; you purchase a policy and one of the main sales arguments advanced is that in addition to gaining needed coverage, you are embarking on a wonderful thrift program. . . . Life insurance has deliberately been made complicated, confusing and unintelligible so that you wind up believing that it is your sacred obligation to buy what they 'sell' you, and to keep paying blindly, faithfully, and uncomplainingly whatever excessive premiums you may have signed up for. Pat

---

[21] Printed in *Best's Review*, October, 1970.
[22] Ralph Hendershot, *The Grim Truth about Life Insurance* (New York: G. P. Putnam's Sons, 1957).

the sacred cow, pay your premiums, and ask no questions. Asking questions will get you nowhere because Bossie knows best!"[23]

Hendershot argued that insurance companies often sell consumers policies they do not need but, because it is difficult to understand what is involved, purchasers are not aware of this fact. He states: "Whereas agents tend to stress the insurance needs for a whole lifetime, who really needs it that long? Why do ordinary life policies endow at 100, an age when most men are dead? Life insurance in principle is to offset the loss of your earning power and to take care of dependents if you're not around to bring home the bacon. Well, at as late an age as 70 earning years are usually at an end, and at that age who are your dependents? Your children will be all grown up (and no doubt be bank or corporation presidents) and you have neither their food, shelter nor education to provide. So actually you will at 70 need far less insurance than you did at 50. So you may safely drop some that you've been struggling through the years to carry. The cash value on your dropped policies might buy a good annuity or create a substantial paid-up estate, assuming income is not needed."[24]

The consumer movement has expressed growing interest in the entire field of insurance. One of the leaders of this movement, Ralph Nader, has stated: "One of the most important lasting effects of the consumer movement has been the growing awareness that education is an essential component of effective purchasing. The transformation of 'shoppers' into 'consumers' has been the result of an extensive public education effort. . . . That effort has paid off in the development of an entirely new mentality, which approaches a major purchase cautiously, knowledgeably and with every expectation that consumer questions deserve real answers from product manufacturers and sales personnel. A healthy skepticism, carefully nurtured by consumer organizations and columnists, has proven an important antidote to an advertising industry that remains impervious to notions of public responsibility. There are important exceptions. Life insurance purchasers—which includes 2 out of 3 Americans—are among the least knowledgeable consumers of virtually any product offered in the United States. This is true despite the fact that nearly 12% of most families' disposable income goes to pay insurance bills. In fact, insurance is the fourth

[23]Ibid., pp. 15–16.
[24]Ibid., pp. 105–106.

140   *Legislative Trends*

leading household purchase, right behind food, housing, and taxes. Of all types of insurance you are likely to pay for over the course of your lifetime, the life insurance bill is the highest." [25]

Nader argued: "Given the size of the average American's investment in this product, it is critical that people begin to think of themselves as 'insurance consumers' by adopting a critical attitude to policy purchases. Against this healthy self-interest, there is a multi-billion dollar industry banking that insurance buyers will never figure out exactly what they're paying for. In 1980, under pressure from one of the strongest and richest lobbies in the country, Congress passed legislation which effectively prevented the Federal Trade Commission from investigating the insurance business. That move cut off consumers from one of the most important sources of information on who is and who isn't providing good policies. It is ironic that the multi-million dollar lobby that cut off the consumer's right to know was paid for with the policy-holders own money." [26]

It has been Nader's view that the life insurance industry had good reasons for withholding information about their product from policy purchasers: "Life insurance agents make ten or more times as much selling cash value life insurance policies as they do selling term insurance policies (which are less expensive, pure protection policies) of the same face amounts, yet no disclosure of this fact is made to consumers. Policies are not sold on the basis of consumer need but on the basis of industry greed. In this context, people tend to be manipulated in the process of buying insurance. Sales presentations abound with deceptive illustrations geared to fool consumers into buying cash value policies. The process of deciding what type of policy to buy, and how much of it, can be extremely confusing." [27]

Various consumer groups, emulating the "shoppers guide" for the purchase of insurance published by Insurance Commissioner Denenberg in Pennsylvania, have been publishing material to better inform consumers about insurance. One typical publication is *Taking The Bite Out of Insurance*, by James H. Hunt, director of the National Insurance Consumer Organization, and former state insurance commissioner of Vermont.

Mr. Hunt sets forth the purpose of his guide this way: "Life insurance

[25] Ralph Nader, introduction to *Taking the Bite out of Insurance*, by James Hunt (Alexandria, Va.: National Insurance Consumer Organization, 1983).
[26] Ibid.
[27] Ibid.

is a complicated business. There are hundreds of companies selling thousands of different policies. In this guide, the National Insurance Consumers Organization (NICO) wants to help you buy the right kind of life insurance policy at a price you can afford. There is one policy that fits our criteria—annual renewable term life insurance. It is the simplest and most understandable policy of all those sold by life insurance companies. It provides the most life insurance for the lowest current cost. The competition among companies is vigorous enough so that prices tend to be lower than for other policies. You don't lose anything if you have to drop your policy within a few years." [28]

The advice contained in *Taking The Bite Out of Insurance*, Hunt stated: "will fit the needs of most Americans, but there will be exceptions. This is not a guide on how to use life insurance for business purposes, for estate tax purposes, or for other complex financial purposes. If your needs are complicated, retaining a fee-only financial planner—one who accepts no insurance commissions—might be wise. But be cautious: most so-called financial planners sell insurance for a living, and many who charge a fee also receive commissions; moreover, fee-only financial planners are expensive. . . . NICO urges readers to be careful about books on life insurance with catchy titles. Many of these 'exposés' contain both good and bad advice, and if you know how to tell the difference, you don't need to waste your money on them." [29]

Hunt emphasized that the name of an insurance company may reveal something important about it: "Companies with 'Mutual' in the name are cooperatives of a kind; there are no stockholders who need to be paid. Generally, NICO recommends mutual companies. Companies from Canada usually are low cost, reliable life insurers. Companies that resort to self-praise in their names bear some skepticism: the Old Reliable Life may be old and reliable, but its policies are still high-priced; the Ideal National Life is not ideal; the Preferred Risk Life sells only to non-drinkers but we don't know why they'd want to pay more, and so forth. Policies featuring the President of the company are uniformly to be avoided: President's Special; President's Endowment, and so forth. On the other hand, policies prefaced by 'econo-' are sometimes good buys if you want whole life insurance. Preferred risk policies sometimes are and sometimes aren't. Non-

---

[28] James Hunt, *Taking the Bite out of Insurance* (Alexandria, Va.: National Insurance Consumer Organization, 1983), p. 1.
[29] Ibid.

smoker discounts are always good, but non-smoker policies in high-cost companies are only better than smoker policies in those companies; they are likely worse than standard policies in low cost companies." [30]

It is the view of Hunt and many other critics of the life insurance industry that traditional whole life insurance policies have largely been misrepresented to consumers and are now largely unnecessary and counterproductive for many Americans.

In his consumer guide, Hunt made his case this way: "While life insurance was developed so the policyholders could continue their life insurance protection beyond those ages (probably 65 or 70 today, but lower in the past) at which the cost of term life insurance becomes prohibitive, if you ask an agent about term insurance, he or she is likely to say that because term insurance is temporary it can only serve temporary needs, and it thereby follows that if you want whole life insurance to be in force when you die you should buy whole life insurance. Because most people buying life insurance in their thirties and forties will live well into their seventies and eighties, the agent will be right. If you want insurance in force when you die and are willing to pay a lot for the privilege now, then whole life is for you. But why do you want it? If you have no special estate tax or other unusual needs, which describes most persons, why do you want life insurance in force at your death at an old age? What will a $100,000 policy be worth in thirty or forty years at today's inflation rates?" [31]

If an individual plans to have enough assets by the time he retires to cover not only retirement income needs but also to provide for the costs of dying (burial, final medical expenses not covered by Medicare and private health insurance, and probate costs, etc.), according to Hunt, he will not need life insurance. "Your spouse will continue to receive Social Security retirement benefits; if you have a pension and elect a joint and survivor income option, your spouse will get that too. If you are making enough money to think about buying whole life, you'll likely have some savings to use for final expenses. It just does not make sense to buy life insurance against the possibility of dying at or beyond the normal life span; you're going to pay the life insurance company too much money for the protection, money that could be better invested. Life insurance is protection against *premature* death. Its purpose is to protect your family against the

[30] Ibid., p. 7.
[31] Ibid.

loss of its income. After retirement, any decrease in income to your surviving spouse may be offset by your own personal expenses that no longer exist." [32]

Many states have adopted the Model Life Insurance Solicitation Regulation, and in other states insurance companies have voluntarily agreed to abide by its provisions. Because it is relatively easy to compare the costs of term policies by comparing one schedule of rates with another, the regulation's main purpose is to facilitate comparisons between policies that combine protection and savings, such as whole life. The Model Regulation provides that when an individual purchases life insurance, the company upon delivery of the policy must provide the purchaser with financial information about the policy, including six key index numbers for dividend-paying policies and four for others.

Hunt has argued that the Model Regulation does not adequately serve the needs of consumers. The idea of the regulation, he has said, "is that somehow you'll know or learn what constitutes a set of index numbers favorable for your age, sex, plan of insurance, and amount of insurance. Then, if the index numbers in your policy don't measure up you can turn it in and get a refund. The Model Regulation is completely useless to consumers. Instead, a committee of the National Association of Insurance Commissioners—the body that formulates model insurance laws and regulations for adoption by state legislatures and insurance commissions—in a rare moment of candor called it 'seriously flawed and fatally defective.' Although its adoption was spurred by consumer pressures for more meaningful cost comparison information, its final form was worked out by an industry committee in a compromise designed to appease competing industry factions. Thus, the index numbers, which are technically deficient to begin with, can be manipulated by companies and agents to get you to buy the wrong policy. . . . The reason the Model Regulation can't be used to compare policies is that the methodology permits the comparison only of similar policies; dissimilar policies, such as term and whole life or even different types of whole life, can't be compared. Therefore, unless you're willing to become a student of the business, you'll find the Model Regulation unworkable."

In 1979, the Federal Trade Commission recommended that insurance companies be required to disclose rates of return on cash value policies. A

[32] Ibid.

rate of return for any period of years is an estimate of the average annual interest rate earned on the cash values of a life insurance policy.

After studying the insurance industry, Congressman John E. Moss stated: "We found that the insurance delivery system does not naturally provide life insurance purchasers with the information they need to be effective consumers. The adverse consequences for consumers are grave. The regulatory initiatives undertaken recently by the states have been too long delayed and are inadequate to the task." [33] Many observers have said that what is needed is "Truth in Life Insurance" legislation along the lines of truth in lending and truth in packaging regulations that have been promulgated in the recent past.

Discussing whole life insurance in 1877, Massachusetts reformer Elizur Wright declared: "As things are mixed in the policy which ought to be kept separate (the protection element and the savings element), and as the knowledge of what is going on under it from year to year is necessarily almost wholly on one side, if anywhere, the facility for swindling in life-insurance is so great, that the wonder is that it should ever be conducted with any degree of honesty." Overall, Wright, like many mid-twentieth-century critics, did not doubt the value of life insurance. He simply felt that the average consumer was in no position to understand the merits and demerits of competing policies and was in no position to make an informed judgment. [34]

Thus, Wright stated: "Provided the game is fairly understood on both sides, fairly played, and no risk run, except what is necessary to secure the desired indemnity, human science has never devised a more admirable plan for securing at the same time the benefit of association and the independence of the individual." [35]

In its 1979 report, the Federal Trade Commission analyzed rates of return on the savings portion of whole life policies available to a thirty-five-year-old male in 1977. It found that the average rates of return from the policies it examined, depending on the length of time they were held, were as follows: after five years, minus 8.36 percent; after ten, 1.43 percent; after twenty, 4.12 percent; and after thirty years, 4.5 percent. These were the rates for participating policies. The rates on nonparticipating policies were lower.

[33] Quoted in Tobias, *Invisible Bankers*, p. 274.
[34] Ibid., pp. 298–99.
[35] Ibid., p. 298.

Consumers Union surveyed 110 of the leading life insurers to analyze the rates of return of their whole life policies. It used a table of term insurance rates developed by the Society of Actuaries, one which is considered low by many observers.[36]

For $25,000 nonparticipating policies, the yield after twenty-nine years, for example, was as follows for a selection of the companies surveyed: Travelers Ordinary Life (age twenty-five), 3.14 percent; Connecticut General Ordinary Life (age twenty-five), 2.28 percent; Aetna Whole Life (age thirty-five), 3.19 percent; J.C. Penney Value Select (age forty-five), 3.33 percent; and Hartford Whole Life (age forty-five), 2.79 percent.

For $25,000 participating policies: Massachusetts SBLI (age twenty-five), 7.85 percent; New England Mutual (age twenty-five), 6.45 percent; Massachusetts Mutual Convertible Life 3 (age twenty-five), 6.08 percent; Prudential Modified Life 3 (age twenty-five), 5.54 percent; and New York Life (age twenty-five), 5.54 percent.

For $100,000 participating policies: Northwestern Mutual (age twenty-five), 5.98 percent; Equitable Adjustable Whole Life (age twenty-five), 5.55 percent; Metropolitan Life, Whole Life (age twenty-five), 5.06 percent; Phoenix Mutual, nonsmokers, (age thirty-five), 5.94 percent; and State Farm Whole Life (age forty-five), 4.40 percent.[37]

Insurance spokesmen, discussing the apparently low interest received by policyholders, point out that interest earned on whole life insurance policies is sheltered from taxes. An individual pays no tax until the policy is surrendered, and then is taxed only on the amount by which what is received exceeds what was paid in, less dividends. In most cases, little or no tax is due. Neither is tax due if the policyholder dies. A policyholder in the 50 percent tax bracket, earning 4 percent tax free, insurance spokesmen argue, is in as good a financial position as if he were receiving 8 percent before taxes.

In recent years, the whole life insurance policy has been challenged by a number of newer approaches to life insurance that have been introduced to the market. Part of the reason for this is recent inflation, according to Tobias. "The worst sustained inflation in the nation's history had pushed interest rates to unthinkable levels. The whole life policyholder who had slaved to pay the premiums on a $25,000 policy now found,

[36] *The Consumers Union Report on Life Insurance*, 4th edition (New York: Holt Rinehart and Winston, 1980).
[37] Tobias, *Invisible Bankers*, p. 298.

twenty or thirty years later, that his slaving had been largely in vain. The $25,000 would still be paid if he died—but what was $25,000 in 1981? The great middle class, long content with whole life's tax-free 2 or 3 per cent yield even if 5 per cent were available down the street (few knew the disparity, and what difference did it really make?), suddenly couldn't pass a bank window without seeing promises of 15 per cent and 18 per cent interest on sums as small as $1,000. The yields on good whole life policies had climbed to a tax-sheltered 6 or 7 per cent, if held for ten or twenty years, but how attractive was that? And who could afford whole life premiums, anyway, now that a pound of hamburger cost $2.39? (And who could tell a good whole life policy from a bad one?)" [38]

Although the insurance industry has escaped direct scrutiny and supervision by the Federal Trade Commission with regard to the question of full disclosure, the future, if today's atmosphere is any indication, may be far different.

The modern statutory base of the Federal Trade Commission (FTC) can be found in several federal laws. The Fur Products Labeling Act, approved August 8, 1951, protects consumers and others against misbranding, false advertising, and false invoicing of furs and fur products. The Textile Fiber Products Identification Act, approved September 2, 1958, protects producers and consumers against misbranding and false advertising of the fiber content of textile fiber products. The Fair Packaging and Labeling Act, approved November 3, 1966, prevents unfair or deceptive packaging or labeling of certain consumer commodities.

The Truth in Lending Act, approved July 1, 1969, requires full disclosure of related credit terms before a consumer credit account is opened or a credit transaction is completed. The act requires that, if any of certain credit terms are specified in advertising, others must be also. An amendment to the act limits the liability for unauthorized use of any credit card to fifty dollars on cards issued on or before January 25, 1971, and no liability on cards issued after that time unless the credit card issuer takes several steps such as: notifying the cardholder of limited liability, providing a postage-free means of notification of loss, and providing a means of identification, such as signature, thumbprint, or photograph. The Fair Credit Reporting Act, approved October 26, 1970, is designed to ensure that a consumer's credit report will contain only accurate, relevant, and recent in-

[38] Ibid.

formation and will be confidential unless requested for an appropriate reason by a proper party.

The Magnuson-Moss Warranty-Federal Trade Commission Act, approved January 4, 1975, extends the commission's authority to represent itself in court (including the U.S. Supreme Court), to promulgate substantive Trade Regulation Rules in the consumer protection area, to obtain civil penalties and consumer redress for violations of the Federal Trade Commission Act, and to pursue any unlawful act "affecting commerce" rather than only those acts defined as "in commerce." The Fair Credit Billing Act became law October 28, 1975. This act is designed to ensure that consumers are not denied credit for reason of sex, marital status, age, race, religion, or national origin.

In the study *Mandate for Leadership in a Conservative Administration*, the conservative view of the proper role to be played by the Federal Trade Commission was presented to President Reagan. It differed from the views of the consumer movement, which would increase governmental authority of business and industry to a much greater extent, but the differences may, in fact, be more a matter of degree than of philosophy.

The author of the segment of the report which concerned itself with the Federal Trade Commission was Kendall Fleeharty. He stated: "The FTC needs to develop a new philosophical underpinning for its fraudulent advertising cases and rulemaking proceedings. In those instances in which it would be reasonable to expect that a consumer of normal competence could readily discover the misstatements of fact in the advertising, and in which it would be an effective marketplace remedy for the consumer to refuse to make further purchases of the product, then the FTC probably ought not to issue prohibitory rules. If, however, the challenged advertising claims (or the product's intrinsic deficiency) were of such a nature that a consumer lacking specific technical expertise could not discover the defect for himself, the promulgation of prohibitory rules would be justified." [39]

Fleeharty stated: "Two examples should suffice to illustrate the point. It ought not to be necessary for the FTC to tell soup companies not to put marbles in the soup bowl for purposes of filming a television commercial, or to stop putting aspirin tablets (or was it salt tablets) in a glass of beer, in order to make it foam more than it ordinarily would. In both instances the

[39] Kendall Fleeharty in *Mandate for Leadership in a Conservative Administration*, ed. Charles L. Heatherly (Washington, D.C.: Heritage Foundation, 1981).

consumer could, after a single purchase, determine that the vegetable content of the soup, or the 'foaminess' of the beer were not as advertised. Their available remedy would be adequate and effective; stop buying that brand. The manufacturer would get the message very quickly and mend his ways—or eventually go out of business. On the other side, if a 'protein' bread were being advertised as having a specific level of nutritional value or a brand of mouthwash were advertised as having specific medicinal properties that it did not possess, the FTC intervention, including stiff fines and mandatory advertising disclaimers are entirely appropriate." [40]

Fleeharty concluded: "If the trade practice were so unfair or deceptive, and the ability of the consumer to respond by refusing to buy the product were an inadequate remedy, then the issuance of prohibitory trade regulation rules would be justified. For example, there is no effective remedy available to a consumer when a funeral home refuses to provide him with an itemized bill, or when it induces a family to purchase an unwanted package of services and goods for a funeral. In those instances, the bereaved family has no adequate market-place remedy. The discipline of the marketplace is inadequate when a customer's purchases are substantial, few and far between. In those cases, rules and regulations appear to be the only alternative." [41]

Insurance, it seems, would clearly fit into the category which even conservatives would consider of legitimate concern to government with regard to false or misleading advertising.

Richard Holton, professor of business administration at the University of California's Berkeley campus, in an essay concerning government regulation of business, pointed out: "If we go beyond regulation of the physical product to regulation of information about the product, we face the array of problems in the regulation of advertising. One obvious way to maximize the efficiency of consumers' information processing is to be sure the information received through advertising is reasonably accurate. Unfortunately, we cannot expect advertising to provide complete information as well; that simply is not feasible." [42]

The Federal Trade Commission, Holton argued, serves as "our principal watchdog regarding false and misleading advertising. But its powers have been limited in many respects. . . . The FTC's ability to stop false and misleading advertising has been substantially enhanced by the FTC

[40] Ibid.
[41] Ibid.
[42] Richard Holton in ibid.

Improvement Act of 1975. The commission can now move against practices 'in or affecting commerce,' not just those 'in commerce'—which brings within the commission's reach cases which would earlier have been considered intrastate commerce. The commission's rulemaking authority, covering whole sets of industry practices, has been clarified. The commission can now fund the participation of consumer groups in FTC proceedings, and can levy fines for knowing violations of FTC rules or of a cease and desist order (formerly, only the latter was covered). In what may be one of the most important changes, the act provides that a cease and desist order, once obtained against a particular company for a particular act or practice, applies to anyone engaging in such acts or practice. Thus, a company which was not subject to the cease and desist order can now be fined for violating the order. This power can obviously have a substantial multiplier effect on the commission's cease and desist orders. Of even greater consequence may be the FTC's power to obtain equitable relief for consumers. Formerly a company could be subject to a cease and desist order without having to pay for its past sins, so to speak. Now the FTC can seek relief through recision or reformation of contracts, refund of money or return of property, payment of compensatory damages, and public notification. Thus, the possible penalties for false and misleading advertising have been increased substantially." [43]

In an important case, the FTC determined in 1975 that the Warner-Lambert product Listerine did not prevent or cure colds, as had been advertised. The FTC ordered that Listerine advertisements in the future include the statement, "Contrary to prior advertising, Listerine will not prevent colds or sore throats or lessen their severity." A federal appeals court upheld the FTC, but said that the statement "contrary to prior advertising" need not be included.

In addition to action by the FTC, there have also been private efforts to minimize false and misleading advertising. One of these had been conducted by the National Advertising Division (NAD) of the Council of Better Business Bureaus. The NAD monitors advertising, investigates alleged abuses, and works with advertisers to gain voluntary corrections of claims.

Holton has pointed out that, "a major topic in discussions of public regulation of marketing practices in recent years has been the minimum disclosures that should be made in advertising, on labels and in other ve-

---

[43] Ibid.

hicles, such as point-of-sale material. An overwhelming majority, nearly 90 per cent, of the executives covered in one large survey agree that 'advertising should include adequate information for logical buying decisions, whether or not consumers choose to use it' (Greyser and Diamond, 1976–77). This would appear to be a reasonable standard, although the debate about how much information is required for a 'logical' buying decision might well rival that surrounding the concept of the 'prudent man' in the law. And one can scarcely expect the sixty-second television commercial for vegetable soup to list the ingredients in the detail provided on the label. Perhaps we should only ask that the information required for logical buying decisions be readily accessible, at least on the label if not in the advertising itself. The Truth-in-Lending legislation calls for disclosure of credit terms in considerable details, and actually prohibits the advertising of credit terms unless all details are provided. One can well ask whether the net effect of that part of the legislation was in the community interest. The assumption was that the consumer would read and comprehend the full disclosure statement when it was encountered elsewhere than in the advertising. It is apparent that minimum disclosure is indeed a conceptual thicket."[44]

It has been argued that the efficiency of information provided to consumers can be improved by the use of standardized terminology. Thus, in the case of automobile tires the term *first line* was used to suggest the highest quality, but its precise meaning was not clear with regard to performance characteristics. The FTC's tire advertising and labeling guides are said to have made the definition somewhat more precise. There have also been efforts to standardize the terms used to describe the quality of fresh fruits and vegetables. The top grades applied through voluntary grade labeling traditionally carried at least four different designations (U.S. Extra No. 1 for potatoes, U.S. Extra Fancy for apples, U.S. Fancy for oranges, and U.S. No. 1 for onions). Such variations, it is generally agreed, complicated the consumer information process.

In addition, the move toward unit pricing is viewed as one means of improving the efficiency with which the consumer can make sense of the information available. Some consumers are interested in the price per pound or ounce. Since the consumer is faced with a variety of package sizes and weights, his ability to quickly make accurate price comparisons is enhanced by unit pricing.

Assessing the needs of consumers, as promoted by the increasingly

[44] Ibid.

vocal and active consumer movement and its advocates within the government, and the needs of business, Mary Gardiner Jones, vice-president for consumer affairs of the Western Union Telegraph Corporation and a former commissioner of the Federal Trade Commission, has stated: "Today's consumer concerns about health and safety issues in the marketplace places . . . in central focus the importance of information if [consumers] are to deal in any respect with the proliferation of conflicting and controversial claims about the potential dangers to themselves or to the environment of an increasing number of products. . . . The issue . . . is essentially one of ensuring to individual citizens the freedom to choose and live a lifestyle of his/her choice while not imposing counterproductive restraints on the business community, or conferring unnecessary power on government. . . .

"In many cases, the available product and service information provides either too little or too much detail to the consumer. . . . Consumers will typically not use unit pricing until they understand how it will help them. Nutritional information, unrelated to consumer health, can be noninformation to many consumers. A mere listing of chemical or other ingredients conveys little useful information to most consumers. . . . If information is to be of real value . . . consumers must be able to locate it . . . when it is needed. Point of sale information . . . is seldom of the quality which enables most customers to perform the type of thoughtful, comparative evaluations which they need. . . . More objective and detailed information prepared by manufacturers or retailers . . . reflects the publisher's priorities, interest, or perceptions of important product categories or product features of interest to consumers. . . . Unless consumers know about these sources of information *and* have both a good memory and reliable filing system, putting their hands on the report or the data at the moment of decision is perhaps their most serious obstacle . . . at the moment of purchase." [45]

Jones concluded: "Information is a natural resource, comparable in importance and need to the vast outpouring of goods which has characterized our economy for the past hundred years. [If] access to information determines where the power in our society will reside, consumers have traditionally been at the lowest end of the power spectrum. . . . Today the technology exists to eliminate this disparity in power in the area or marketplace information. Yet . . . society must take affirmative steps to see . . . that con-

[45] Quoted in *Regulating Business: The Search for an Optimum* (San Francisco: Institute for Contemporary Studies, 1978), p. 152.

sumer information data bases develop and . . . that the hardware is in place to enable consumers to have access to the telecommunications technology which is so rapidly emerging in the commercial world. . . .

"Americans today are living in an electronically based information society. Information, like any other product, is no better than its delivery systems and availability. . . . Unless we can develop national storage, retrieval, and delivery systems for the information and knowledge required by consumers and citizens to function in our society, we will perpetuate . . . the already serious power imbalances and injustices which exist throughout our society today between individuals and institutions as well as between rich and poor. . . . It is time we turned our attention to putting these technological advances to work for consumers. . . .

"The interrelationship of computer, home terminal, and telecommunications network technologies opens up a vast area of memory storage and relay services for individuals."[46]

Under the Reagan administration, the Federal Trade Commission has shifted from a policy of compelling businesses to follow particular policies and approaches to one of encouraging voluntary compliance with the law.

While the insurance industry has, in many respects, avoided the full brunt of congressional and Federal Trade Commission demands for full and complete disclosure, there can be little doubt that it remains an important target of consumer groups and activist government officials. Under a conservative administration these demands meet a countervailing opposition to increased power for government agencies. Under a more liberal administration, however, such demands are likely to result in more stringent legislation and regulations in this regard.

Andrew Tobias has suggested, for example, that "for competition to work, life insurers should be required to disclose, in a simple, prominent, standardized format, what they were charging each year for the . . . insurance protection and, on policies that include a savings component, the rate of interest they were crediting each year. . . . So long as the industry insists this can't be done, consumers should buy inexpensive term insurance and do their savings elsewhere."[47]

Tobias, in proposing his own ideal insurance system, went even further than full disclosure. He suggested: "It's not enough to print on an in-

[46] Ibid., pp. 152, 153.
[47] Tobias, *Invisible Bankers*.

surance policy that only 20 cents of each premium dollar will be paid in claims if the prospect can barely read. Why not ban sales of whole life policies under $10,000 and term insurance under $25,000? Policies smaller than that are ordinarily so uneconomical as to represent, ipso facto, a terrible buy. Exceptions would be made where it could be demonstrated that at least 60 cents of each premium dollar would be paid in claims and that, with respect to savings, interest would be at least 3 per cent for policies kept in force five years or more. If stockbrokers can be required to 'know their customers' and not to sell them securities inappropriate to their financial situations, why should not life insurers be prevented from selling to the poor policies that pay out 30 cents on the dollar or earn a negative rate of interest for the first ten years?"[48]

In the view of Tobias and other critics of the life insurance industry, "The only legitimate argument *against* adequate life insurance cost disclosure and wide open competition from the banks, et al., is this: Less might be sold. With life insurance recognized for what it is, a financial commodity, its price would be lower. Many would thus find their insurance dollars stretching to buy greater coverage. . . . the one—and only—legitimate argument against life insurance reform is that it would damage the nation's enormous and costly life insurance sales force and ultimately impair the nation's ability to generate capital through the sale of whole life insurance."[49]

It is certain that this question will be the subject of much debate in the future, and it is likely the insurance industry will be as subject to the demands of the consumer movement for full disclosure as other businesses and industries in American society.

Many insurance companies appear to recognize this fact and have been voluntarily moving toward full disclosure and toward offering a variety of policies that are competing in the marketplace. To the extent that the industry itself corrects what are generally perceived to be its shortcomings in this area, the demand for legislative and regulatory oversight might lessen, particularly when the administration in office has a philosophical predilection against such governmental involvement in the economy.

[48] Ibid.
[49] Ibid.

7

Rate Regulation and Rate Bureaus

Discussing the evolution of rate regulation in the insurance field, John G. Day, in a study prepared for the U.S. Department of Transportation entitled *Economic Regulation of Insurance in The United States*, noted that during the latter part of the nineteenth century, insurance companies fixed the level of rates and commissions in order to exercise control over the agents. Their efforts failed, largely because participating companies did not adhere to the rate schedule. In addition, some states adopted anticompact laws that prohibited such concerted activity, reflecting the public sentiment against excessive rates.[1]

By 1911, Day reported, some state legislators appeared to be more sympathetic to the problem of inadequate (below cost) rates and considered it a major cause of insurance company insolvency. In that year, the Merritt Committee of the New York Legislature recommended state-supervised joint rate making as a means of preventing inadequate and discriminatory rates. Despite these developments, by 1944 the practice of price fixing by private rate bureaus, which was widespread, was largely uncontrolled by the states. It was also thought to be insulated from the federal antitrust laws since the Supreme Court had ruled that the business of insurance was not interstate commerce.

That changed in 1944 when the Supreme Court held that insurance

---

[1] John G. Day, *Economic Regulation of Insurance in the United States* (Washington, D.C.: U.S. Department of Transportation, 1970).

transactions across state lines constituted interstate commerce and thus were subject to the federal antitrust laws.[2] The court rejected the argument that the only relevant part of the insurance transaction was the sales contract.

The effect of the *United States* v. *South-Eastern Underwriters Association* decision was dealt with in the McCarran-Ferguson Act, which in Section 2(b) gave the insurance industry and its state regulators the opportunity to preempt the federal antitrust laws with state regulation. By 1955, most states had adopted the "All Industry" model legislation under which rates prepared by the private rate bureaus were submitted to the insurance commissioner and deemed effective if not disapproved within a specified period.

Some states, however, have relied upon market forces to determine the level of insurance prices and, at present, there are increasing calls to open insurance to free competition and eliminate the influence of rate bureaus. The Department of Justice's 1977 report to President Gerald Ford compared economic data on the effects of regulation on private passenger automobile insurance in three states. California was selected as representing a regulatory system that relied on market forces to determine the level of prices, and New Jersey and Pennsylvania were selected as systems representing affirmative state involvement in the rate-making process.

A 1974 report issued by the California Department of Insurance pointed out that in California there was no requirement of "advance approval or specific approval of rates by the regulatory authorities." In fact, there was no provision for the filing of rates by any insurer or rating bureau. The state authorities periodically examined company records but took "affirmative action only when adopted rates [did] not comply with the standards of the rate law."[3]

Under this system, prices can adjust to changes in market conditions and operating costs in all segments of the market. Nonstandard insurers are able to charge substantially higher rates to drivers considered high risks, and the assigned risks plan is operated approximately on a self-sustaining basis, although rates and rating classifications are subject to prior-approval regulation.

New Jersey is deeply involved in the rate-making process, and there is minimal reliance on market forces. The rating and classification systems

[2] 322 U.S. 533 (1944).
[3] Cited in Paul W. MacAvoy, ed., *Federal-State Regulation of the Pricing and Marketing of Insurance* (Washington, D.C.: American Free Enterprise Institute, 1977), p. 23.

are subject to prior approval by state authorities, a process that has delayed the implementation of rate changes. Individual insurers may obtain approval from the state authorities to deviate from the bureau by a fixed percentage for all classes of risk or to adopt an independent schedule of rates. However, an independent filing requires that the insurer bear the cost of obtaining regulatory approval and the burden of justifying a rate structure at variance with the bureau. The sale of nonstandard insurance in the state is prohibited, and rates in the assigned risk plan are artificially suppressed at the bureau level.

Pennsylvania has a similar system of prior-approval regulation, which differs, however, in certain respects from New Jersey's in the manner of implementation and the degree of state involvement. State regulators in Pennsylvania, unlike those in New Jersey, have permitted substantially higher rates for high-risk drivers, both in the nonstandard market and in the assigned risk plan.

These states do not by any means represent the full range of approaches to rate making. This range includes major deregulation, as in Illinois, and state-made rates, as in Massachusetts. California, New Jersey, and Pennsylvania were chosen for comparison because of the structure and implementation of their rating laws and the reasonable uniformity of their laws over the previous decade. The three states together account for approximately one-fifth of the total private passenger automobile insurance business conducted in the United States in 1975.

One comparison made among the three states was for loss ratio. This was designed to evaluate the stability of losses to premiums over the long term, an indicator of the ability of insurers to respond to changes in loss experience through higher or lower rates.

In a highly regulated system, there are greater year-to-year variations in the loss ratios because of the inherent delays in adjusting rates under a regulatory process in which the state is involved in rate making. For example, the Insurance Services Office (ISO) has described the administrative delays in New Jersey as follows: "The rate level filings average approximately six months pending. The other filings average about the same. However, some General Liability rate filings are refilings of previously pending filings. If the dates of the original filings are considered, the average pending time for rate level filings becomes approximately 9 months. . . . The role of the Public Advocate in insurance matters promises to add an additional period of time, possibly months onto the existing delays."

One company reported that in 1975 its independent filing for a rate adjustment took approximately six months to process.[4]

Combining the experience of all eleven insurers in each state, the results show that the loss ratios in New Jersey and Pennsylvania were much more volatile than those in California over the ten-year period. In New Jersey, the loss ratios varied 92 percent more than in California, while the ratios in Pennsylvania showed 40 percent more variation than in California.

Over a ten-year period, the eleven insurers saw an average price change in California auto insurance rates of 5.9 percent every eleven months. The same companies, by contrast, experienced an average price change in New Jersey of approximately 9.6 percent every twenty-one months, and in Pennsylvania of 10.0 percent every twenty-four months.

One insurer described the effects of state rate regulation on its operations during this ten-year period this way: "In California, as the experience turned bad in 1968 and 1969, we were able to take corrective action twice, in April and again in December of 1969. Similarly, we were able to take two rate increases in 1975 as the experience during that year worsened steadily. During the profitable years of the cycle, 1970 through 1974, millions of dollars were returned to California policyholders by way of dividends. . . . Under ordinary circumstances, the company would undoubtedly have reduced its auto insurance rates in California in 1971, and in larger amounts than the modest decreases actually taken in 1972 and 1973.

"On the other hand, in New Jersey, the response to the bad experience was much slower, a small increase in May of 1969 and finally a large increase in May of 1970. Again, despite our efforts during 1974 and 1975, no increase was effected in New Jersey until January 15, 1976. A somewhat similar pattern prevails in Pennsylvania, late response to the bad experience in 1966, 1967, 1968, and 1969, and similar problems in 1975. The 1975 pattern is complicated by a mandatory rate decrease legislatively imposed in July of 1975. This decrease cut squarely against the grain of steadily worsening experience."[5]

While the price changes represented average price increases over the ten-year period, there were a number of statewide price decreases during this period, especially in California. Approximately 55 percent of all price decreases, including the mandatory decreases in New Jersey and Pennsyl-

[4]Ibid., p. 28.
[5]Ibid., pp. 28, 30.

vania, were experienced in California. About 90 percent of all voluntary price decreases during the ten-year period were executed in California, ranging from a small statewide decrease of 0.1 percent to a more significant decrease of 8.6 percent.

These figures may understate the potential for price decreases in California because federal wage-price controls were in effect at that time. Their effect on price decreases during 1971–74 was described by one California insurer: "At a time when . . . [our] historical practice would have called for substantial rate cuts, we elected instead to return unneeded premiums to policyholders by way of dividends, because of the prospect of federal price controls and rigid administration of state prior approval laws."[6]

Another area in which the three states were compared was that of the availability of insurance, which was defined as the ability of consumers to purchase adequate insurance protection in the open market at a price reasonably related to cost—an "actuarially fair" price.

In California, a driver who is considered by the insurance industry as a standard, or preferred, risk will be charged the prevailing market price based on the class experience of individuals with similar rating characteristics. A driver who is viewed as marginal or high risk may be rejected by standard insurers because the rates are considered inadequate as a matter of underwriting judgment. Even in an open-competition state such as California, high-cost insurance is sold by specialty companies or affiliates of standard companies in order to comply with the state's rating laws against unfair price discrimination. A study entitled *The Role of Risk Classifications in Property and Casualty Insurance: A Study of the Risk Assessment Process* stated: "The public and regulators do not necessarily want to reflect cost differences with exactly proportional price differences. Many basic insurance coverages have become a necessity."[7] Sometimes the risk is great enough to necessitate risk-sharing. As a result, the rejected driver may have to seek coverage from nonstandard insurers or the assigned-risk plan.

In California nonstandard insurance rates may exceed standard rates by 50 percent or more. The nonstandard market offers both liability and physical damage insurance; these types have been estimated to account for approximately 10 percent of the insured market in California.

[6] Ibid., p. 30.
[7] Ibid., p. 32.

The assigned-risk plan represents an involuntary market in which the state requires the participation on a pro rata basis of all insurers licensed to sell automobile insurance, in order to cover drivers who cannot qualify in the voluntary market. The assigned-risk population in California in 1974 was about 1.9 percent of the insured market, compared with the nationwide average of about 3.7 percent.

It was found that the California experience was sharply different from that of New Jersey, where the assigned-risk group represented about 10 percent of the insured market in 1974. This was partially explained by the rigid state regulation in the voluntary market, the prohibition of nonstandard insurance, a subsidized rate structure in the assigned-risk plan in which rates were keyed to the voluntary market, and a compulsory system of insurance protection. In New Jersey, every owner of an automobile registered or principally garaged in the state must maintain liability insurance.

In Pennsylvania, the assigned-risk population was comparable to that of California—1.7 percent of the insured market—because of the competitive nonstandard market in liability and physical damage insurance and an assigned-risk plan administered by the state on a self-sustaining basis. There was minimal subsidization of the assigned-risk rates by the voluntary market, enabling the nonstandard market to serve as a competitive alternative.

Advocates of direct state control of prices and of the risk assessment process have argued that these statistics are misleading, overemphasizing the assigned-risk population as a measure of the residual market. They challenge the reliability of the open-market mechanism in California as a method of identifying marginal drivers. They believe that good risks are denied coverage at the standard rate and are forced to pay higher rates in the nonstandard and assigned-risk markets. The Federal Insurance Administration report, *Full Insurance Availability* (1974), argued that a large number of so-called clean risks in the assigned risk plan are evidence of the unreliability of the free market approach.

Advocates of state control also argue that insurance priced strictly on a cost basis would violate concepts of social fairness by imposing a "regressive tax" on low-income drivers, or by forcing such individuals to drive without coverage. They point to the large uninsured market in California as evidence of the affordability problem inherent in a competitive system.

Discussing the argument about clean risks being placed in the nonstandard and assigned risk markets, the Justice Department study declared: "There is little dispute that a significant portion of the drivers forced into the assigned risk plans are clean risks. However, we do not believe that this fact alone is evidence that the marketplace is an unreliable mechanism for identifying high or marginal risks. A driver with a clean record may still constitute a marginal or high risk." [8]

The Stanford Research Institute found that the three-year experience of a driver in Massachusetts would explain only about 13 percent of actual losses, leaving a random factor of approximately 87 percent. The SRI concluded: "The weak correlation between actual losses and expected losses makes it difficult to infer the latter from the former. In particular, and contrary to many naive theories, loss experience on an individual basis does not have a conclusive value. A 'clean risk,' meaning someone who has not reported any accident during the year, is not necessarily a low risk." [9]

The Justice Department study said that, "Under these circumstances, where business judgment is such an important factor in evaluating risks, we would normally expect a competitive market to serve as the most effective and reliable mechanism for identifying high or marginal risks. As far as we can determine, it is the independent judgment of individual insurers that forces so-called clean risks into the assigned risk plans. In other words, in a state like California which imposes minimal interference with the market mechanism, the size and composition of the assigned risk plan simply reflects the collective judgment of the marketplace that these individuals should be insured on a risk-sharing basis. In addition, there is some evidence that the so-called clean risks are in fact high risks." [10]

Data from the Automobile Insurance Plans Service Office indicate that many of the "clean" risks in the assigned risk plans are in fact not "good" risks. So-called clean risks have, on the average, yielded a loss ratio much in excess of the "break-even" loss ratio set by the state. In New Jersey, the companies participating in the plan in 1974 actually paid out, on the average, $178 per policy for losses on clean risks, or $103 more than the state insurance department permitted them to charge to cover those losses. The subsidy was about $21 per policy for each clean risk in the California plan and about $10 in Pennsylvania.

Does a free-market mechanism for setting automobile insurance rates

[8] Ibid., p. 35.
[9] Ibid.
[10] Ibid., p. 36.

lead to inequities, in which large numbers of lower-income drivers are unable to afford insurance? Assessing this problem, the Justice Department declared: "The California experience provides some evidence that a fully competitive market may serve as a reliable mechanism for assessing risks and controlling prices. The experience also highlights the fact that a system in which prices are reasonably related to costs may create a serious affordability problem, causing some drivers to forego insurance protection or imposing socially unfair burdens on those individuals who can least afford the high cost of protection." [11]

Those who are concerned about the affordability problem and believe that direct state control is the best solution advocate the imposition of a simplified classification system, a uniform rate structure for the voluntary and involuntary markets, and mandatory underwriting in which insurers must accept all applicants, some of whom may be ceded to a reinsurance facility.

Such "full insurance availability" programs have been instituted, at least in part, in such states as South Carolina, North Carolina, and Massachusetts. The Justice Department, after reviewing the available evidence, stated: "The experience of these systems to date has not been very favorable. There is some evidence that they have resulted in substantial cross-subsidization of high-risk drivers by low-risk drivers. For example, the Massachusetts Insurance Commissioner is reputed to have described his state's automobile property damage laws as 'the worst in the nation' resulting in the 'transfer of dollars from good drivers in the state to the bad.' He estimated that the motoring public in certain areas was paying an average subsidy of more than $100 to the bad drivers in the reinsurance facility. . . . New Jersey's system of rate regulation also results in a subsidy of high-risk drivers by the voluntary market. The New Jersey Insurance Department estimates that in 1974 the average subsidy paid by insured drivers in the voluntary market was twelve dollars per driver. However, the subsidy may vary sharply between territories so that a driver in a large metropolitan area may pay a subsidy substantially higher than the twelve-dollar average." [12]

Alfred E. Kahn has stated that the reliance on an "internal" subsidy in New Jersey and Massachusetts to drivers in the assigned-risks plan pro-

[11] Ibid.
[12] Ibid., p. 39.

vides a "highly imperfect" and "very crude device for egalitarian objectives." [13] In addition, the "internal" subsidy interferes with the operation of the free market in relating the price of insurance to the cost of protection. Kahn is quoted as saying that an "external" subsidy could satisfy the state objectives for social fairness without interfering with the market objectives of economic fairness.

This also seems to be the conclusion of the Stanford Research Institute, which declared: "We suggest that transfer payments (cross-subsidies) be explicitly promulgated by legislators. The public and the industry would be well served by additional research into ways of implementing transfer payments that would interfere minimally with the free market forces." [14]

Cross-subsidization may take several forms. For example, the insured market may be viewed as subsidizing the uninsured market through uninsured motorists insurance, which in California added from about eight dollars to about twenty-five dollars to premiums. In New Jersey, the additional cost was about two dollars. An official of the Federal Insurance Administration described another form of subsidy: "To any extent that the class differentials in use vary from the differentials actually indicated by class relativity tests, one or more classes may well be subsidizing some other class or classes." [15] Another form of subsidy between states was suggested by a former director of insurance in Illinois. Robert B. Wilcox, addressing the American Insurance Association Seminar on Anti-Trust and Trade Practices, declared, "It seems inescapable to me that Illinois policyholders are subsidizing the several states where regulation is imposing inadequate rates." [16]

The Justice Department concluded: "It is recognized that a fully competitive system cannot eliminate the availability problem, which is a function of various factors, such as the loss and investment experience and expectations of individual insurers, the level of consumer knowledge, and the degree of competitive pressures. However, our own study of the California experience and the conclusions of the Stanford Research Institute suggest that the elimination of the artificial restraints on the risk assessment process and pricing mechanism would produce greater operating stability and

[13] Ibid.
[14] Ibid.
[15] Ibid.
[16] Ibid.

predictability, which in turn may serve to minimize the availability problem. The classification of risks and underwriting selectivity are not processes that can be severed from the competitive system; they are an integral part of the free market mechanism in establishing an economic and actuarial 'fair' price for insurance protection." [17]

The findings of the Stanford Research Institute and other studies indicate that there is "room for improvement in the risk assessment process" and that the validity of some of the class relativities currently in use is questionable. According to the Justice Department, "a fully competitive system should serve to correct some of these inequities in the risk assessment process. Nevertheless, to the extent that the market mechanism fails to prevent such inequities, we recommend that insurance companies be subjected to a federal standard against invidious discrimination." [18]

The Stanford Research Institute defined a "fair" insurance price in a competitive market as the "expected loss" of insuring a risk plus a provision for profits and expenses. The expected loss may be based upon the individual's own experience or the experience of a class of individuals with similar risk characteristics. SRI, however, noted that there is substantial uncertainty in assessing expected losses of individual risks: "The estimation of [individual] expected losses is difficult because expected losses must be inferred from actual losses and . . . actual losses have a large random component. . . . Individual records of a large number of insureds over long periods of time are necessary to determine expected loss variability with some degree of confidence. Data of this kind are not commonly available." [19]

The average expected loss for a risk class is a common basis for predicting costs. SRI noted, "If a group of policies is sufficiently large, the group's average experience is credible and their average is an accurate estimate of the group's risk." [20]

The goal is to establish homogeneous risk groups to as great an extent as possible. In *Casualty Insurance*, Kulp and Hall wrote: "Generally, the larger the number of groups and subgroups, the more nearly homogeneous will be the insureds within each category. Rates for the various rate groupings are generally made upon the basis of past experience. Given a suffi-

[17] Ibid., p. 40.
[18] Ibid.
[19] Ibid., pp. 48–49.
[20] Ibid.

cient volume of experience, the more nearly homogeneous the composition of a group, the more reliable will be the experience indications of that group, for its composition remains relatively constant as between the experience period and the period of rate application. However, as the number of rate groupings increases, the volume of experience within each rate grouping declines." [21]

In order to enhance credibility, insurers pool their loss experience on a nationwide basis for establishing and testing the driver classification system, and on a statewide basis for formulating "base" rates. The Insurance Services Office (ISO) described its testing procedure in these terms: "In the context of classification . . . ISO generally uses the latest available year of country-wide loss experience in its review of automobile classification relativities. . . . The underlying assumption is that the relationships between the rates for the different classifications are going to be very similar regardless of the state or territory." [22]

Insurance companies justify the use of bureau rates on this rationale. Smaller companies argue that they are heavily dependent upon the bureau rate because of their inability to obtain the professional expertise to evaluate the composite industry data and because of the lack of credibility of their own company's experience. There is, however, some disagreement about the collective rate bureau approach to assessing expected losses of individual risks. A study conducted by the Stanford Research Institute on the efficiency of the risk assessment process concluded that the classification systems used by the bureau contained a large random component: "Current risk assessment processes in automobile insurance explain about 30 per cent of the variance of the expected loss distribution among drivers. . . . 22 per cent is explained by rating, and 8 per cent is explained by selection. . . . Saying that 30 per cent of the expected loss uncertainty is explained by current risk assessment in automobile insurance means that on the average, 70 per cent remains unexplained within risk classes." [23]

The Justice Department assessed the rate bureau classification system this way: "Regardless of the efficiency of the classification system, there is also a question as to the reliability of the average loss and expense experience of disparate companies. Companies may differ substantially in their mix of business, as determined by their marketing and underwriting poli-

[21] Ibid., p. 89.
[22] Ibid., p. 49.
[23] Ibid., p. 50.

cies. They may also differ in their efficiency in administering claims and controlling operating and production costs. The reliability problem is compounded by the fact that the formulation of rates involves a substantial element of judgment. The bureau rate represents the collective judgment of a large number of competing insurers, aided by a professional staff of actuaries, as to the average future losses and expenses for the industry." [24]

How would rate bureaus be viewed if the insurance industry exemption from federal antitrust laws were eliminated? Could such bureaus continue to operate as they have in the past? Would they alter their methods of operation or cease to exist entirely? In terms of Section 1 of the Sherman Act, a rate bureau would most likely be viewed as either a "trade association," collecting and disseminating cost and price information, or a "joint venture," performing a support function for its members.

Public policy favors the exchange of cost and price information in a competitive environment. In *Maple Flooring Association* v. *United States*, it was stated: "The public interest is served by the gathering and dissemination, in the widest possible manner, of information with respect to the production and distribution, cost and prices in actual sales, of market commodities, because the making available of such information tends to stabilize trade and industry, to produce fairer price levels and to avoid waste which inevitably attends the unintelligent conduct of economic enterprise." [25]

In the case of *Cement Manufacturers Protective Association* v. *United States*, it is stated, however, that this policy is premised on the notion that "complete independence of judgment" by informed sellers rather than concerted action contributes to fairer prices and maximum efficiency. [26]

The Supreme Court has prohibited the collective exchange of sensitive data among competitors for use in formulating prospective prices. In the case of *American Column Company* v. *United States*, the court made this point: "Genuine competitors . . . do not submit the details of their business to the analysis of an expert, jointly employed, and obtain from him a 'harmonized' estimate of the market it is and, in his specially informed judgment, it promises to be." [27]

It is generally believed that a rating bureau, where it deals with future

---

[24] Ibid., p. 52.
[25] 268 U.S. 563, 582–83 (1925).
[26] 268 U.S. 588, 605 (1925).
[27] 257 U.S. 377, 410 (1921).

pricing data, including the projection of losses and expenses and the formulation of prospective average rates, would be likely to violate Section 1 of the Sherman Act in the absence of the current McCarran-Ferguson Act exemption. It is also thought that the formulation of prospective pure premiums, representing a major component of the rate structure could be held to violate Section 1, although the courts have addressed this issue only by way of dictum.[28]

Court cases indicate the rate bureaus would not necessarily be insulated from antitrust attack for such activities just because their staffs had been delegated authority to formulate rates "independent" of the membership, given the possible indirect effect of the members' interest on staff decision making.[29] Neither would rate bureaus be protected by the voluntary nature of the arrangement or by the fact that a large proportion of the members priced independently of, or deviated by a fixed percentage from, the bureau rate.[30]

Some rate bureau activities, however, might be permissible under the Sherman Act. Thus, the Justice Department argued: "Where the bureau deals with data on past experience, it would be on safer ground, even though such data may help insurers formulate their future rates. This involves some considerations which may be unique to the insurance industry—with its special need for loss data. Essentially, we believe that the bureau can collect loss and expense data from competing insurers, a function that, as a practical matter, cannot be performed by individual companies. In this connection, the bureau can develop classification standards with respect to coverage, drivers, territories, and automobiles. The bureau also provides standard policy forms, and it prints rate manuals and pages for members, including those companies that price independent of, or deviate from, the bureau rates. It appears that these concerted activities could be conducted in a manner that would satisfy the federal antitrust standards for the exchange of cost information. Collected data could be limited to past loss and expense experience. This restriction should not preclude the bureau from estimating actual losses (that is, adjusting loss experience by

[28] Jacobi v. Bache and Company, Inc., 377 F. Supp. 86, 93–96 (S.D. N.Y., 1974), affirmed 520 F. 2d 1231 (2nd Circuit, 1975), Certiorari denied, 96 S. Ct. 784 (1976).
[29] U.S. v. Masonite Corporation, 316 U.S. 265, 276 (1942).
[30] Northern California Pharmaceutical Association v. U.S., 306 F. 2d 379, 391 (9th Circuit, 1962).

a development factor), preparing backup data for trend analysis, or estimating actual countrywide expenses or 'hypothetical' profit returns."[31]

There seems to be a widespread consensus that it is necessary to pool and project loss experience within the insurance business. In *Casualty Insurance*, Kulp and Hall noted, "The very reason for insurance is that it permits the insured to substitute for his casual and unpredictable individual loss experience the certainty of the average experience in the classification."[32] It is widely believed that there may be a practical necessity for permitting a bureau to collect and compile data, since a certain amount of cooperation among competing insurers is needed to establish and implement a statistical plan.

It is generally believed that the antitrust laws permit the joint performance of certain functions, including the formulation of a classification system and statistical plan, and the collection, compilation, and dissemination of past loss and expense data. The projection of future rates, or any large component of them, would more than likely fall within the prohibitions of the Sherman Act.

With regard to the question of whether auto insurers would be able to operate without bureau rates, the Department of Justice concluded: "The available evidence clearly suggests that with access to trended (or 'developed') loss cost data based on the aggregate experience of competing insurers most insurers would be able individually to determine their own rate structure in a competitive environment. The experience in Illinois may provide the best available evidence of the feasibility of limiting advisory services to loss cost data. In Illinois, automobile insurers are provided trended loss cost data (including a schedule or pure premiums) which 'must be loaded for appropriate expenses to obtain gross (manual) rates.'"[33]

This also appears to be the conclusion of the Insurance Services Office (ISO) in its response to the Justice Department's questions on the ability of small insurers to compete effectively with access only to developed loss cost data: "As a matter of opinion, if the regulatory system were to permit departures from ISO advisory pure premiums based on judgment rather than requiring strict actuarial or empirical justification for such departures, we believe that, for the major personal lines, most companies

---

[31] MacAvoy, *Federal-State Regulation*, p. 52.
[32] Cited in ibid., p. 54.
[33] Ibid., p. 58.

could effectively compete. Additionally, most specialty companies might reasonably be expected to fare well." [34]

The available evidence, the Justice Department declared, "does not support the conclusion that small insurers or new entrants could not operate without the bureau's schedule of rates. The access to past industry-wide experience, trended losses, and current price data should be sufficient to enable all companies to construct their own rates independently. In conclusion, the market characteristics of the automobile insurance industry provide an appropriate framework for the exchange of cost and price information necessary to the conduct of business and consistent with federal antitrust standards. We do not believe that a special exemption from the federal antitrust laws for the pooling of statistical data would be necessary or appropriate." [35]

In the case of pricing commercial fire insurance, the rate bureaus in most states perform a major role In formulating the final rate or starting point for pricing. They develop the relativity factors and formulate the class rates for the smaller commercial risks. Where analytical rating is required, the bureaus classify individual properties and provide conversion tables and rate adjustment information for the formulation of rates. In most states, rating laws for commercial fire insurance provide each insurer with the flexibility to price individual risks based on the company's own loss and expense experience and expectations. The individual-insured rating plans serve as a competitive device in which insurers may deviate substantially from the bureau rates.

In addition to rate bureaus, there are two other widely used means of setting commercial fire insurance rates: (1) ad hoc joint ventures in the form of a placement or reinsurance arrangement and (2) the more permanent type of joint venture arrangement in the form of a syndicate or "pool."

The Justice Department, reviewing these forms of concerted activity, concluded that "the pricing activities of all three of these entities can and should operate pursuant to the federal antitrust laws, as a substitute for state regulation. We believe that the bureau as a trade association or joint venture can continue to perform certain concerted activities in connection with the pricing of commercial fire insurance that either are necessary to the conduct of business or result in significant economies of scale without

---

[34] Ibid.
[35] Ibid., pp. 59–60.

substantially lessening price competition. . . . The efficient pricing of commercial fire insurance, like automobile insurance, appears to depend ultimately on the judgment of individual insurers, not on the collective judgment of a bureau. . . . We believe that there is sufficient precedent in the federal antitrust laws to permit the perpetuation of the placement and reinsurance arrangements that are necessary to the conduct of business and that are reasonably structured. . . ." [36]

A subject of growing controversy in the entire discussion of how insurance rates are set is the relationship of those rates to the investment income of insurance companies. The National Association of Insurance Commissioners Task Force on Profitability and Investment has been cautioned against any precipitous regulatory action in this area because "neither the property-casualty industry nor its regulators is possessed of any broad experience base from which to derive conclusions with respect to the most reasonable regulatory approach." [37]

This advice was given in the Advisory Committee Report to the NAIC Task Force. The report declared that "the state of the art" in total rate of return regulation is "indeed embryonic" and that "rate of return regulation is exceedingly difficult, costly and complex" and "brings with it some uncertainty as to outcome." A separate report was issued by two of the thirteen members of the advisory committee, John W. Wilson and J. Robert Hunter. It contained a legal analysis by Robert A. Jablon, Daniel J. Guttman, and Ron M. Landsman. [38]

While the majority of the industry-oriented advisory committee members maintained that antitrust exemptions and collectively supported rate bureaus are necessary and desirable features of the insurance industry, stating that the competition between companies is actually so vigorous that consumers are adequately protected by free-market forces, "the need to regulate rates disappears, taking with it concern over the role of investment income." [39]

Wilson and Hunter sharply disagreed. They declared: "The time has clearly come for insurance industry regulators to explicitly include invest-

[36] Ibid., p. 61.

[37] Private memorandum, National Association of Insurance Commissioners.

[38] John W. Wilson and J. Robert Hunter, *Investment Income and Profitability in Property/Casualty Insurance Ratemaking*, report prepared for the National Association of Insurance Commissioners Task Force on Profitability and Investment Income. (Available from J. W. Wilson & Associates, 1010 Wisconsin Ave., Washington, D.C. 20007.)

[39] Ibid.

ment income in the ratemaking and approval process. Both the underwriting practices of insurance companies and dramatic increases in the level of investment income (to the point where it now greatly exceeds the level of underwriting income for most lines) clearly demonstrate that the '1921 Standard Profit Formula' is no longer relevant." Wilson and Hunter also stated that failure to include investment income explicitly in the ratemaking and approval process was tantamount to "not regulating insurance industry profits at all."

The Wilson and Hunter report also concluded: "While some imperfections will always remain in the regulatory application of a total return approach (as they will in any human endeavor), they will be far less significant than the immense error of failing to incorporate investment income explicitly. Moreover, the regulatory process and the judgments involved will be no more difficult than what has been required in traditional ratemaking and approval practices. Even if there is legitimacy in the contention that rate of return regulation is not yet adequately tested and researched to settle upon the ultimate adoption of a specific approach, that does not invalidate this conclusion. It would be far better for insurance regulators to be approximately right than precisely wrong."

When it adopted the "1921 Standard Profit Formula," the National Convention of Insurance Commissioners specified a 5 percent underwriting margin which is still used today. NCIC at that time declared, "No part of the so-called banking profit (or loss) should be considered in arriving at the underwriting profit (or loss)."

While the NCIC did not explain its basis for adopting the 5 percent underwriting factor or for excluding investment income in the rate-making process, the National Board of Fire Underwriters (NBFU) presented its reasons for opposing the explicit recognition of investment income: (1) discounts on three-year and five-year term policies already implicitly recognize investment income; (2) there may be untold legal complications if companies admit such an entirely new principle; (3) investment income is simply not part of underwriting, it is not the property of policyholders. It is derived in part from reserves belonging to stockholders and is needed by companies to fund reserve growth that would otherwise have to be funded by stockholders; and (4) it would be expensive to calculate the correct credit to rate-payers (National Board of Fire Underwriters, *Proceedings*, 1921, p. 51).

Hunter and Wilson argued, "the industry has profited enormously more from investment income than could ever have been contemplated when the still traditional '1921 Standard Profit Formula' was implemented. When investment income is properly recognized, it is clear that the industry's total return has significantly outpaced other business sectors and, as a result, the industry's stock market performance has greatly exceeded other enterprises in our economy. There is mounting evidence that business and financial risks (and therefore profit requirements) in the property/casualty insurance industry are relatively low in comparison with other industries in our economy. In today's economy, traditional underwriting profit allowances, coupled with investment income, would produce total returns that greatly exceed the industry's cost of capital."

After the passage of the McCarran-Ferguson Act, the NAIC, with assistance from the insurance industry, developed the "All Industry Rate Regulatory Bills," discussions for which raised the issue of investment income. New York became the first state to take investment income into account in automobile insurance rate making by reducing the 5.0 percent underwriting profit provision to 3.5 percent in recognition of investment income's contribution to total return.[40] According to state senate hearings in 1976, New York returned to the 5 percent profit allowance years later, after a series of private meetings between insurance company officials and New York Insurance Department staff. More recently, New York has again taken to examining investment income in reviewing private passenger automobile insurance filings.

The 1947 report of Roy C. McCullough of the New York Insurance Department to the NAIC is considered a significant document in the early debate on this subject. This report, which was opposed by the industry, recommended (1) withdrawing approval of the "1921 Standard Profit Formula" and (2) developing revised flexible profit standards which would explicitly recognize investment income in determining the required underwriting profit.

Prior to the NAIC's 1970 staff report on investment income, the Virginia State Corporation Commission, in a contested rate case, required that investment income arising from unearned premium reserves be re-

<hr />

[40] C. A. William, *Determining Excess Profit Refunds on New York State Automobile Insurance* (Albany: New York State Department of Insurance, 1979).

flected in rate making. The Supreme Court of Virginia, hearing the case on appeal, went further, requiring the reflection of investment income arising out of loss reserves as well.

The Supreme Court of Virginia declared: "A premium is designed to pay casualty losses and provide for operating expenses and underwriting profit. Contrary to the Commission's view, premium income does not become stockholders' profit by the mere passage of time, without any charge for the payment of casualty losses. Nor is the loss reserve derived from funds belonging to the stockholders. The loss reserve represents that part of the premium paid by the policyholders that, it is expected, will be devoted to the payment of losses." [41]

There has been a growing recognition that the old 5 percent standard must be altered. Following the 1972 New Jersey Insurance Department determination that investment income should be explicitly recognized in rate making, the NAIC conducted further study and concluded: "Few will quarrel with the finding about lack of documentation for the 5% profit allowance. . . . The 1947 McCullough Report, never seriously challenged by the business, demonstrated quite conclusively that the 5% was simply a negotiated figure, with scant statistical 'back up.' Considering the social nature of the coverage provided by the property and casualty insurance business, the insuring public is entitled to have the profitability factor in the rate structure measured by a realistic yardstick; the return on net worth which considers income from all sources is a standard method for this purpose." [42]

In 1975, the Massachusetts Insurance Department undertook a review of profitability issues that had an impact on insurers and concluded: "It is absolutely incomprehensible . . . how the industry could have successfully argued for so long that an underwriting profit margin should be programmed into the rates without regard for the investment implications of the business. It does not take an economist to know that if someone takes a dollar from you and returns $.95 one year later, his profit on the transaction was the sum of five cents directly taken and the gain from the use of your money for the year's period."

In the late 1970s and early 1980s, as investment yields increased, the issue of profitability and investment income became subject to increasing

[41] Virginia AFL-CIO v. Corporation Commission, 107 SE 2d 322.

[42] "An Early Look at the Decision in the New Jersey Remand Case" (National Association of Insurance Commissioners, May, 1972), pp. 9, 19.

discussion and concern. Minnesota developed a profitability–investment income system for workers' compensation based on analysis of internal rates of return. North Carolina received total return testimony in several rate cases. The City Council of the District of Columbia passed a bill requiring that the superintendent "mathematically" take investment income into account. The Florida Insurance Department issued new investment income requirements in response to its legislature's enactment of investment income requirements. The Texas Insurance Department undertook a major study of the issue, and an NAIC Task Force on the subject was organized.

According to the Industry Members' Advisory Report, adopted by the majority of the committee, "the era of sidestepping the issue of investment income is over." This is so, they say, because "property/casualty insurers . . . have (already) included investment income in determining insurance prices." While maintaining that the insurance industry "is above average risk," the Industry Advisors argued that more than 80 percent of the nation's other industries earned greater profits. As a result, they state, the industry now has a deplorable record of low profits, and its risks are among the highest in the economy. The Industry Members' Report declared: "There is no evidence of excessive profitability in the property-casualty insurance industry. . . . Over eighty per cent of the non-insurance industries had . . . [an] average return larger than [property-casualty] insurance."

In their minority report, Hunter and Wilson disagreed. They declared: "Since 1969, which is the base index year for Best's Property/Casualty Stock Index [i.e., 1969 equals 100], property/casualty industry stock prices have more than tripled while the Dow Jones Industrials were up only 30 per cent and the S and P 500 were up 54 per cent. No one can deny that this is quite a remarkable showing for one of our economy's highest risk and lowest profit performers. Investors have certainly been fooled." [43]

In each of the five years from 1976 to 1980, the return on average equity has been higher for the property-casualty industry than for the Fortune 500. In 1980, for example, the property-casualty industry had an 18.2 percent return while the Fortune 500 had a 14.4 percent return. The average for this five-year period was: property-casualty, 19.3 percent; Fortune 500, 14.3 percent.

The rate bureau structure, Hunter and Wilson argued, was inappropriate for a competitive atmosphere and instead simply served the interests of

[43] Wilson and Hunter, *Investment Income and Profitability*.

companies involved. They stated: "Traditional cartel activities continue to stifle the remaining potential outlets for enhanced competitive rivalry. The agenda of rate bureaus does not include supplying information to buyers. The exchange of detailed information and the provision of pricing recommendations is reserved for the benefit of 'rival' sellers. In view of the fact that information dissemination is reserved for the bureau's seller-members, it is clear that these efforts, especially pricing guidance, are more essential for cooperative than for competitive market organizations. Rate bureaus have not been designed merely to ensure an intelligent and informed business rivalry by which competitive relationships may be established. On the contrary, they involve a cooperative interpretation and dissemination of market data and at least a strong effort at the coordination of market policy designed to bring security and profits to underwriters at the expense of those who purchase coverage. These bureaus provide their members with a forum for obtaining intimate knowledge of the pricing guidance that is dispensed to rival suppliers. It is thus hardly appropriate to view the property-casualty industry as a group of unrelated atomistic competitors when they proceed to march forth into markets in united cadence to deal with widely separated and unorganized consumers who are frequently ignorant of the true conditions under which personal lines coverages are sold or the alternatives available to them in the marketplace."

Hunter and Wilson concluded: "Whether rate bureaus prepare and promulgate proposed or suggested final rates or stop just short of that ultimate step, merely leading the herd to the trough of rates through the preparation and distribution of uniform data on trending, experience periods, class selection, territories, differentials, etc.—the detailed underpinnings which permit and encourage consciously parallel 'independent' rate determinations—their anti-competitive impact can not be construed as benign." [44]

Still, Hunter and Wilson argued that this did not mean that all potential rate bureau activities were or ought to be "per se unlawful." They believed: "Such organizations, or alternative government entities, may be able to perform useful public activities; for example, the dissemination of necessary market information to consumers. But if we are to rely upon enterprise and competition as the disciplinary forces within our economy, concerted industry action through rate bureaus, particularly in areas re-

[44] Ibid.

lated to pricing is dangerous. If, on the other hand, cooperative endeavors are to exist in the area of pricing (especially pricing guidance), responsibility and authority should go hand in hand. That is, regulatory authorities with ultimate responsibility to protect consumer interests should exercise control in the ratemaking process."[45]

On January 5, 1983, the Insurance Services Office (ISO) issued a press release announcing that it would develop "only prospective loss costs" in competitive rating states, although it would continue to "develop advisory rates" and file rates in behalf of members in noncompetitive rating states. While ISO stated that "the insurance industry has always been highly competitive," it expressed the view that this move would "further stimulate independent pricing decisions." Critics argue, however, that this step is debilitated by ISO's announcement that it will determine the "average loss experience . . . as well as the loss development and trend factors" in states that have competitive rating systems.

It is generally agreed the kind of joint rate making engaged in by insurance companies would be prohibited as illegal price fixing for industries not enjoying antitrust immunity. When Congress gave its approval to joint rate making in its consideration of the McCarran-Ferguson Act, it did so on the understanding that the rates would ultimately be made by state officials or that they would be directly subject to state approval. This was the practice advocated by the original NAIC model rate regulation acts. Thus, joint rate making was approved because competition was not to be the principal determinant of insurance rates because of the industry's asserted need to conduct joint activities not permitted under antitrust laws.

In other areas of law, price fixing among would-be competitors is considered the clearest form of anticompetitive and antitrust behavior. One of the Supreme Court's most recent statements with regard to price fixing came in a summary per curiam reversal of a decision holding that an agreement among wholesalers not to extend credit to retailers was not price fixing, that is, not per se illegal. In the case of *Catalano, Inc.* v. *Target Sales, Inc.*, the court declared that an "agreement to fix prices is the archetypal example" of "certain agreements or practices that are so plainly anticompetitive that they are conclusively presumed illegal without further examination."[46]

---

[45] Ibid.
[46] 446 U.S. 643, 646–47 (1980).

It seems that no explicit or even implicit agreement to adhere to set prices is required to cross the line between permissible information collection and impermissible price fixing.[47] In addition, because price is the "central nervous system of the economy,"[48] the antitrust laws have been applied to a wide range of agreements among sellers designed to tamper with price competition, usually by giving sellers detailed knowledge of what their competitors are doing and putting customers at a disadvantage. Even arrangements to share information on a seller-only basis can be per se violations of the antitrust laws becuase they dampen price competition.

Competition, many observers point out, is greater in commercial lines of insurance than in personal lines. A front-page article in the *National Underwriter* reported: "A large commercial umbrella risk came up for renewal and was rated at $105,000, about the same time as the previous year. But the insured was not satisfied. Aware of the aggressive rate competition in the commercial lines market today, he decided to shop around. He approached a second agent, who submitted the very same risk to a different company, which offered to write it for just $20,000. But the insured still was not happy. He continued shopping and eventually the original company, which initially wanted $105,000, came back and took the business [for] $5,000. That's right, $5,000."[49]

Robert A. Bailey, writing for *Best's Insurance Damages Reports*, made this point: "While this industry aggregate is profitable, those profits are not evenly spread. The premium growth this year comes entirely from personal lines. Commercial lines premium is flat. Consequently, results for commercial lines are deteriorating much more seriously. Expense ratios, while relatively flat in personal lines for the past five years, have risen substantially for commercial lines and continued to do so."[50]

Hunter and Wilson said in their report that at present, "after more than half a century of sidestepping the issue of investment income in the ratemaking and approval process, property/casualty carriers are increasingly being forced by regulators to give the issue detailed attention. And it is clear that they must. Investment income accounts for virtually all of the industry's profits. Failure to give it explicit regulatory focus is tantamount to discarding price regulation altogether."[51]

---

[47] U.S. v. National Association of Real Estate Boards, 339 U.S. 485 (1950).

[48] Society of Professional Engineers v. U.S., 435 U.S. 679 (1978).

[49] *National Underwriter*, November 20, 1981.

[50] *Best's Insurance Damage Reports*, December 6, 1982.

[51] Wilson and Hunter, *Investment Income and Profitability*.

In a legal analysis of the NAIC Advisory Committee Report on Investment Income and Profitability, attorneys Robert A. Jablon, Daniel Guttman, and Ron M. Landsman declared: "The idea that casualty insurance rates can be regulated without directly taking into account what is, in most cases, the sole source of net income is difficult to fathom. The substitution of a fixed ratio of profit on sales for analysis of actual income and actual profit needs was characterized by the Massachusetts insurance commissioner as the 'shoddiest component' of insurance ratemaking, 'hanging solely on threads of imagination unsupported as measures of reasonable profit in either hearing evidence or actuarial literature' [quoted in *Attorney General* v. *Insurance Commissioner*, 353 N.E. 2nd 745, 760, Mass. Sup. Jud. Ct., 1976]. Based upon our review of legislation and regulation . . . it appears that state legislatures have in recent years taken the lead in correcting this practice to the extent it caused disregard of investment income. With or without express direction from their legislators, however, it also appears that most insurance commissioners have the authority to do so, and some have even taken the lead in protecting the public on this issue. . . . The alternative of totally competitive rate-making continues to be of doubtful benefit to consumers. To the extent practicable, competition is a complement to rate regulation and is to be encouraged. To that extent, rate regulatory systems that give insurers substantial freedom to reduce rates would be appropriate. But freedom for insurers to change rates should be combined with authority for commissioners to suspend rate increases or to permit increases to go into effect subject to refund pending regulatory hearings and review." [52]

The views of the insurance industry, its critics, and its regulators are very much at odds with regard to the role now being played by and ideally to be played by rate bureaus, as well as the proper means of setting rates and the part to be played by investment income. If the industry's antitrust exemption is eliminated, much that is accepted practice today would come to an almost immediate end. Even if such a step is not taken, the debate over the proper role in rate formulation of investment income is certain to produce important changes in the future, as will the growing concern over what is perceived as the anti-consumer collusion involved in the rate bureau process.

[52] Ibid.

8

....

Tax Legislation Affecting
the Insurance Industry

ONE of the hot topics in Washington in the mid-1980s was the perceived need to alter tax codes to a significant degree. Speaking in January, 1984, Donald T. Regan, secretary of the Treasury, said that if President Reagan were reelected, he would be likely to propose far-reaching changes in the nation's tax system. The changes, Secretary Regan said, could include a "simplified" tax system that would eliminate many income tax deductions and also lower tax rates.

In his budget message presented to the Congress early in 1984, President Reagan reaffirmed his faith in "supply-side" tax cut policies. The budget repeated the president's proposal that the federal tax code be made "simpler and fairer," and he directed the Treasury Department to recommend tax code revisions by the end of 1984.

The main goals of the tax simplification study were to close tax loopholes, improve taxpayer compliance, and broaden the tax base so that rates could be cut, he said. The Treasury Department was to study three major options: a "consumed income" tax, which would have the effect of taxing what an individual spends rather than what he earns; a broad-based income tax, eliminating many deductions, exclusions, and exemptions; and a value-added or retail sales tax.

Prior to the president's announcement of the tax reform proposals, the House Ways and Means Committee had in 1983 considered legislation intended to overhaul the tax laws governing the life insurance industry. The issue with which Congress was attempting to come to grips reflects the fact that life insurance companies serve two functions: providing life insurance and providing savings or investment. The profit from the provision of life insurance is called underwriting income. On the investment side, companies invest funds paid by the policyholders between the time the money is received and the time it is paid out to beneficiaries. The profit is referred to as investment income.

Until recently, the investment part of life insurance played a secondary role for most consumers. The savings portion was limited, and the rate of return was usually lower than the prevailing interest rates. Now, many new investment opportunities have been created. Insurance companies have fought to meet new competition from banks and brokerage houses by creating new types of life insurance products. The newer policies provide returns closer to the market rate, and the balance between the insurance element and the investment element of a policy has shifted. In some instances, the investment portion of the policy is now considered dominant. In "universal life" policies, for example, policyholders are given a choice about the timing and amount of premium payments. Such policies are considered closer to simple investments than they are to traditional insurance policies.

Congressional Quarterly has reported: "Creation of these investment-oriented forms of life insurance exacerbated problems within the life insurance industry between stock companies and mutual companies. Stock life insurance companies essentially are ordinary corporations. They are owned by their stockholders and their policyholders are their customers. Mutual insurance companies, however, are owned by their customers or policyholders. Someone who buys a life insurance policy from a mutual company gets a life insurance policy and the right to share in the profits of the company. A former U.S. Court of Claims judge once described the maze of life insurance tax laws—written in large part by the industry itself—this way: 'These complex and obscure provisions bear all the earmarks of a conspiracy in restraint of understanding.'" [1]

The judge was referring to the 1959 insurance tax law, still in effect in 1985. Congress began deliberations on that bill in 1954, and took five years to achieve the kind of balance that proved acceptable to both elements of the industry. The 1959 provisions were designed to balance the tax burden between the two segments of the industry. Mutual companies were

[1] *Congressional Quarterly*, October 8, 1983.

taxed mostly on the basis of investment income and stock companies largely on underwriting income.

When interest rates began to increase sharply in the late 1970s, so did the tax burden of the mutual companies. Using a special provision in the 1959 act called modified coinsurance ("Modco"), mutuals were able to redefine much of their investment income as underwriting and thus to reduce their tax burden or in some cases to avoid it altogether. To eliminate this redefinition under "Modco," the 1982 tax-increase bill did away with that special provision but included temporary relief that was to expire at the end of 1983.

In an address to the American Council of Life Insurance in Washington, D.C., in November, 1983, Regan discussed the Life Insurance Tax Act of 1983. He noted: "This bill proposes a major overhaul in the way life insurance companies and their products are taxed. Generally, the approach taken by the Act is simpler and fairer than the present system. In particular, there will no longer be three 'phases' of tax for life companies and the often artificial distinction between investment and underwriting income will be eliminated." [2]

Regan declared that "some complexity is inevitable. This stems primarily from the fact the industry consists of two competing segments: stock and mutual companies. Since a distribution from a mutual company to its policyholders consists in part of corporate profits, the profits must be measured and made subject to tax at the corporate level if stocks and mutuals are to be able to compete on an equal basis. The Act also makes several changes in the taxation of life insurance products. The principal innovation here is that for the first time a general definition of life insurance is provided. The role of the definition is to exclude those policies which have too much investment when compared to the amount of insurance protection provided. We are generally satisfied with the way the definition turned out—the tax system continues to encourage long-term savings through life insurance but the limitations imposed should eliminate the use of life insurance primarily as a tax shelter or investment vehicle." [3]

Insurance companies have experienced a number of changes in the way they are taxed. According to one insurance guide, "before 1921, life

[2] Donald T. Regan, press release of speech to American Council of Life Insurance, Washington, D.C., November, 1983.
[3] Ibid.

insurance companies were taxed in much the same way as any other corporation. From 1921 through 1957, however, a life insurance company was taxed on investment income only. Premiums were excluded from the income computation, as were losses and expenses incurred in underwriting operations and gains and losses from the sale of investment assets. In addition, various formulae excluded from taxation the portion of investment income necessary to satisfy the company's obligations to policyholders and, though the formulae varied from time to time, their purpose always was to compute that portion of investment income allocable to policyholders. This approach of taxing income only to the extent not needed to fund current and projected liabilities to policyholders as determined under state laws was called taxing a company on *free investment income*. Present law—adopted in the Life Insurance Company Tax Act of 1959 (#801–820)—significantly changed prior law by attempting to measure the *total income* of a life insurance company rather than just its *free investment income*." [4]

Another tax question of interest to the insurance industry relates to the question of the Internal Revenue Service's position concerning whether retroactive "insurance" qualifies for tax deductions. The National Insurance Consumer Organization has charged that "foot dragging" by the IRS on this question "has cost taxpayers hundreds of millions of dollars." [5]

In a letter to Roscoe Egger, a commissioner of the IRS, Robert Hunter, president of NICO and formerly the Federal Insurance Administration, said that it had been almost three years since NICO requested that the IRS look at this matter and almost two years since the IRS had agreed to give the matter "active" attention. Retroactive "insurance," Hunter argued, was not insurance at all, since both parties were aware that the claim had already occurred and thus no transfer of risk could take place, only transfer of claims. Without transfer of risk, insurance did not exist, according to all insurance reference texts, Hunter declared. [6]

MGM was the first major retroactive insurance case. The catastrophic fire at the MGM Grand Hotel in Las Vegas in November, 1980, resulted in an extremely complicated legal battle. MGM had purchased only $39 million in liability insurance, which was not nearly sufficient to handle claims.

[4] "Insurance Guide," Bulletin 12 (Englewood Cliffs, N.J.: Prentice-Hall, 1983).
[5] Robert J. Hunter, letter to Roscoe Egger, October 6, 1983.
[6] Ibid.

Broker F. B. Hall then arranged for the hotel to purchase an additional $200 million in retroactive coverage in order to profit by investing the premiums in the lengthy period before the claims would be settled.

The *Journal of Commerce* reported: "MGM surprised the insurers by settling most of the claims within two years instead of the anticipated five-to-seven years. To make matters worse, Hall had estimated that claims would total between $40 million and $60 million, however, in July 1983, a U.S. District Court judge settled most of the claims for a total of $138 million, and there are 37 suits still pending. Hall is suing MGM for settling the claims so quickly. Thomas G. O'Brien III, Hall's general counsel, said, 'The company figured it was playing with someone else's money. Had they taken what we consider a business-like approach the settlements wouldn't have been either so high or so quick.'" [7]

NICO has maintained that tax considerations drove the deal since insurance premiums would be immediately deductible (in 1981) for MGM and loss reserves retroactively deductible (back to 1980) for insurance companies. If MGM paid the claims, they would not be deductible until actually paid. Hunter said the "unwarranted" tax write-offs in 1980 and 1981 from the MGM deal alone were in the range of $100 million. "And that is just the tip of the iceberg," Hunter maintained. "Doctors, hospitals, firms with toxic tort claims and others with inadequate insurance following claims are queuing up to buy this coverage . . . with taxpayers' money. [The] IRS is fiddling while our money burns and our nation's deficits mount. . . . The decision has taken on a new urgency because of the MGM fiasco which confirms NICO's predictions that insurer's profit considerations dictate deferring, just as long as possible, the settlement of losses." [8]

Unlike true insurance, where many insureds are covered but only a few have claims and payment is anticipated fairly quickly for most claims, retroactive insurance, Hunter charged, was a "one-insured deal, requiring that a specific time pass before claims are settled if the insurer is to profit. That's why the insurers are suing MGM for settling those cases." [9] Hunter also wrote to the Federal Trade Commission and the Justice Department, asking them to take jurisdiction over retroactive insurance, which, he maintained, was in violation of antitrust laws.

In his letter to James C. Miller III, FTC chairman, Hunter stated: "It

[7] *Journal of Commerce*, October 3, 1983, p. 3D.
[8] Hunter letter to Egger.
[9] Ibid.

appears clear . . . to us that public policy issues abound in connection with such retroactive provision of coverage to large entities which have been caught short on their liability coverage but which are enabled to emerge relatively unscathed because of this nunc pro tunc 'insurance' protection. It has always been thought to be contrary to public policy for an individual to purport to buy insurance for a loss which he or she knows has already occurred. To be sure, it has correctly been held not to contravene public policy to purchase ocean marine or life insurance covering a loss event which has already occurred so long as neither the insured nor the insurer actually knew that the event had already occurred. However, where the loss event has not only already occurred but is known by both parties to have occurred, it would seem to be clear that there has been no transfer of risk. If it be argued that the actual amount which will become payable as a result of the occurrence is 'uncertain' or the time when such losses will be paid is 'uncertain' then, of course, that same argument could be made by the un-insured driver who seeks coverage for an automobile accident which has already occurred. Since insurance inherently contemplates the transfer of 'risk,' retroactive coverage would not appear to constitute 'insurance' within the meaning of the various state insurance laws or within the meaning of the Federal statutes, including the Internal Revenue Code and the McCarran-Ferguson Act." [10]

The brokerage community takes a far different position and feels optimistic about providing retroactive insurance despite the apparent failure of the MGM Grand Hotel deal. Andrew H. Marks, senior vice-president of Reed Stenhouse, Inc., has said that retroactive coverage will continue to be a usable financial device.[11] Many companies that experienced losses as a result of Hurricane Alicia, which struck the Gulf Coast in 1983, were able to purchase retroactive coverage even after the MGM case.

Tax reform proposals relating to the insurance industry were being considered in Congress in 1984, and John B. Crosby, vice-president and general counsel of the National Association of Independent Insurers, said: "Bad legislation . . . could adversely affect every single company in America and could cost big bucks now and forever, because once on the books, tax laws are the closest thing we'll ever see to immortality." [12]

One reason for the insistence upon a change in tax rules and regula-

---

[10] Robert J. Hunter, letter to James C. Miller III, October 12, 1983.

[11] *Journal of Commerce*, October 3, 1983.

[12] John B. Crosby speech to Insurance Institution of Indiana, September 7, 1983.

tions with regard to insurance, Crosby said, was the need for additional government revenue. "Senator Robert Dole (R-Kansas) as much as said that because of the pressure the government is under to reduce the deficit, the insurance industry had better be prepared to pony up," Crosby said. "It remains to be seen if and how much the industry might have to pony up, but it is important to note that the proponents of a new taxation policy for insurance do not look on what they're doing as tax increase or insurance-bashing. They consider it tax compliance. The GAO says the industry's effective tax rate has been zero in recent years and many have seized on that as proof that insurers aren't paying their fair share because of the special tax treatment of reserves, acquisition expense and so on. In response to that, we've been hammering home that the industry's tax liabilities are reduced because insurers have been awash in red ink for years. Those severe losses, plus the fact that we are heavily invested in tax-exempt municipal securities, which is itself an important public service we provide, are the real reasons for the low effective tax rate. . . . Congress is reaching and grabbing at the tail of something, but they don't know yet what they've got hold of, or what to do with it. From my experience in Washington, any time you've got Treasury, GAO, important figures like Dole, bipartisanship like Stark-Moore, you've got a lot of cars and a lot of locomotive. And with so many ideas, options and suggestions in the air, writing a tax bill becomes a bit like a crazy quilt party." [13]

Discussing the position of the National Association of Independent Insurers, Crosby stated: "We and the rest of the industry have been stressing that changes in taxation aren't needed or wise. They will translate immediately into higher prices for consumers, and threaten the solvency of the industry and the states' authority to regulate solvency. In addition, we argue that new tax burdens on U.S. insurers would send business to foreign companies." [14]

The insurance industry has been expanding its influence and presence in the nation's capital as government considers a wide variety of legislation and regulations affecting insurance. The current president of the American Council of Life Insurance (ACLI) is a former senator and former secretary of Health and Human Services, Richard Schweiker.

The ACLI, whose 601 members provide about 95 percent of the nation's life insurance coverage, employs fifteen registered lobbyists. "Until

[13] Ibid.
[14] Ibid.

very recently," said the head of one of ACLI's member companies, "the industry didn't really understand what it meant to be involved in political activity. We were regulated, historically, by the states and still are. Our activity in Washington was innocuous." [15]

Insurance and taxes were very much in the news as the Congress reconvened in January, 1984. On January 31, Vice-President George Bush's Task Group on Regulation of Financial Services unanimously recommended a plan for a comprehensive overhaul of the financial regulatory system and creation of a new Federal Banking Agency within the Treasury Department. Federal Reserve Board Chairman Volcker and Federal Deposit Insurance Corporation Chairman William Isaac both indicated that they were pleased with the plan.

Four of the key recommendations were noteworthy.

1. The number of banking agencies handling day-to-day bank supervision would be reduced from three to two and the new Federal Banking Agency, which would regulate all national banks, would replace the comptroller of the Treasury.

2. The Federal Reserve would lose to the new Federal Banking Agency the responsibility for determining permissible activities for bank holding companies, including the development of regulations and modification of the "laundry list" of investment powers available to banks. The Fed would have veto power in this area if two-thirds of the Fed governors agreed.

3. The Fed would have regulatory responsibility over approximately fifty international-class bank holding companies, while subsidiary banks would be regulated by the new agency within the Treasury.

4. The Fed would regulate approximately nine thousand state-chartered banks, up from the one thousand institutions that are now members of the Fed. A new certification program would be established for shifting regulatory responsibility to qualified states.

A presidential election would normally preclude enactment of new tax legislation. Nonetheless, Congress did pass the Tax Reform Act of 1984, which was signed into law (Public Law 98-369) by the president on July 18, 1984. Appendix A gives an analysis of the new law's provisions governing insurance. [16]

---

[15] *Philadelphia Inquirer*, February 6, 1984.
[16] Excerpted from "Tax Reform Act of 1984," an analysis prepared by Arthur Andersen & Co.

9

....

Review of Litigation
Relating to Insurance

LITIGATION and government regulation with regard to the insurance industry have been mounting in recent years. A brief review of some of the important areas of consideration makes this abundantly clear.

On July 6, 1983, the U.S. Supreme Court declared that an employer's retirement plan may not provide smaller benefits to women workers than to comparably situated male employees. This ruling has sweeping implications for the insurance industry, which has traditionally used sex-based actuarial tables, and is likely to lead to new activity to pass legislation now pending in Congress that would outlaw sex-based bias in all forms of insurance.

Title VII of the 1964 Civil Rights Act prohibits employers from discriminating against "any individual with respect to his compensation, terms, conditions or privileges of employment because of such individual's race, color, religion, sex or national origin." This means that workers are to be treated as individuals, not as members of groups. The fact that women as a group live longer than men is not a permissible basis for paying them different monthly retirement benefits.

Justice Sandra Day O'Connor provided the key vote in the five to four decision in the case of *Arizona Governing Committee for Tax Deferred Annuity and Deferred Compensation Plans* v. *Norris*. She was joined by Justices Thurgood Marshall, William J. Brennan, Jr., John Paul Stevens, and Byron R. White.[1] The case involved a life annuity plan made available by

[1] 103 S. Ct. 3492 (1983).

Arizona as one of several retirement options for its employees. Such a plan provides a fixed monthly benefit for as long as a retiree lives.

Noting that the court had ruled in the 1978 case of *Los Angeles Department of Water and Power* v. *Manhart* that Title VII barred employers from requiring women to make larger contributions than men to a pension fund, Justice Marshall, writing for the majority, said: "The classification of employees on the basis of sex is no more permissible at the pay-out stage of a retirement plan than at the pay-in stage." [2]

On the question of whether the relief granted as a result of this decision should be retroactive, and thus available to current retirees, Justice O'Connor switched sides. She joined Chief Justice Warren Burger and Justices Harry A. Blackmun, Lewis F. Powell, Jr., and William H. Rehnquist—who had dissented from the main decision—in ruling that only retirement benefits derived from contributions made after this decision must be calculated on a unisex basis.

The court majority said that the assumption that gender may be used to predict longevity "is flatly inconsistent with the basic teaching of Manhart: that Title VII requires employers to treat their employees as individuals, not 'as simply components of a racial, religious, sexual or national class.'" The court stated: "The use of sex-segregated actuarial tables to calculate retirement benefits violates Title VII whether or not the tables reflect an accurate prediction of the longevity of women as a class for under the statute 'even a true generalization about a class' cannot justify class-based treatment." [3]

Justice Marshall noted that actuarial studies "could unquestionably identify differences in life expectancy based on race or national origin, as well as sex." If Arizona's reasoning in the Norris case were adopted, he said, "such studies could be used as a justification for paying employees of one race lower monthly benefits than employees of another race." [4]

Dissenters Powell, Burger, Blackmun, and Rehnquist warned of the decision's "far-reaching effect on the operation of insurance and pension plans." Writing for himself and his three colleagues, Powell said: "Employers may be forced to discontinue offering life annuities, or potentially disruptive changes may be required in long-established methods of calculating insurance and pensions. Either course will work a major change in the way

[2] 435 U.S. 702, 98 S. Ct. 1370 (1978).
[3] Ibid.
[4] Ibid.

the cost of insurance is determined—to the probable detriment of all employees." [5]

The focus on the individual that Title VII requires, Justice Powell said, cannot be squared with the whole concept of insurance. He explained: "Insurance and life annuities exist because it is impossible to measure accurately how long any one individual will live. Insurance companies cannot make individual determinations of life expectancy; they must consider instead the life expectancy of identifiable groups. . . . Explicit sexual classifications, to be sure, require close examination, but they are not automatically invalid. Sex-based mortality tables reflect objective actuarial experience. Because their use does not entail discrimination in any normal understanding of that term, a court should hesitate to invalidate this long-approved practice on the basis of its own policy judgment. Congress may choose to forbid the use of any sexual classifications in insurance, but nothing suggests that it intended to do so in Title VII." [6]

In a separate opinion, Justice O'Connor said that the court had not weighed whether sex could be considered in all insurance plans, including individually purchased insurance. The Norris decision had no necessary effect on that issue, she wrote. O'Connor also explained the practical reasons for her joining the dissenters to form a majority limiting the relief available as a result of the court's decision. To make the new system of calculating these benefits retroactive would not be fair, she wrote. A court order that employers must now pay out larger annuity benefits each month to retired women workers than had been anticipated could jeopardize an entire pension fund. Should such a fund collapse, innocent people would be harmed, she said. "This real danger of bankrupting pension funds requires that our decisions be made prospective," she concluded. [7]

In separate orders announced July 6, 1983, the court sent back to courts of appeals three other cases involving sex-based pension differentials. One case concerned California's retirement plan for its employees; two others, from Long Island University and from Wayne State University, involved the retirement system provided for college teachers by the Teachers Insurance Annuity Association and College Retirement Equities Fund. The Supreme Court directed the appeals courts to reconsider these cases in light of its decision in the Norris case. Women's groups and the insurance industry appeared to have mixed feelings about the court ruling.

[5] Ibid.
[6] Ibid.
[7] Ibid.

For the women's groups, the ruling established that employers cannot discriminate in retirement benefits because of a worker's gender. While the ruling applies only to employer-sponsored pension programs, representatives of women's groups predicted that the decision would, in the long run, result in the elimination of sex as a factor in all types of insurance in the general marketplace.

Judy Goldsmith, president of the National Organization for Women, called the ruling "a victory for women's rights." Some women activists, however, were critical of the court's decision to require unisex benefit calculations only for contributions made after August 1, 1983—the effective date of the ruling. They contended that employers had known since at least the 1978 Manhart ruling that benefits should not be calculated on the basis of sex. Goldsmith also argued that retirement plans for women were governed by a double standard as a result of the court ruling because the decision did nothing to preclude insurance companies from continuing to sell sex-based individual policies.

Insurance industry officials were pleased that the ruling did not require that benefits be recalculated for current retirees or for contributions made to retirement plans prior to August 1. Richard Schweiker, president of the American Council of Life Insurance (ACLI) declared that retroactivity would have resulted in "devastating costs to employers."[8] Justice Powell said that a 1983 Labor Department study showed that the added cost of annuities with equalized benefits would range from $85 million to $676 million a year for at least the next fifteen years, depending on the method used for adjusting benefits.

At this time, it remains unclear whether companies that offer annuity plans will have the option of reducing men's benefits and increasing women's until they are equal, or whether they will have to "top up" women's benefits to the level of the men. There is also a third option, one that Arizona has chosen. Employers can refuse to offer any kind of annuity plan for their retirees.

Schweiker has said that annuities as a benefit alternative may be eliminated by many employers because of the cost of equalizing benefits. He said that the ruling "did not revolutionize the business of insurance" because it applied only to employer-provided programs, not to insurance companies selling annuity policies to individuals. Also, insurance companies could consider the gender makeup of a company's work force in de-

---

[8] Press release of speech by Richard Schweiker, June 27, 1983.

termining the price of a pension program, he said. According to the ACLI, between one million and three million women and eight million men are in employer-sponsored plans with benefits calculated on the basis of gender. Another four million women with individual annuity contracts bought on the open market would not be affected by the ruling, ACLI officials said.

According to the Employee Benefit Research Institute, a nonprofit research group funded by actuarial firms, insurance companies, and others, the court ruling will have an impact on 25 million people in 450,000 pension plans. The group sees ramifications for a wide range of retirement plans.

Congressional Quarterly reported: "The impact of the court ruling on pending legislation to outlaw sex discrimination in all forms of insurance was unclear. Both women's groups and insurance industry officials said the ruling should help them in Congress and they will continue their lobbying efforts. . . . Unlike the court decision, the bills would affect all types of insurance and pension policies—annuities, life, health, disability, and auto—whether provided by employers or bought individually. Also, the legislation would require companies to increase the benefits of current retirees and others who already have begun paying premiums if their contracts provide for lower benefits or higher rates because of sex-based tables."[9]

Insurance industry officials say that court ruling should reduce the pressure for the legislation. They argue that pension benefits had been the main focus of concern in Congress. "Our strategy doesn't change. We're against the bill in its present form," said Richard Schweiker.[10]

Others, however, do not view the ruling as the end of legislative proposals to eliminate gender as a factor for determining premiums or benefits. Senate Commerce Committee Chairman Robert Packwood (R-Oregon) said that the Supreme Court decision "takes care of only part of the problem, making the need for legislation to bar discrimination in insurance based on sex even more important. It is now up to the Congress to make non-discrimination on the basis of sex the standard in all insurance for all people."

The debate over banking regulation revolves around the question of whether the role in the economy of banks, by which we generally mean

---

[9] *Congressional Quarterly*, July 9, 1983.
[10] Schweiker speech, June 27, 1983.

depository institutions, justifies treating them differently from other providers of financial services. Do the benefits of freer competition outweigh what critics of deregulation see as the inherent dangers—excessive risktaking, conflicts of interest, and undue concentration of economic power?

Sen. William Proxmire (D-Wisconsin), former chairman and ranking minority member of the Senate Banking Committee, has explained the reasoning of those who argue that banks are special and unique. "The essence of banking is to allocate a scarce resource—credit—to those enterprises where it can be most productively employed," he said. "If bankers do their job well, the entire society benefits through higher economic growth. If bankers do poorly, society loses through lower rates of growth and productivity." This, Senator Proxmire said, is the logic behind the laws that have sought "to separate the business of banking from other commercial endeavors, and especially from the securities industry. This is why we do not permit banks to buy stocks and why we confine their activities to areas that are closely related to banking. We want to be sure that bankers are as impartial as they can possibly be in allocating credit among alternative uses." [11]

Those who support deregulation take a more liberal view of the distinction between depository institutions and the rest of the financial services industry. C. Todd Conover, comptroller of the currency, for example, has stated: "I think it is important to separate banking from commerce, but I define banking . . . to include a whole host of financial services." [12]

A discussion of this issue in the 1982 annual report of the Federal Reserve Bank of Minnesota stated: "Efforts to distinguish among kinds of institutions are both futile and unnecessary . . . many financial services offered by various classes of institutions are so complementary to (or such close substitutes for) one another that institutional distinctions are rendered useless. Implicit in this view is the assumption that banks are not special." [13]

Testifying before the Senate Banking Committee, Secretary of the Treasury Regan stated: "The laws and policies that govern or are related to banking—deposit insurance, comprehensive regulation and supervision, government liquidity assistance, and exemptions from [certain] securities laws—are designed to encourage savers to deposit their funds in banks, in preference to other investment media. Permitting banks to make other uses

[11] Text of William Proxmire speech, printed in *Congressional Quarterly*, September 10, 1983, p. 1904.
[12] Ibid.
[13] Ibid., p. 1900.

of these combined savings flows—to allow them, for example, to capitalize subsidiaries engaged in non-banking businesses—alters and diminishes their necessary and intended role as intermediaries between savers and productive users of credit." [14]

The Reagan administration did not propose to permit banks to go directly into nonbanking services; it would let them do so only through subsidiaries or affiliates. Regan stated, "The administration believes that banks should be able to associate themselves with organizations that may legally offer a broad range of financial services, so that banks may take advantage of the access to customers that such an affiliation provides." [15]

Treasury Department General Counsel Wallison explained: "If you have an American Express card, then you get in the mail all the time material inviting you to buy traveler's checks, insurance [and other services]. It turns out to be a very effective marketing tool." Wallison said that the Reagan administration wanted to let banks "eliminate that marketing disadvantage." [16] The way to achieve deregulation and still maintain the safety and soundness of the banks, the administration seemed to be saying, was to permit their holding companies to engage in such functions.

While many in the Reagan administration believed that expanding bank powers through their holding companies was a perfect solution, opponents of deregulation considered this a dangerous approach. They believed that it was the practice of letting banks affiliate with non-banking entities, especially securities firms, that led to the events which prompted the regulations under discussion.

Of particular concern to many in the insurance industry is what is perceived as a lowering of federal automobile safety standards. In December, 1983, the U.S. Court of Appeals for the District of Columbia heard oral arguments in the State Farm/Allstate case challenging the weakness of the government's auto bumper standard. The insurers argued that the Transportation Department's estimates of costs to the auto industry were overstated and benefits to consumers and insurers understated and that real-world experience data failed to support its cost-benefit assessment. For this reason, the government had no basis to downgrade the standard, according to the insurers.

---

[14] Donald Regan testimony of April 6, 1983, printed in *Congressional Quarterly*, September 10, 1983, p. 1904.

[15] Ibid.

[16] *Congressional Quarterly*, September 10, 1983, p. 1905.

Discussing this in the U.S. Department of Transportation hearings, Lowell R. Beck, president of the National Association of Independent Insurers, stated: "In view of the Supreme Court's recent ruling that the previous [National Highway Transportation Safety Administration] Administrator acted unlawfully in rescinding the 208 standard, we are asking the Department of Transportation Secretary to implement the rule as expeditiously as possible. When the NAII brought its action before the Court of Appeals, and then proceeded to the Supreme Court, we did not believe the Administrator had made a case for rescission; and if there *were* sufficient reasons for abandoning the standard, they were not presented to the Court. In reviewing the testimony that has been presented so far at these hearings, we submit that the case for rescission still has not been made, and respectfully urge this panel to take appropriate action to reinstate the standard." [17]

Beck stated: "If a major airliner crashed every day during the week prior to hearings on aviation safety and there were a known way to save the lives of passengers in such crashes, I have no doubt the government would take immediate action to ensure the safety of passengers on future flights. Sadly, we are losing an equivalent number of people each day, every day, 365 days a year, in motor vehicle accidents although the technology exists to cut this death toll significantly, as well as reduce serious injuries, with automatic occupant crash protection systems. . . . Our companies have been alarmed for years by the number of deaths and injuries occurring on our nation's highways, not only because of the impact on our companies financially, but more importantly because of the extent of human suffering involved which our members witness on a daily basis." [18]

Beck cited the latest statistical data. Each year 45,000 to 50,000 Americans die as a result of motor vehicle accidents. In 1982, 36,000 motor vehicle occupants were killed, 24,000 in passenger cars. Over 90 percent of those were front seat occupants. And 1.7 million suffered disabling injuries. Auto crashes were the leading cause of death for young Americans under the age of thirty-four, the major source of brain damage and head injury, a significant cause of epilepsy and spinal cord injury (paraplegia and quadriplegia), and a contributor to other serious dis-

[17] U.S. Department of Transportation Hearings on FMVSS 208 (Occupant Crash Protection), December 4, 1983. (Transcript, "Oral Remarks of Lowell R. Beck before the U.S. Department of Transportation," available from National Association of Independent Insurers.)
[18] Ibid.

abilities such as blindness. The economic loss to society from motor vehicle accidents has been estimated to be $57.2 billion per year, according to the Department of Transportation's own figures. Nearly nine out of ten automobile occupants in America today do not protect themselves from injury by using manual seat belts. Air bags and automatic seat belts have been proven reliable, acceptable to the public, and cost-effective in reducing fatalities and serious injuries. As standard equipment, automatic crash protection systems would save many thousands of lives and tens of thousands of serious injuries each year, by conservative estimates. Installed in all new cars, air bags would increase the sticker price between $200 (estimated by air bag manufacturers) and $320 (estimated by NHTSA), and automatic belts about $80 (NHTSA). This cost would be more than offset by reduced insurance rates and medical, welfare, and other societal savings.

Beck stated: "The most compelling evidence comes from the testimony of just a few of the survivors of motor vehicle crashes who have suffered permanently disabling injuries and from those who have avoided death and serious injury because they were fortunate enough to have been driving one of the few cars on the road with automatic air cushion restraints. . . . We in the insurance industry have a strong economic interest in the reduction of death and injury on our nation's roads and highways. The cost of automobile insurance is, today, high and rising, and the future promises new cost pressures unparalleled in recent times. No businessman wants to face the prospect of being in a position of offering an unaffordable product, and our problem here is that we know that, absent significant government action, the auto insurance affordability problem will worsen significantly. These cost pressures, which are common to the industry, continue to mount. Future auto insurance costs will increase because of inflation and because of the shift to smaller, lighter, less safe and less damage-resistant cars. The significant insurance cost savings to insurance companies and consumers which would result from implementation of the automatic crash protection rule are clear." [19]

Beck noted that in addition to its own business interests, the insurance industry also had a substantial "humanitarian interest" in this question. He stated: "The insurance industry deals personally with the families of the deceased victims. We know on a first-hand basis of their pain, suffering, anguish, and of the grief and permanent family trauma which results from

[19] Ibid.

injury and death caused by automobile accidents. This facet of our job is not a pleasant one, and it is most frustrating to know that, had cost-beneficial occupant restraint technology been employed at the earliest possible date, much of this pain . . . could, indeed, have been avoided. . . . While the Department's program to increase voluntary usage has commendable motives, its potential effectiveness has severe limitations. Mandatory seat belt usage laws requiring criminal or civil penalties for nonusage do not appear politically feasible and they would be nearly impossible to police and enforce, even if they could be passed in every state. The evidence to date on use laws in other countries suggests that unless a belt use law is vigorously enforced with real penalties for noncompliance, the effects on injuries and deaths will remain relatively small. . . . Rather than attempting in vain to change the habit patterns of millions of motorists by increased usage of an inferior safety mechanism, DOT should proceed as soon as possible to implement the existing passive restraint standard. Requiring a small change in the production techniques of a handful of automobile manufacturers will be far easier and far more productive than attempting to change the habits of millions of people. . . . The case for automatic crash protection has been fully documented and the Supreme Court recently ruled that there were insufficient reasons for abandoning the requirement. It is now up to the Department of Transportation to begin implementing the rule to fulfill its mandate to save lives and reduce injuries. Further delay for studies, demonstrations and so on, in our opinion, are totally unwarranted and will only result in many more needless deaths and injuries, and will be inconsistent with the mandate of the Supreme Court." [20]

Following is a review of some of the insurance cases that have been reported in the recent past. This cannot be considered a complete report of all cases in the insurance field, but it does review some of the most important ones.

Accidental Death Benefits

In *O'Toole* v. *New York Life Insurance Co.*, an action for accidental death benefits where the insured died from a self-administered injection of cocaine, the court affirmed judgment for the plaintiff and held that, although the insured intentionally injected himself with cocaine, he did not intend to cause, or anticipate that the injection would cause, his death, say-

[20] Ibid.

ing that if the insurer had wished to exclude death resulting from the self-administration of drugs, it should have expressly so provided in the policy. (671 F. 2d 913 [5th Circuit, 1982])

Williams v. *New England Mutual Life Insurance Company* dealt with a Florida statute which provided that, as a matter of public policy, alcoholism was to be regarded as a disease. At issue was a provision in an accidental death policy which excluded from coverage death caused directly or indirectly by disease. The court held that the Florida statute was not dispositive and that, for the purposes of insurance, alcoholism was not a disease. (419 So. 2d 766 [Florida Ct. Appeals, 1982])

In *Croteau* v. *John Hancock Mutual Life Insurance Company*, an unambiguous intoxication exclusion was held applicable, precluding recovery of accidental death benefits. The trial court erred in instructing the jury that it might find the exclusion inapplicable if the reasonable expectations of the insured were that accidental death coverage would be afforded without limitation. The unambiguous language of the policy governed whether or not the insured read the insurance policy, in the absence of a finding that the parties' prior dealing led the insured to form a reasonable belief that the policy provided the claimed coverage. (461 A. 2d 111 [1983])

Causation

Goodwin v. *Nationwide Insurance Company* involved a plaintiff who was insured under a group policy providing benefits for disability arising out of accidental injury and was involved in an automobile accident. He sustained a cut over his left eye and was unconscious for nearly an hour. Subsequently, he developed chronic headaches which, he claimed, resulted in total disability. The only evidence linking the headaches to the auto accident was the insured's own lay testimony that the headaches began immediately following the auto accident. The court held such testimony sufficient to support the trial court's finding that the predominant cause of the headaches was the accident. (104 Idaho 74, 656 P. 2d 135 [1982]).

In *Russell* v. *Metropolitan Life Insurance Company*, suit was brought against a life insurer to recover accidental death benefits. The insured, an alcoholic, died after consuming a lethal quantity of alcohol. The court affirmed the trial court's finding, as a matter of law, that death resulted "solely through accidental means," stating that foreseeability was the test of whether an insured's death so resulted. The court also held that the insured's death was not caused by disease, nor did the disease contribute to his death within the meaning of the exclusion, reasoning that the immediate cause of death was the lethal amount of alcohol in the insured's body and that his alcoholism could only be considered a "remote" cause of his death and not a "contributing cause." Significantly, the court observed that if the insurer had submitted evidence that alcoholism had rendered the insured's body less capable of surviving the dose of alcohol ingested, there would have been a question as to whether disease contributed to his death. (108 Ill. App. 3d 417, 439 [N.E. 2d, 1982] Appeal denied.)

Disease and Treatment Exclusions

In *Sekel* v. *Aetna Life Insurance Company*, the accidental death of an insured, occurring when he fell and struck his head, was held precluded from coverage under a group life and accidental health policy because the insured's cardiovascular disease contributed to or caused the fall. (704 F. 2d 135 [1983])

Voluntary Exposure to Danger

Crumpton v. *Confederation Life Insurance Company* involved the fatal shooting of the insured by his neighbor, who charged that the insured had raped her five days earlier. The death was held accidental since the insured could not reasonably anticipate that she would shoot him. (672 F. 2d 1248 [1982])

Workmen's Compensation Exclusion

Tobin v. *Beneficial Standard Life Insurance Company* concerned a cab driver who was killed in an armed robbery during the course of his employment. The policy excluded benefits payable "because of injury for which compensation is payable under any Workmen's Compensation Law." The court, reversing summary judgment for the insurer, held that the term "injury" in the exclusion was ambiguous as to whether it extended to fatal injuries and that construing the exclusion most strongly in favor of the plaintiff entitled his survivors to accidental death benefits. (625 F. 2d 606 [1982])

Insurer's Liability for Agent's Misrepresentation of Tort

Weaver v. *Metropolitan Life Insurance Company* was an action against an insurer to recover damages as a result of the alleged misrepresentations of the insurer's agent concerning the existence of waiver of premium disability benefits. Although the plaintiff was not entitled to such benefits because of his age and work history, the court held that the insurer, by accepting premiums sufficient to cover waiver of premium benefits and by the use of ambiguous "sale aid" to demonstrate the features of its policies to the plaintiff, ratified the representations of its agent. The court held the insurer liable in tort for the acts of its agent under the theory of respondeat superior. The court held that although the level of culpability did not justify punitive damages, the insurer was liable for compensation damages in an amount equal to the difference between the actual paid-up value of the policy and the cash value received by the plaintiff upon surrender of the policy. (545 F. Supp. 74 [E.D. Mo., 1982])

Unlicensed Agents

In *Idle Assets, Inc.* v. *State Department of Insurance*, the court affirmed an order of the Florida Insurance Department ruling that certain activities of bank employees not licensed as insurance agents violated a Florida statute as to activities of unlicensed persons. The employees reviewed customers' policies and encouraged them to borrow against the policies, invest in certificates of deposit, and loss insurance with term insurance. (424 So. 2d 902 [1982])

Antitrust

In *Blue Shield of Virginia* v. *McCready*, Blue Shield reimbursed subscribers for services provided by psychiatrists but not for services provided by psychologists unless treatment was supervised by and billed through a physician. The plaintiff brought a class action suit against Blue Shield and the Neuropsychiatric Society of Virginia, alleging unlawful conspiracy in violation of the Sherman Antitrust Act and seeking treble damages under Section 4 of the Clayton Antitrust Act. The district court granted the defendant's motions to dismiss, holding that the plaintiff had no standing under Section 4 to maintain her suit. The court of appeals reversed, and the Supreme Court affirmed reversal. The Supreme Court held that the plaintiff's suit was consistent with Congress's expansive remedial purpose in enacting Section 4 to create a private enforcement mechanism to deter violaters and to deprive them of the fruits of their illegal actions. It further held that the plaintiff's injury was not too remote to permit the maintenance of her suit for the reason that denying reimbursement to subscribers for the cost of treatment by psychologists was the very means by which Blue

Cross allegedly sought to achieve its illegal ends and that the plaintiff's injury was precisely the type of loss which the claimed violations would be likely to cause. (457 U.S. 465, 73 L.)

The refusal of Virginia Blue Cross and Blue Shield to offer a health insurance policy that would cover a husband and his child without also covering his wife was held the "business of insurance" regulated by state law within the meaning of the McCarran-Ferguson Act's exemption from the antitrust laws and was also held to be a legal boycott (*Anglin* v. *Blue Shield of Virginia*). (693 F. 2d 315 [1982])

Disqualification

In *Harper* v. *Prudential Insurance Company of America*, an insurer which had paid the primary beneficiary ten days after receiving its investigation report was held liable to the contingent beneficiary when the primary beneficiary was convicted over two years later of the murder of the insured. The court said that the insurer should either have delayed payment to protect the interests of the contingent beneficiary or filed an interpleader. The court reviewed Kansas decisions and concluded that the rule that a beneficiary must be convicted in order to be disqualified was ill conceived and should no longer be followed. The court adopted the "common-law rule which is almost universally followed in this country and which bars the beneficiary of a life insurance policy who feloniously kills the insured from recovering under the policy whether convicted or not." (233 Kan. 358, 662 P. 2d 1264, 1271 [1983])

Divorce

In *Bersch* v. *Van Kleeck*, the court pointed out the difference between the interests of the owner of a policy and the interests of the beneficiary. A court order in divorce proceedings restraining the insured's husband from "transferring . . . or in any way disposing of any property . . ." was held not to prevent the insured from changing the beneficiary of his group term life insurance. That policy did not constitute property subject to the order because it had no present value. Thus, upon the death of the insured, the proceeds of the policy were payable to his mother, whom he named beneficiary in lieu of his wife. (334 N.W. 2d 114 [1983])

In *Briece* v. *Briece*, an insured had changed his beneficiary designation from his wife, upon learning of her divorce action against him. The wife obtained a court order directing the insured to reinstate her as his beneficiary. The insured died four days later without knowing or complying with the order. The court held that the insured's change of beneficiary designation was valid, and the divorce action and the interlocutory order abated upon the insured's death. A dissenting judge might have applied the maxim, "Equity considers as done that which ought to be done." (703 F. 2d 1045 [1983])

Conditional Receipts

In *Gdovic* v. *Catholic Knights of St. George*, the court held that an insured had a reasonable expectation of coverage from the date of payment of the first premium for a disability policy and he was entitled to coverage from that date rather than from the later policy date. (453 A. 2d 1040 [1982])

In *Bierer* v. *Nationwide Insurance Company*, although the original policy, an option rider, an application, and the new policy all stated a June effective date, it was held that the additional life insurance taken by an insured pursuant to the rider became effective in April when he signed the application and paid two months' premiums and thus covered his death, which occurred in May. The court held that the insured reasonably expected to have immediate coverage as of April under the additional insurance and the insurer did not prove otherwise. (1983 CCH Life Cases 309 [1983])

In *Cain* v. *Aetna Life Insurance Company*, a conditional receipt given to an employee in connection with an application for group health insurance was held to provide temporary insurance coverage. The court expressly limited its rule to contracts for group health insurance. The court said that its holding "reflects what we believe to be the reasonable expectation of the applicant." (135 Ariz. 189, 659 P. 2d 1334, 1340 [1983])

Contestable—Time Limit On Certain Defenses

In *North Miami General Hospital* v. *Central National Life Insurance Company*, suit was brought under a policy which provided that "no claim for loss incurred commencing after two years from the date a person becomes covered under this policy shall be reduced or denied on the grounds that a disease or physical condition not excluded from coverage . . . had existed prior to the effective date of coverage." One year after issuance of the policy, the insured was hospitalized and treated for a preexisting condition, but the insured filed his claim after the two-year period had run. The court, affirming entry of summary judgment for the insurer, held that the two-year contestability provision referred to the date on which the loss was incurred, which, in this case, was within two years of the date of coverage, and that the date on which the claim was filed was irrelevant to contestability.

In *Holtzclaw* v. *Bankers Mutual Insurance Company*, the court held, reversing summary judgment for the defendant insurer, that where the policy had been in force two years, a jury determination must be made whether the insured's misrepresentations were fraudulent before the defendant would have a defense under the clause placing time limits on certain defenses. (448 N.E. 55 [1983])

Conversion

In *Goldwater* v. *Jackson National Life Insurance Company*, the waiver-of-premium rider in an endowment policy issued as a conversion of a term life policy was held to relate back to the date of issuance of the term policy. Thus, the insured could take advantage of the waiver-of-premium benefit with respect to a disability suffered after the date of conversion, even though the disabling disease preexisted the conversion date (but not the date of issue of the term policy). (555 F. Supp. 1022 [1983])

Defamation

In *Slaughter* v. *Friedman*, the insurer, explaining reasons for denial of certain dental claims, sent letters describing a dentist's procedures as being "unnecessary" and claimed that the dentist was "overcharging." The dentist sued the insurer for libel. The Supreme Court reversed dismissal of the action. While acknowledging the insurer's statutory obligation to provide explanations for claim denials, the court refused to consider such explanation privileged. (649 P. 2d 886 [1982])

Setoff of Collateral Benefits

In *Bell* v. *Allstate Insurance Company*, Social Security benefits paid to the wife and children of the insured under a group disability policy were held properly setoff by the insurer against benefits paid to the insured. The contract provided for a setoff of all "benefits available under governmental benefit programs" and stated that "benefits will be considered as available to an employee under these programs if (s)he is entitled to claim payment (including payment due members of his/her immediate family on account of his/her disability." The court found this policy language clear and unambiguous. (451 A. 2d 1152 [1982])

Extracontractual Damages

In *Peel* v. *American Fidelity Assurance Company*, the insurer, after paying disability benefits to the plaintiff from March, 1974, to November, 1976, terminated benefits based upon a physician's report which concluded that the plaintiff's condition had improved to the extent that she could return to work. The plaintiff was held entitled to policy benefits but not extracontractual damages. The court held that based upon the physician's report, the insurer had an "arguable defense" that precluded recovery of punitive damages and that the plaintiff was not entitled to extracontractual compensatory damages based upon a tortious breach of conduct for the reason that the insurer did not act recklessly as to evince utter indifference to the consequences. (680 F. 2d 374 [1982])

In *Austero* v. *Washington National Insurance Company*, the court held that in first-party "bad faith" insurance litigation, there is no "bad faith" exception to the general rule that each party bears its own attorney's fees. (132 Cal. App. 3d 408 [1982])

Mello v. *Occidental Life Insurance Company of California* was an action for benefits under a disability policy, alleging a tort for unlawful termination of the policy. The court considered the same issues that were considered in Austero but came to a different conclusion. It held that because it is the tortious conduct of the insurer that requires the insured to incur the expense of obtaining the services of counsel, the services of counsel are included in the amount that will compensate for "all the detriment proximately caused by tort." (137 Cal. App. 3d 510 [1982])

In *Harris* v. *American General Life Insurance Company of Delaware*, the insurer admitted liability for the accidental death benefit. The insurer sent the beneficiary a check for the face amount with a restrictive endorsement stating that it was accepted in full and final settlement of all claims under the policy. The Montana Insurance Code provides that it is an unfair claims settlement practice to fail to settle claims promptly under one portion of a policy, where liability has become clear, in order to influence settlements under other portions of the same policy. Demand for a new check without the restrictive endorsement was not met for approximately three months. After trial, accidental death benefits were denied, but punitive damages were awarded. The court affirmed, holding that only minimal actual damages need be shown and that because the insurer had failed to recalculate the interest due from the time the first check was tendered until the second check without the restrictive endorsement was tendered, a substantial punitive damages award could stand, based upon an implied right of action of a first-party claimant for violations of the Insurance Code. (658 P. 2d 1089 [1983])

In *Jarvis v. Prudential Insurance Company of America*, the court held, among other things, that an insurer has no independent (i.e., extra-contractual) duty to deal fairly with its insured, which could support a cause of required services. The court also rejected as failing to state causes of action the plaintiff's claims based on theories of intentional and negligent inflicting of emotional distress. But the court did recognize that an insurer's failures to pay insurance benefits could constitute a bad-faith breach of contract if the terms of the health insurance policy in fact covered the disputed medical services. (448 A. 2d 407 [1982])

In *Metropolitan Life Insurance Company v. McCarson*, a group health insurer was held liable for damages in a wrongful death action based on wrongful termination of home nursing care benefits, which caused the insured to be placed in a nursing home where her health rapidly deteriorated and she died. (429 So. 2d 1287 [1983])

In *Hoskins v. Aetna Life Insurance Company*, the court held that based upon the relationship between an insurer and its insured, an insurer has the duty to act in good faith in handling and payment of the claims of its insured. A breach of this duty will give rise to a cause of action in tort against the insurer. Punitive damages may be recovered against an insurer who breaches its duty of good faith in refusing to pay a claim of its insured, upon proof of actual malice, fraud, or insult on the part of the insurer. (6 Ohio St. 3d 272 [1983])

Failure to Obtain Insurance

In *Beal v. Lomas and Nettleton Company*, an insurance agency was found to have misled the insureds to believe they were getting the same coverage under a new policy that they had under an old one. The agency was held liable on the ground of negligent misrepresentation for the amount of accident insurance under the old policy after the insured died accidentally. (410 So. 2d 318 [1982])

In *Sur v. Glidden-Durkee, a Division of S.C.M. Corporation*, an employee terminated his employment and converted his group health coverage to an individual policy which, unlike the group policy, did not contain major medical insurance. The court held that the employer could be liable to him for breach of its duty to inform him of conversion rights and benefits, and the insurer could be liable by estoppel because its booklet could be found by a jury to be misleading. Summary judgments in favor of both defendants were reversed. (681 F. 2d 490 [1982])

Misrepresentation by Employer

In *Woodman Company, Inc.* v. *Adair*, the defendant employer erroneously informed the plaintiff employee that the policy would be in effect for a period of thirty days after the termination of his employment and apparently failed to inform him of his conversion rights. The court held that the employer, by misadvising the plaintiff of his policy rights, breached its liable to the plaintiff for the medical expenses incurred within thirty days of the termination of the plaintiff's employment. (294 S.E. 2d 579 [1982])

Notice of Cancellation

In *Brown* v. *Blue Cross and Blue Shield of Mississippi, Inc.*, the plaintiff's employer and the insurer had canceled a group health insurance contract by agreement during the plaintiff's pregnancy. The plaintiff's claim for maternity benefits was denied. The court found that the plaintiff had a cause of action against the insurer because it held that allowing the plaintiff's employer and the defendant to cancel the policy of insurance without notification of or consultation with the plaintiff would be against public policy. The court stated that plaintiff's reasonable expectations with respect to his insurance outweighed the importance of the employer's and insurer's ability to contract. (427 So. 2d 1939 [1983])

Health Insurance—Psychiatric Charges Exclusion

In *Beaugureau* v. *Equitable Life Assurance Society*, a major medical policy excluded coverage for charges incurred in connection with "nervous or mental disease or disorder, except such charges incurred during confinement in a hospital other than an institution specializing in the treatment of such disease or disorder." The court held that a psychiatric hospital's exchange of services contract and affiliation agreement with a full-service hospital and the insured's technical admission to the full-service hospital as a condition of admission to the psychiatric hospital were not sufficient to take the insured's treatment outside of the exclusion of the policy. (647 P. 2d 1194 [1982])

Double Benefits

In *Edwards* v. *Aetna Life Insurance Company*, an insured claimed disability benefits under his employer's group policy on the grounds his tuberculosis was not service-related after receiving benefits from the Veterans Administration on the contrary ground. He was held not judicially estopped since the Veterans Administration administrative settlement was not a judicial endorsement. (690 F. 2d 595 [1982])

Hospital or Convalescent Facility

In *Hoskins* v. *Aetna Life Insurance Company*, an insured suffered a stroke and was admitted to the medical-surgical unit of a hospital. To facilitate use of a large apparatus used for physical therapy prescribed for her, she was moved to a room in the skilled nursing unit. The court held that she was entitled to benefits under the hospital expense clause of her policy rather than the lesser benefits under the convalescent facility expense clause. (6 Ohio St. 3d 272 [1983])

Recurrent Illness

In *Giancarli* v. *Nationwide Mutual Insurance Company*, the insured was treated for cancer in his shoulder for two years. After an eight-month period during which there was no clinical evidence of cancer, metastasis was found in his lung, and he was treated for another two-year period. The court held it was a question of fact for the jury whether there were two sicknesses (entitling the insured to a second benefit period under the policy) or one. (5 Ohio App. 3d 68 [1982])

Materiality

In *Pennsylvania Life Insurance Company* v. *Tanner*, application questions concerning the insured's total life and disability insurance then in effect either were not answered or were answered incompletely. Upon the death of the insured, the insurer denied benefits, claiming that material misrepresentations were made as to these questions. Judgment for the plaintiff was affirmed. The court found that the omitted facts could not have been material to the acceptance of the risk where the insurer took a calculated risk in accepting the policy despite glaringly omitted information. (293 S.E. 2d 520 [1982])

Premium Notice or Notice of Termination

In *First United Life Insurance Company* v. *Northern Indiana Bank and Trust Company*, a provision in a life insurance policy requiring notice before the insurer could void the policy for excessive loans was held not to prevent the lapse of the policy for nonpayment of premiums without notice by the insurer. (444 N.E. 2d 1241 [1983])

Reasonable Expectations

In *Robin* v. *Blue Cross Hospital Services, Inc.*, the court rejected the plaintiff's claim and declined to adopt the reasonable expectations rule. It held that the group policy sued on was a product of negotiation between equally strong parties—the plaintiff's employer and the insurance company—and that therefore, the policy was not a contract of adhesion. The court therefore adhered to the rule of construction that policy language should be given its plain meaning, and it held that according to such plain meaning, the plaintiff was not entitled to benefits. (637 S.W. 2d 695 [1982])

In *Cain* v. *Aetna Life Insurance Company*, a conditional receipt given to an employee in connection with an application for group health insurance was held to provide temporary insurance coverage. The court said that its holding "reflects what we believe to be the reasonable expectation of the applicant." (659 P. 2d 1334 [1983])

In *Hemenway* v. *MFA Life Insurance Company*, the reasonable expectation rule of interpretation was applied in determining the effective date of a health policy to be the date of the conditional receipt. (318 N.W. 2d 70 [1982])

Reinstatement

In *Depositors Trust Company* v. *Farm Family Life Insurance Company*, the court held that a clause on the reinstatement application form purporting to make reinstatement conditional on approval by the insurer was invalid as a unilateral attempt by the insurer to modify, without consideration, the terms of the original insurance contract, under which reinstatement was not dependent on the insurer's acting on or accepting the application. Therefore, the policy was in force when the insured died, even though the insured had not accepted the reinsurance application. (445 A. 2d 1014 [1982])

Sex Discrimination

In *Newport News Shipbuilding and Dry Dock Company* v. *Equal Employment Opportunity Commission*, an employer's health plan, which provided pregnancy-related hospitalization benefits for its female employees but did not include those benefits for the spouses of its male employees, was held discriminatory and in violation of Title VII of the Civil Rights Act as amended by the Pregnancy Discrimination Act. The otherwise inclusive plan discriminated against the wives of the male employees and, consequently, against the male employees. There was a dissent. (103 S. Ct. 2622, 77 L. Ed. 2d 89 [1983])

Suicide

In *Travelers Insurance Company* v. *Summers*, the insured was given a conditional receipt and a policy was thereafter issued. Under the policy suicide clause the insurer's liability was limited to the amount of premiums paid if the insured committed suicide within two years from the "date of issue." The court held that the various documents were ambiguous as to "date of issue" and, construing the ambiguity in favor of the insured, held that the suicide exclusion period ran from the effective date of the conditional receipt, hence had expired when the insured committed suicide. (696 F. 2d 1311 [1983])

Parchman v. *United Liberty Life Insurance Company* dealt with the insured's suicide more than two years after the conditional receipt was delivered but less than two years after it became effective. The court held that, even construing the policy most favorably to the insured, the insured's death occurred within the suicide exclusion period and there was no coverage. (640 S.W. 2d 694 [1982])

Waiver of Premiums

In *Goldwater* v. *Jackson National Life Insurance Company*, the plaintiff converted his term life insurance policy to an endowment policy and, under a right granted by the term policy, chose the date of conversion as the issue date of the endowment policy. Shortly after conversion, the plaintiff became disabled due to a disease which preexisted the conversion date. The court held that the endowment policy, which contained a similar waiver of premium provision as that in the term policy, was a continuation of and related back to the issue date of the term policy and that, therefore, the plaintiff was entitled to the benefit of the waiver of premium provision in the endowment policy. (555 F. Supp 1022 [1983])

In *Barber* v. *Old Republic Life Insurance Company*, the court held that the provisions of group policies concerning termination of insurance, including those for termination of the policies and separate ones permitting disabled persons to continue being covered although they were no longer "covered persons," were clear and unambiguous and not in conflict with one another. Therefore, it held that the coverage of such persons did not continue after termination of the policies. (647 P. 2d 1200 [1982])

10

....

The Insurance Industry
and the Future

THE insurance industry faces many challenges in the years ahead. Among them are bank deregulation, the antitrust exemption, unisex insurance, and financial difficulties. Each of these deserves an overview.

Bank Deregulation

In 1984 the Reagan administration expressed its support of pending legislation that would permit affiliates of firms that own banks or savings and loan associations to underwrite and deal in municipal revenue bonds; sponsor and manage mutual funds; underwrite and sell insurance; and develop, own, and sell real estate.

Under laws passed beginning in 1933, banks and firms that own banks—bank holding companies—have been barred from nonfinancial businesses and most aspects of nonbanking financial pursuits such as securities, insurance, and real estate.

Since the 1970s, when high interest rates and new technologies made traditional banking activities possible and profitable, securities firms, insurance companies, and conglomerates that combine financial with nonfinancial products have been merging these bank-style services with other products. The prototype in this area is Sears Roebuck and Company, which had set a goal of opening financial centers in 250 of its stores by 1984. Toward that goal it acquired in 1981 the real estate firm of Coldwell Banker and Company and the securities firm Dean Witter Reynolds. Sears also owns the Allstate Savings and Loan of California and planned to purchase other banking institutions across the country.

Banks, concerned about competition from firms not governed by strict banking regulations, have been seeking ways to enter fields that were traditionally off limits. The Reagan administration led the call to permit banks to compete more freely. In 1982, it proposed that Congress enable banks to deal in securities, insurance, and real estate. Congress, at that time, refused to take such action. It did enact PL 92-320, which bolstered the faltering savings and loan industry and gave both savings and loans and banks the ability to compete with money market funds by creating the Money Market Deposit Account.

Pressure for Congress to act on the question of bank deregulation has been rising. Actions taken by C. Todd Conover, comptroller of the currency, and by the South Dakota legislature are examples of such pressure. In February, 1983, over objections from the Federal Reserve Board, Conover's office approved applications by two large mutual fund companies, the Dreyfus Corporation and J. and W. Seligman and Company, for national bank charters to operate what have come to be called "nonbank banks." The nonbank bank is a vehicle to which nonbank firms have been turning in recent days. The goal is to own a bank but, through a legal loophole, to remain exempt from the 1956 Bank Holding Company Act, which gives the Federal Reserve power to limit the activities of bank holding companies.

The act defines a bank as an institution that both takes deposits and makes commercial loans. Nonbank firms, while desiring the benefits of a national bank charter and federal deposit insurance, have argued that they are exempt from the Bank Holding Act if they abstain from commercial lending. Conover agreed.

In the Dreyfus and Seligman cases, the Federal Reserve reacted by stating that it would reinterpret the term "commercial lending" as used in the Bank Holding Company Act to include the sale of various financial instruments such as certificates of deposit. Thus, if the Dreyfus and Seligman banks engaged in such common banking activities, the Fed could assert that they had become bank holding companies under the act and were subject to authority of the Federal Reserve Board.

In March, 1983, Conover was asked by Dimension Financial Corporation, a new Denver-based firm chartered in Delaware by a subsidiary of the Valley Federal Savings and Loan Association of Hutchinson, Kansas, to grant it charters for thirty-one nonbank banks in twenty-five states. At that point, Conover said that his office was imposing a moratorium on new nonbank charters to encourage debate and to hold banking innovations in check while Congress reviewed the situation.

At the same time, the holding company for a major bank, Citicorp, which owns Citibank, n.a., and other financial firms, launched its own counterattack against nonbank competitors. It persuaded the legislature of South Dakota to pass two laws: (1) authorizing out-of-state bank holding companies such as Citicorp to acquire or charter a state bank in South Dakota (a move permissible under federal law with specific state approval), and (2) giving any state-chartered South Dakota bank authority to own an insurance firm if the insurance arm operated only outside the state. Gov. William J. Janklow signed this legislation into law on March 4, 1983. Shortly after this, Citicorp announced that it would seek to acquire the American State Bank of Rapid City, South Dakota, and use the state-chartered bank to enter the insurance business.

The insurance industry vigorously opposed such an action, and the Federal Reserve Board was disturbed by what it saw as a circumvention of federal law. Four insurance trade associations—the Alliance of American Insurers, the American Council on Life Insurance, the American Insurance Association, and the National Association of Independent Insurers—asked the Federal Reserve to declare Citicorp's move a violation of federal law.

The controversy continues. Peter J. Wallison, general counsel of the Treasury Department, said that with South Dakota's action "a lot of people started to get a little frightened."[1] In April, 1983, Jake Garn, chairman of the Senate Banking Committee, opened hearings on the question. The Fed's chairman, Paul Volcker, testified on April 26, telling the committee that the comptroller's moratorium on new nonbank charters was welcome but inadequate. He asked the Congress to close the nonbank bank loophole in the Bank Holding Company Act by redefining the term "bank." He also suggested that Congress override state laws like South Dakota's.

On May 9, the three-member board of the Federal Deposit Insurance Corporation, which included its chairman, William M. Isaac, who sup-

---

[1] Unless otherwise indicated, quotations and other information in this chapter were extracted from unpublished internal documents made available to members of insurance trade associations.

ported banking deregulation; comptroller Conover; and former FDIC chairman Irving H. Sprague, proposed to spell out new FDIC regulations on securities activities of state-chartered and nonmember banks.

The securities industry vigorously opposed this proposal, arguing that the 1983 Glass-Steagall Act expressly barred banks from having securities affiliates. The board plan itself flowed from a 1982 FDIC opinion that the Glass-Steagall Act did not apply to the banks in question. Don Crawford, senior vice president of the Securities Industry Association, called the FDIC plan outrageous. David Sulver, president of the Investment Company Institute, a mutual fund trade association, described it as "statutory book burning." Such critics warned that the FDIC's proposal could lead national banks to switch to state charters and Federal Reserve System member banks to leave the Fed system.

The FDIC action resulted in the Fed's presenting a specific moratorium proposal to Congress, and on June 23 Senator Garn introduced such legislation. The Treasury Department presented its new legislation with additional provisions to close the nonbank bank loophole.

Senator Garn's banking deregulation legislation, "The Financial Services Competitive Equity Act," became the focus of discussion in the Congress. The Vice-Presidential Task Group on Regulation of Financial Services met on December 22, 1983, and agreed to a number of recommendations: functional regulation of securities and antitrust laws, requiring thrift institutions that function like banks to be regulated as banks, reform of the federal deposit insurance system to ensure that institutions pay higher insurance premiums if they engage in risky activities, and a reduction in duplication by federal and state banking authorities.

On January 6, 1984, the Federal Reserve Board blocked three major banks' plans to acquire banks in South Dakota, which would allow the sale of insurance outside the state, on the grounds that it would be appropriate to wait for Congress to act on pending legislation concerning the extent to which bank holding companies may engage in insurance underwriting brokerage.

The National Association of Independent Insurers issued a joint statement with the American Council on Life Insurance in support of the Fed decision. The insurance groups said: "As we contended last July in our filing with the Fed, approval of the banks' applications to acquire South Dakota banks would have run counter to longstanding federal law. We believe the Fed's decision is correct, and that it should signal the end of efforts by individual states to circumvent federal banking law."

The applications by Citicorp, First Interstate Bancorp, and Bank-America to acquire state-chartered banks in South Dakota were designed to take advantage of the recent legislation permitting out-of-state bank holding companies to acquire banks in that state for the purpose of engaging in insurance activities outside South Dakota. In refusing to approve the transactions, the Fed also cited the "significant legal questions concerning the applicability of the Bank Holding Company Act to state-chartered banks and/or their subsidiaries." Because of the states' rights issue and the prospect of congressional action, the three banks requested the Fed to suspend the processing of their applications.

When the Senate Banking Committee held field hearings in Salt Lake City on Senator Garn's financial services deregulation bill, Treasury Secretary Donald Regan testified, "[The] administration is not convinced that 'bigness is badness,' or that current antitrust laws are inadequate."

Both Regan and Federal Reserve Board Chairman Volcker, who also testified at the hearing, expressed concerns about Senator Garn's attempts to prevent possible tying of bank credit or other activities to the sale of products or services provided by the bank holding companies' other affiliates. Volcker said that existing laws and Federal Reserve regulations already contained safeguards against such practices. He added, however, that one way to ensure equality, since Senator Garn's proposal did not cover thrift holding companies, would be to extend more stringent anti-tying provisions to thrift holding companies and curtail the ability of other businesses to buy nonbanks or consumer banks to which these provisions would not apply.

Volcker stressed the urgent need for Congress to act quickly on financial services legislation, adding that in many cases there already existed a core of consensus. "The present arrangements are in disarray, and events, willy-nilly, are forcing change that may, or may not, be consistent with considered judgments about public interest."

An indication of current trends may be seen in the recommendation by a high-level state commission in New York that banks in that state be given broad powers to enter the insurance business. The proposal would allow state-chartered commercial banks to sell and underwrite a wide range of insurance and also to own insurance companies. On February 14,

1984, the Temporary State Commission on Banking, Insurance, and Financial Services voted twelve to four in support of this proposal. The *Wall Street Journal* noted: "[This action] sets the stage for a test between New York's insurance banking lobbies. If adopted, the proposals would further blur the lines among the banking, insurance and securities businesses and could lead to a conflict with federal banking regulators. . . . The commission action may increase pressure on Congress to deal with banks' demands for more powers and could lead to a confrontation with the Fed, which has already acted on the South Dakota law. New York officials say commercial banks chartered in New York, under the proposal, could sell insurance without federal approval but would need the Fed's consent to underwrite." [2]

Insurers have voiced criticisms of the plan. Robert M. Best, chairman and chief executive officer of Security Mutual Life Insurance Company of New York, warned that the proposals "threaten the very existence" of many small life insurance companies. Banks, on the other hand, argue that they can sell insurance less expensively than insurance agents can. Insurers, however, claim that the move would mean only higher costs to consumers. One representative of the agents warned that the proposals could jeopardize eighty thousand to one hundred thousand insurance jobs in New York State.

The outlook for reform of the regulatory structure of the nation's banking system remains uncertain. Writing in the *New York Times*, Robert A. Bennett noted: "Much of the uncertainty reflects the need for Congressional approval of the suggested changes. Indeed, if the past is any indication, such approval is doubtful; Congress has ignored similar reports that were issued in 1971, 1961, 1949, and 1937. But some say that the fate of the Bush report (issued by the task force headed by Vice President George Bush) might be different because its goals are more modest and it represents a compromise among the regulators themselves. Unlike its predecessors, the Bush report does not recommend consolidation of all the Federal banking agencies. The recommendation that could have the greatest impact is one that would shift the decision-making power concerning what bank holding companies may or may not do from the Federal Reserve System to a proposed Federal Banking Agency. The new agency would be similar to

[2] Daniel Hertzberg, "New York Commission Backs Move into Insurance," *Wall Street Journal*, February 15, 1984, p. 6.

the Office of the Comptroller of the Currency, which is part of the Treasury Department and headed by a Presidential appointee. The Bush panel has recommended that the position of Comptroller be eliminated. . . . But even if that shift in power to a new agency were adopted, its impact would depend heavily on the passage of another, more controversial bill that would expand the powers of banks in such fields as insurance, securities, and real estate development." [3]

William Isaac, chairman of the Federal Deposit Insurance Corporation, said that he supported the recommendations of the Bush Commission, even though they would curtail his agency's powers. Isaac, a member of the panel, said that the FDIC "wanted to be relieved of the day-to-day regulatory responsibilities it had been given by Congress [so it could] focus on its role as insurer of bank deposits." [4]

Isaac did, however, express disappointment with two major proposals. He said that he would have preferred to see the Fed's role as bank regulator and supervisor eliminated and to see the Federal Banking Agency made an independent agency. Under the recommendations, the Fed would surrender to the Federal Banking Agency regulation of most bank holding companies and its ability to determine what activities bank holding companies could involve themselves in. But the Fed would pick up from the FDIC the responsibility for state banks that are not members of the Federal Reserve System, would regulate the fifty largest bank holding companies, and would have veto power over the agency's decisions on permissible bank activities. The Fed "is certainly not out [of banking regulation] to the degree I had advocated," Isaac said, but it "did give some ground in this process. I don't think it would be fair to say that the Fed walked away with everything it had and then some. In my judgment, there's been a substantial reshuffling of authority." [5]

Isaac also said that he had concerns about giving the Treasury Department, whose comptroller of the currency regulated national banks, control of the new FBA. "If it were an independent agency headed by a board (instead of an individual) there would be less chance that the agency would become politicized," he said. [6]

[3] Robert Bennett, "Assessing the Bush Report," *New York Times*, February 2, 1984, p. P-1.
[4] Quoted in *Washington Times*, February 2, 1984.
[5] Ibid.
[6] Ibid.

The momentum for some form of banking deregulation which would facilitate banks' entry into the insurance field in the mid-eighties appeared to be growing, but solutions to the debate may continue to be out of reach for both industry and government.

The Future of the McCarran-Ferguson Antitrust Exemption

In December, 1983, Peter Rodino (D-New Jersey), chairman of the House Judiciary Committee, directed the staff of the subcommittee with jurisdiction over the McCarran-Ferguson Act to prepare for in-depth hearings in 1984 on antitrust aspects of the insurance industry. In making this announcement, Rodino said: "The National Commission for the Review of the Anti-Trust Laws and Procedures . . . recommended in 1979 a re-examination of the insurance industry's exemption from the Federal competition laws with an eye toward narrowing its scope. Congress has yet to undertake this inquiry. It is time we do so." Rodino added that the inquiry would examine "all relevant competitive aspects of the industry, including the high costs of many types of insurance and the responsiveness of the industry to changing needs and conditions among consumers who purchase insurance."

In his farewell press conference on December 15, 1983, William F. Baxter, who resigned as head of the Justice Department's Anti-Trust division, called for the repeal of the insurance industry's antitrust immunity under the McCarran-Ferguson Act. Baxter said there was no justification for the act's protection for certain insurance industry activities.

J. Paul McGrath, who replaced Baxter as the Reagan administration's new antitrust chief, said in his inaugural press conference early in January, 1984, that he was studying the question of possible repeal of the McCarran-Ferguson Act, but he declined to endorse Baxter's call for its repeal. Later in January, McGrath said he doubted that the antitrust division of the Justice Department would seek repeal of the McCarran-Ferguson Act. He also said he would continue the division's efforts to combat horizontal price fixing and would push for passage of the Reagan administration's antitrust legislative package.

Informed observers in Washington believed that, while congressional hearings on the subject of repealing the McCarran-Ferguson Act would likely stir much publicity and debate, any congressional action in this area was unlikely in the foreseeable future.

Unisex Insurance

The debate over unisex insurance is likely to have a significant impact in partisan politics, since both parties view this as a "women's issue." In their desire to gain women's votes, both parties are likely to give serious consideration to supporting such legislation.

In January, 1984, the General Accounting Office (GAO) issued a report on the economic effects of unisex insurance. The GAO concluded that in the short term, unisex insurance could cause insolvencies for some life insurance companies but suggested that the adverse effects could be avoided if Congress excluded existing insurance policies and allowed a full year for transition to the new system.

Writing in the *Washington Post*, Nancy L. Ross noted: "Non-discrimination in insurance began as an equity issue, championed by civil rights and feminist lobbies. The insurance industry countered with fierce opposition on economic grounds, claiming that a ban on the use of sex to determine rates and benefits would be financially ruinous for carriers and would not benefit the women it was designed to help. After various attempts at compromise, the committee [U.S. Senate] adjourned last year without taking action and agreed to meet again when, they hoped, the GAO report would have clarified the economic issues." After the report was issued, both sides in the dispute claimed that it bolstered their own position. The American Insurance Association stated: "The draft appears to reinforce the economic arguments made since the introduction of the unisex insurance legislation: namely, that this legislation would create a far greater adverse economic impact on women than it would alleviate." State Farm Insurance Company declared the draft "an important confirmation of the insurance industry's contention that this legislation would create economic havoc in the insurance marketplace."[7] The American Council of Life Insurance said: "It makes clear that substantial changes need to be made in [the bill] and that careful study needs to be given to the potential economic consequences before Congress takes any action."[8]

After congressional hearings ended in June, 1983, the cause supported by the feminist movement received major support in the Supreme Court's decision in the *Norris* case that employer retirement and pension

[7] Nancy Ross, "GAO's Unisex Insurance Study Is Inconclusive," *Washington Post*, January 30, 1984, p. 23.
[8] Ibid.

plans could no longer calculate benefits differently for men and women. In that decision, only future contributions and benefits would be affected. Justice Lewis F. Powell, Jr., said that retroactivity might bankrupt insurance companies.

Mary W. Gray, professor of mathematics at American University in Washington, D.C., speaking for the coalition supporting unisex legislation, said that the GAO report vindicated the unisex position because the GAO recognized that the industry could use a nondiscriminatory standard and at the same time avoid insolvencies by adopting one of several suggested alternatives, something she said the industry claimed was impossible.

A staff attorney for the Senate Commerce Committee said that the GAO report "doesn't hurt the unisex bill. We can now move forward with it." On the other hand, Barbara Lautzenheiser, who headed the Committee for Fair Insurance Rates, an insurance industry lobbying group, said the report reaffirmed the complexity of the economic issue. But "legislators are probably going to be disappointed and frustrated" that the report does not forthrightly endorse one side or the other, she said.[9]

In the report, the GAO authors admitted that it was "impossible to say what the consequences of the bill would be because they would depend on the actions taken by insurance companies, pension plan sponsors, and state insurance regulators in response to the legislation." The conclusions, based on various scenarios, were written such that each side could use them to defend its own position.

The report stated, for example, that unisex insurance would increase unfunded liabilities by between $14 billion and $32 billion. This would create a danger of short-term insolvencies for life insurance companies because they are required by law to cover any unfunded liabilities with reserves. The report predicted that if premiums were increased, insolvencies could be avoided, but if all companies were to equalize coverage by cutting premiums rather than increasing benefits, then the increase in reserves would amount to only $6.6 billion.

Regarding automobile insurance, the GAO said industry arguments that unisex insurance would cost women $700 million more a year in premiums were as exaggerated as consumer estimates that it would save $1 billion in women's premiums. The effect, it said, would probably be somewhere in the middle, which would mean little or no difference at all.

[9] Ibid.

The GAO report said that substitution of mileage ratings for sex-based ones, suggested by the National Insurance Consumer Organization, would be difficult to verify and could deter some firms from using it. Andre Maisonpierre of the Alliance of American Insurers called a mileage rating unrealistic and said that drivers would lie about how much they drove in order to get lower rates.

With regard to health and disability insurance, the Health Insurance Association of America quoted the GAO's conclusion that mandatory maternity coverage provisions "would cause health and disability insurance to rise, imposing a net cost on those who do not bear children, to the benefit of those who do." The report also estimated that the actual rise would be about one-third of that projected by the insurance industry.

The Women's Equity Action League agreed to exempt paid-up contracts and said it would consider exempting life insurance policies on which payments are still due, but not existing pension contracts. The GAO suggested exempting both. The industry consensus was that the elimination of existing contracts as a condition of supporting unisex standards in the future was unacceptable. It was reported that Senator Packwood was prepared to consider the exemption of existing contracts.

The unisex issue has produced criticism of the insurance industry's lobbying activities. A group called the Committee for Fair Insurance Rates, made up of more than a dozen property and casualty insurance companies, has spent approximately $1 million thus far on a campaign to defeat unisex insurance legislation. In this effort it has enlisted the assistance of the public relations firm headed by former White House aide Peter D. Hannaford.

Describing this massive lobbying effort, *Congressional Quarterly* reported: "In addition to sending 500,000 letters to voters in selected congressional districts, the Committee for Fair Insurance Rates also sponsored radio and newspaper ads in May [1983] that appeared in the states and districts of 16 senators and 15 representatives. The targeted senators included every member of the Commerce Committee, which has jurisdiction except for its chairman, Bob Packwood (R-Ore.), the sponsor and chief advocate of the unisex bill. In the House, the insurance group singled out 15 of the 42 members of the Energy and Commerce Committee. Insurance industry critics say that the intense lobbying effort by the industry demonstrates its opposition to sexual equality. Molly Yard, a lobbyist for the National Organization of Women (NOW), states: 'Our belief is that the insurance industry is determined to keep sex discrimination legal. They will fight this to the end. But how long can they afford to antagonize the public?' " [10]

Congressional Quarterly noted: "So far, NOW and other supporters have not been able to match the insurance industry's massive public relations campaign. But with some members of Congress fuming over the industry's tactics, insurance companies could pay a heavy price, even if they succeed in blocking passage of the unisex bills. One immediate concern is how Congress might resolve the issue of how best to tax insurance companies. Although the companies have enjoyed generous tax breaks in the past, Congress could crack down harder on them this year, perhaps partly in retaliation for the aggressive lobbying against the unisex bills. Congress 'will rise up in wrath against these kinds of tactics,' warned Packwood after the industry began firing its salvos in May." [11]

Some insurance officials, while vigorously opposing unisex legislation, are concerned about the industry's lobbying campaign. Leslie Cheek III, vice-president of legislative affairs for Crum and Forester Corporation, a leading property and casualty insurance company, said, "Many insurers believe that a substantial amount of ill will is being created by lobbying on both sides of this issue, but that the issue is worth the tough fight." [12]

The House Energy and Commerce Committee has already sent a clear reminder to the insurance industry that it has no intention of staying out of the industry's affairs. In a resolution approved May 12, 1983, the committee asked the Federal Trade Commission to look into a variety of insurance practices with an eye toward determining whether consumers know enough about insurance before they purchase it. It is believed that Chairman John Dingell (D-Michigan) and Congressman Florio might have pushed for the FTC probe even if insurance companies had not embarked upon their lobbying drive. But congressional anger over the industry campaign prodded the committee's action, according to committee sources.

The chief sponsors of the unisex legislation have pledged to continue their effort to achieve passage of the bill. Congressmen Dingell and Florio, and Congresswoman Barbara Mukulski (D-Maryland), in a letter to the Energy and Commerce committee members in May, 1983, declared, "While we are prepared to negotiate in good faith and address legitimate concerns,

[10] *Congressional Quarterly*, July 9, 1983, p. 1401.
[11] Ibid., p. 1402.

we remain committed to [enactment] and will resist tactics of delay, obfusca-tion and distortion designed to paralyze the legislative process."

Mukulski said she was disturbed that groups supporting the unisex legislation were not being heard "because they don't have the multi-million dollar war chest that the industry has."

Nonetheless, the vigorous campaign launched by the insurance indus-try did seem to reduce the likelihood of quick passage of the unisex bills. Originally, the Senate committee had hoped to approve Senator Packwood's bill in June, 1983. Then it decided to wait for the results of the GAO study. The House committee also delayed its consideration of the unisex legisla-tion. Congressman Norman Lent (R-New York) stated: "If the insurance industry had not gone to work and begun the job of educating members of the committee as to what the ramifications of this bill were, it is very likely that it would have passed under the guise of civil rights legislation, gone off to the floor and breezed through." [13] Instead, on March 28, 1984, the House Energy and Commerce Committee adopted substitute legislation which had the effect of killing the pending unisex bill.

Opposition to the unisex legislation has also come from the National Association of Insurance Commissioners (NAIC), an organization of state insurance regulators who are concerned that the bills would reduce the au-thority of the states to regulate insurance companies. Five states now ban gender-based auto insurance rates, and some insurance officials think that more will follow. Supporters of the bill argue that the industry would rather leave the issue up to the states since it often has more influence in state capitals than in Washington.

The Washington office of the American Civil Liberties Union has pre-sented the following assessment of the status of unisex insurance legisla-tion: "The insurance industry continues to spend enormous amounts of money it receives from insurance premiums to lobby against the Non-discrimination in Insurance Act. Efforts will be made to protest the use of funds at rate increase hearings. Action will be taken on a state by state basis." [14]

---

[12] Ibid.
[13] Ibid.
[14] *ACLU Civil Liberties Alert*, January, 1984.

The Economic Position of the Insurance Industry

The insurance industry is in a period of serious financial difficulty. As of December, 1982, the industry had lost money on its underwriting every year since 1978. In 1983, its decline continued, with damage claims soaring as a result of Hurricane Alicia in August and the even more costly damage caused by a severe December freeze. Analysts expected combined damages for both to exceed $2 billion, while they estimated overall underwriting losses for the year at $12.2 billion. Maurice R. Greenberg, president and chief executive officer of the American International Group, a major commercial insurer, called it the worst underwriting year on record.

Writing in the *New York Times*, Yla Eason pointed out: "What has rescued the industry from its underwriting losses in the past has been income from investments. But that saving factor can no longer be relied upon. The industry's perennial price-slashing carnival has gone too far, analysts say, while growth of investment income has slowed. . . . Price-slashing, with the aim of obtaining more money to invest—a process called cash-flow underwriting—is the main cause of the industry's troubles according to Allerton Cushman, Jr., a Morgan Stanley officer and a senior insurance analyst. Under this process, higher interest rates allowed the companies to have a much higher investment income and caused them to rely more on this income than on earning from underwriting." Eason quoted Cushman as saying, "They remove policies at lower rates intending to make it up on the investment-income side. As Pogo said, 'We have met the enemy and he is us.' There has been a tendency to accept rising underwriting losses as a way of life. Almost all companies the last three years have indulged in a competitive posture that has contributed to the downturn of the industry." Sanford I. Weill, chairman and chief executive officer of American Express Insurance Services, Inc., stated, "Prices have gone too low relative to investment results, and loss expenses have grown faster than growth in investment income." [15]

Earnings reports for the fourth quarter of 1983 showed that six out of nine insurers posted lower results than a year earlier, and two of them reported losses. Three were more profitable than in 1982, but their commercial casualty underwriting activities were not. John C. Burridge, vice-

[15] Yla Eason, "Insurers' Mounting Troubles," *New York Times*, February 14, 1984, p. D-1.

president of the A. M. Best Company, which follows the insurance industry, stated, "You can have underwriting losses and still have a profit because of investment income." According to Best, underwriting losses rose by 17.5 percent in 1983, while premium income rose by only 4.6 percent. Property and casualty companies wrote premiums totaling $108.4 billion in 1983. Michael Frinquelli, managing director and insurance industry analyst at Salomon Brothers, reported that since 1981 the insurers' losses had been getting progressively worse: "The industry is now losing 12 cents for every dollar on every premium written on average. The fact that there is a loss is not as significant as the magnitude of the loss." [16]

Beyond this, analysts reported that the industry had approximately 10 percent less than it needed in its reserves account to cover losses. By law, companies are supposed to maintain adequate reserves, and when they are deficient, the insurers are forced to take the money from surplus or net worth. The two companies that reported fourth-quarter 1983 losses due to insurance problems were the American Express Company, whose loss was attributable to an addition of $250 million to the reserve account of its subsidiary, the Fireman's Fund, and the Mission Insurance Company of Los Angeles. Mission added $23 million to its loss reserve account to cover losses for closing out its reinsurance line. American Express reported a 1983 fourth-quarter loss of $22 million, compared with a profit of $156 million in the fourth quarter of 1982. Mission Insurance lost $32 million in the 1983 fourth quarter contrasted with a $12 million profit in the same period in 1982.

The *New York Times* stated: "The measure of the health of the insurance industry is the combined ratio that relates losses and underwriting expenses to premium income. It has been slipping steadily since 1978. At 100, it means the industry is breaking even; below that, it signals a profit. Last year [1983] that ratio rose to 112, implying a 12 per cent loss on underwriting. Meanwhile, investment income was about 15 per cent of sales last year, compared with 14.6 per cent in 1982. . . . Analysts say the practice of price slashing must halt before there can be any improvement." [17]

Richard J. Haayen, president of the Allstate Insurance Company, noted: "There is one factor that is starting to appear. The companies which are selling commercial insurance lay off some of their risk to reinsurance

---

[16] Ibid.
[17] Ibid.

companies—which take part of the risk from the primary insurer—and the reinsurance price is going up. That will force companies to raise prices to pay for the cost of reinsurance." [18]

A task force report to the National Association of Insurance Commissioners argued that investment income should be considered along with premium income when insurance rates are approved. The task force also asked the commissioners to eliminate the 5 percent profit built into the premiums, an industry margin set in 1921. In 1983, underwriting losses grew by 17.5 percent to a record $11.4 billion. At the same time, investment income rose an estimated 7.4 percent to a record $16 billion. But the sum of both, or net pre-tax income, shrank to $4.6 billion from $5.2 billion in 1982, according to estimates by the Insurance Information Institute. This was the smallest net income since 1975.

Commenting on a draft of the NAIC report, the American Insurance Association stated: "The draft doesn't acknowledge that the best way to regulate rates in most jurisdictions for most lines is by means of competitive rating. It doesn't acknowledge that various regulatory methods of considering investment income in the rating process today are working."

Currently twenty-three states allow the market to determine rates for personal automobile policies, for example. Of the twenty-seven states that require insurance commissions to give prior approval to rates proposed by companies, nineteen take investment income into account to some degree. The NAIC force remained neutral on the question of whether rates should be regulated or competition should be allowed to prevail. But in those states where regulation was required, it advocated that commissioners "generally have the authority and, in many cases, the duty to consider investment income."

The *Washington Post* reported: "The importance of investment income is shown by the 1983 results of Aetna Life and Casualty and Cigna, the country's largest multiline companies. Aetna's operating income edged up 1.9 per cent to $325 million, but its net income, including realized capital gains, rose by 55.8 per cent to $349 million. During the fourth quarter, its operating earnings slipped by 54.2 per cent, but capital gains kept the net slide to 26.3 per cent. Cigna's 1983 operating income was off 18.3 per cent to $400 million, but its net was up 3.5 per cent to $535 million. Moreover, industry reserves are now about 10 per cent less than needed to cover

[18] Ibid.

claims. If interest rates decline, investment income—and hence net income—could be cut even further." [19]

The NAIC task force stated, "Investment income has grown dramatically as a percentage of the industry's net worth and, as a result, the margin of profit needed from underwriting has declined sharply. In fact, it has become negative." The task force noted that if insurers were actually to earn 5 percent of premium in addition to investment income, their total rate of return on equity after taxes would approximate 25 percent. The report suggested that, with investment income so high, the margin on underwriting actually should be cut by 4.6 percent to keep the return on equity from being "excessive."

Many observers believe that the system of state regulation of insurance has been less than effective. In July, 1983, the Insurance Commissioner of Arkansas seized the life insurance subsidiary of the Baldwin-United Corporation that was headquartered in that state and placed it in "rehabilitation." Benjamin Nelson, the executive director of NAIC, declared that "the Baldwin case proves that the system does indeed work." Others believe the system is seriously deficient. Robert Kennedy, a Kansas insurance regulator, stated, "The sad truth is that even with a company half as smart as Baldwin, moving only half as fast, it could still happen again to any of us."

For a lengthy front-page report in the *Wall Street Journal, Journal* reporter Damon Darlin wrote: "A close look at the handling of Baldwin-United indicates that the critics are right, that state insurance officials are ill-equipped to regulate their increasingly complex segment of the financial-services industry. It also suggests that despite the trend toward deregulation of financial services, stronger regulation may be needed in a world where oil companies, brokerage houses, retailers and even piano makers such as Baldwin are selling insurance." [20]

The article cited the following situations that spell out states' difficulties in handling insurance company insolvencies:

Protracted reviews of investment portfolios. State insurance regulators must review a company's investment portfolio to determine the company's ability to pay its policyholders. However, such reviews are typically

[19] Nancy Ross, "Insurance Company Profits Questioned," *Washington Post*, February 19, 1984, p. G-12.

[20] Damon Darlin, "Baldwin Case Indicates Flaws in States' Ways of Regulating Insurers," *Wall Street Journal*, February 14, 1983, p. 1.

done only triennially, and unless there is reason to suspect inadequacies in the portfolio transactions, a review can take years to complete.

Steps to protect policyholders that inadvertently mislead. Only a month prior to the seizure in Indiana of Baldwin-United subsidiaries, a state insurance official assured policyholders that reserves were adequate and that there was no cause for alarm. The official later said that alarming policyholders by advising them to redeem policies would have accelerated the company's demise and benefited only those who cashed in their policies the quickest.

State emergency funds inadequate to cover policies. Funds set aside in twenty-nine states to guarantee benefits when an insurance company goes out of business may not be sufficient to cover policies, and it might take years to distribute what funds are available.

The Baldwin case is not unique. When Tara Life Insurance Company of Delaware went into rehabilitation in March, 1983, that state's fund could not raise even half the money necessary to reimburse policyholders. William Pugh, Delaware's special deputy commissioner, was quoted as saying, "It's a fraud to have a law that tells the public they have protection when the state doesn't have the funds to make up for reasonable losses." [21]

The *Wall Street Journal* stated: "If more companies do fail, more policyholders may lose money. Unlike banking regulation, which generally catches failures before they happen, insurance regulators try to pick up the pieces afterward. 'Our system of enforcement will always be after the fact,' says Lou Zellner, deputy insurance commissioner of Wisconsin. That is what happened with Baldwin-United, even though regulators tried hard to prevent it. . . . Some state regulators are pessimistic. 'I really don't think that even the Baldwin collapse woke up the commissioners in at least 40 states,' says Thomas Farrell, an Illinois insurance regulator. 'They have a tendency to ride along with the crises. But we are rapidly approaching the point when it will be impossible for us to audit insurance companies.' " [22]

Insurance in the Eighties

Discussing the status of the insurance industry as the 1980s began, Joe Lancaster, executive vice-president of the Tennessee Farmers Mutual

[21] Ibid.
[22] Ibid.

Insurance Company and chairman of the National Association of Independent Insurers, stated: "For the next several years, property-casualty insurers are going to lose a lot of money. . . . The cause of the companies' trouble, of course, is inflation. Its effects can be seen not only in the higher cost of loss settlement, but also in the misleading increases in investment and surplus . . . a statistic that doesn't show up in operating results, but is critically important for companies is loss reserves. This is where inflation hurt us most. . . . The nineteen eighties will not exactly be a picnic for property-casualty insurers. Inflation will continue, not at its current rate, but even if it is cut in half, insurance companies will still have a hard row to hoe. . . . It doesn't take much imagination to foresee that if surplus and reserves are dangerously threatened, underwriting departments throughout the industry will tighten up. The resulting shortage of available and affordable coverage will give new ammunition to consumer activists and bring the government barking at our doors again. There will be another wave of attacks on underwriting criteria and cost-based pricing. And as the 80s progress, we and our customers will be putting heavier emphasis on the role of risk managers and loss control departments." [23]

Demographic changes in the 1980s will have an impact upon the insurance industry. Lancaster declared that "companies will have to . . . change their underwriting philosophy to accommodate the society of the late 80s. The futurists tell us that in the next five years, there will be a 33 per cent increase in the number of people in the 25 to 44 age bracket, and a large increase in the number over 65. There will be more affluent people, more single-issue political pressure groups and more unmarried couples living together." [24]

Lancaster did point to a few possible bright spots in the insurance industry's future. "Asian markets should open up and the new risk exchanges should recapture a good part of the business that has been going overseas to Lloyds. In addition, the long-awaited automation of the industry should begin in earnest during the 80s and generate savings on the expense side of the ledger, but we run the risk of de-personalization of the business more than ever, and that runs counter to a prevailing trend of protecting and fostering the rights and concerns of individuals." [25]

[23] Joe Lancaster, speech to Tennessee chapter CPCU Society, April 17, 1980.
[24] Ibid.
[25] Ibid.

It is no secret that changes in the insurance industry are occurring, and occurring rapidly. A *U.S. News and World Report* article asserted that with "[insurance] markets eroded by high interest rates and financial conglomerates, insurers are making major changes in the services they sell and the way they invest their customers' funds." The article cited prominent examples of insurance company diversifications in the early 1980s: (1) Prudential Insurance's acquisition of the Bache securities firm, (2) Aetna Life and Casualty's involvement in oil exploration and satellite communications, (3) Cigna's introduction of cash-management money-market accounts to its traditional insurance offerings.[26]

A major reason for such diversification, observers point out, is the shrinking popularity of whole-life policies, whose yields cannot compete with larger returns offered by money-market mutual funds or a number of other new forms of investment. This has led insurance companies to offer a variety of new policies. In a *New York Times* article Leonard Sloane wrote: "A new kind of life insurance is on the horizon with the tongue-twisting name of flexible premium variable life insurance. And if this contract is allowed to join the multitude of other products in the highly competitive insurance marketplace, buyers will find that it has some of the characteristics of two other currently popular types of life insurance. This new hybrid combines the features of universal life insurance and variable life insurance. It comes at a time when purchasers of insurance policies have become increasingly concerned with the investment yields obtainable from various financial products."[27]

Sloane pointed out: "With such a policy, an owner could obtain more coverage or less coverage within the same policy at different times in his or her life, thereby lowering the insurer's administrative burdens and potentially reducing the buyer's sales expenses. In addition, the policyholder's cash value may change periodically, in keeping with the investment experience of the funds in the account managed by the insurance company."[28]

The proposed insurance is viewed as a security and therefore cannot be sold until it is cleared by the Securities and Exchange Commission. In addition, each state must approve its distribution. Thus far, only Delaware

---

[26] *U.S. News and World Report*, April 11, 1984.
[27] Leonard Sloane, "Hybrid Life Insurance Plan," *New York Times*, January 28, 1984, p. 30.
[28] Ibid.

has adopted final regulations, but more than two dozen companies prepared themselves to start selling such policies as soon as laws permitted them to. The *Times* article quoted Carl Wilkerson, assistant general counsel of the American Council of Life Insurance, as saying that "momentum seems to be growing. This is a form of life insurance that is responsive to developments in the economy and also very compatible with policyholder needs to increase or decrease insurance coverage." [29]

The National Association of Insurance Commissioners revised its variable life insurance model regulation in December, 1983, to accommodate the flexible premium classification. Richard Barnes, the Colorado insurance commissioner and past chairman of the association's task force on universal life and other new plans, stated, "The NAIC takes the position that it will meet the needs of some people, but it is not a cure-all for all people. Any new product should be properly explained and qualified before it is utilized."

Of growing concern to many in the insurance industry is the tendency of government to use insurance as a "back-door" to social reform. Dwight C. Perkins, former president of the Farmers Mutual Insurance Company of Nebraska and chairman of the National Association of Independent Insurers, described this tendency:

Back-door social reform bothers me because it is a hidden form of taxation without representation. It is a subtle way to redistribute large parts of the national income without having to take such politically unpopular steps as raising general taxes or increasing public spending. As a matter of fact, income redistribution through insurance can be accomplished without many people ever becoming aware of what is going on. In this way, vast sums of private capital can be brought to bear on social ills which the government finds itself unable to remedy. . . .

Under considerable government pressure, the industry created the FAIR Plans following the fiery summer of 1968. Now it would be unfair to blame the government to come up with an instant solution to the deep and persistent problems causing the deterioration of our inner cities. But consider the solution they did come up with. The explosion of the inner city cannot be stopped, but the government insists that insurance be provided to cushion the economic shock waves.

As a corollary to this attitude, FAIR Plan rates are not sufficient to cover the losses and expenses properly chargeable to risks in the Plan. Therefore, the deficiency is made up by charging people not in the Plans higher rates than they would otherwise pay. In other words, the income generated from non-Plan risks is being redistributed in the form of a subsidy for Plan risks . . . the same income redistri-

[29] Ibid.

bution and subsidy are present in the Automobile Insurance Plans. Subsidy of the poor risk by the good risk will also likely characterize the new so-called "facilities" that have been set up in a few states. . . .

The flood and crime insurance programs offer other examples of making insurance the back door to social reform. In each instance, insurance is provided at "affordable" rates that are well below actuarially sound rates. The difference is made up from federal revenues, collected from all those who don't live on the flood plain or in high-crime areas. And once again, no unpopular tax or unpalatable spending program was involved. Just an insurance subsidy.

At present, such "back-doors" to social policy through insurance can be seen in the campaign for no-fault automobile insurance and for unisex insurance legislation. Perkins declared: "As I understand it, insurance is intended to redistribute income by spreading the losses of a few among the many. Insurance buyers are divided in relatively homogeneous classes and each class is charged for its expected losses and expenses. Thus, while those without losses are subsidizing those with losses, the resulting redistribution is largely fortuitous. No one knows ahead of time who, within a class, will be subsidizing whom. The government programs are of a quite different character. They are not based on fortuitous misfortune at all. Instead, they are designed to soften the blow of non-fortuitous misfortune. They seek to ameliorate social conditions beyond the control of the government by pumping in funds that are unlikely to trigger political repercussions. To achieve these goals without stirring up popular discontent, the cost of redistribution must be, to the individual consumer, subtle and slight. Thus, we have the gentle subsidies of the Automobile Insurance Plans, the flood and crime programs and the FAIR Plans. . . . Among the casualties of such an approach would be rating based on exposure, specialty markets, smaller insurers, and the common-sense moral principle that the good risk should pay less for his insurance than the poor risk."

The single-parent household, the two-income family, and the cohabiting couple are some of the ubiquitous signs that U.S. demographics resemble less and less those of the first three-quarters of the century. These demographic changes have their own economic consequences, and as the economy and the century mature, the "traditional" approaches to insurance bear less and less relevance to the increasingly diverse needs of the populace. To achieve fairness in meeting those needs and to keep the insurance industry economically viable, some sides call for deregulation and competitive innovation; others favor government involvement. But unforeseen problems are an inherent danger in any innovation, whether it is a new drug, a new machine, or a new financial tool; thus, increased competitive innovation, and likewise, the government controls to regulate it, suggest that controversy over insurance will be with us as we approach 2000.

Although no statistical crystal ball can be depended on to show us where such trends as diversification or government regulation will lead, it is crystal clear that the insurance industry's tranquil mid-century existence is indeed a thing of the past.

Life Insurance Tax Provisions

The life insurance industry has been taxed under a complex three-phase system since 1959. This system was designed when interest rates were low and relatively stable. As interest rates increased over the years and new life insurance products evolved, the three-phase tax system proved to be inadequate for both the industry and the government.

Stopgap provisions were enacted in 1982 to provide a temporary solution to the shortcomings of the 1959 Act. The 1984 Act contains the permanent provisions affecting life insurance companies as well as their products and policyholders. The new rules are intended to simplify the overall structure governing the taxation of life insurance companies and to update the rules for taxing life insurance products to reflect the modern marketplace.

Tax Treatment of Life Insurance Companies

The entire set of rules governing the taxation of life insurance companies is virtually rewritten to elimi-

nate certain perceived inadequacies and problems identified under the old system, such as:

□ An inappropriate measure of life insurance company income in an environment of increasing interest rates.

□ Certain deductions and deferral items that do not reflect a proper measure of life insurance company income and that provide extraordinary benefits for some companies and no benefits for others.

□ An overstatement of deductions resulting from the computation of liabilities (reserves) using assumptions under state law when compared to the same liabilities measured under more realistic current economic assumptions.

□ A significant shifting of the industry's overall tax liability toward the mutual company segment of the industry.

Specific provisions of the new law address these and other inadequacies.

Definition of a Life Insurance Company—The prior-law test for determining whether an insurance company is a life insurance company is retained. However, the new law adds a statutory definition of an insurance company that basically requires that more than half of the company's business activity during the taxable year is the issuing of insurance or annuity contracts or the reinsuring of risk underwritten by insurance companies. This new determination of a company's primary and predominant business activity is a subjective, facts-and-circumstances determination that may present practical difficulties for some taxpayers.

A special election allows certain accident and health insurance companies to be taxed as casualty insurors rather than as life insurance companies. The election is permanent and must be made on the return filed for the first taxable year beginnning after 1983.

Single-Phase Tax Structure—
The previous three-phase system is replaced by a single-phase tax structure. It generally applies the tax rules applicable to regular corporations and includes certain special rules that address issues unique to the life insurance industry. As under prior law, net capital gain that is taxable to the company may be subject to an alternative tax.

Small Life Insurance Company Deduction—
The new law provides for a "small life insurance company" deduction. The deduction is equal to 60% of the first $3 million of "Tentative Life Insurance Company Taxable Income" (LICTI) and decreases to zero when Tentative LICTI equals or exceeds $15 million. The determination of Tentative LICTI is limited to insurance operations and investment activities traditionally carried on by a life insurance company but excludes noninsurance business. Thus, for companies with diversified investment operations, the determina-

tion of Tentative LICTI will require careful analysis. The deduction is computed on a controlled-group basis.

This deduction is only available to life insurance companies with gross assets of less than $500 million. Eligibility is determined on the basis of a controlled group. First-year transition rules are provided for 1984.

Special Life Insurance Company Deduction—
The special deductions under prior law for nonparticipating contracts and accident and health and group life insurance are eliminated. The new law allows a special life insurance company deduction equal to 20% of the excess Tentative LICTI over the new small life insurance company deduction, if any. This deduction has the effect of reducing a life insurance company's tax rate from 46% to 36.8% (or less if the company qualifies as a small life insurance company).

As with the small life insurance company deduction, the determination of Tentative LICTI for purposes of this deduction is limited to insurance operations and investment activities traditionally carried on by a life insurance company but excludes noninsurance business. The deduction is calculated on a controlled-group basis.

Reinsurance—
The Act specifically expands Treasury's authority to reallocate and/or recharacterize income, deductions, assets, reserves, credits and any other item included in a related-party reinsurance agreement in order to reflect the proper source and character of the items for each taxpayer. The Act also grants Treasury the authority to recast reinsurance transactions entered into by unrelated parties if such transactions have a significant tax avoidance effect with respect to any party to the contract. The determination of whether a reinsurance transaction has a significant tax-avoidance

purpose is very subjective. Accordingly, all new reinsurance transactions will require careful evaluation.

The provision for related party reinsurance is effective with respect to risks reinsured on or after September 27, 1983. The provision for unrelated party reinsurance is effective with respect to risks reinsured after December 31, 1984. It is clear that these provisions apply to casualty insurance companies as well as life insurance companies.

Computation of Reserves— The Act generally requires that a company's insurance reserves be revalued using rules prescribed in the new law as of the beginning of the first taxable year after December 31, 1983. In most cases, a company's revalued reserves will be significantly lower than its prior-law tax reserves. Companies can exclude from their taxable income any decrease in reserves resulting from the revaluation under a fresh-start rule. The fresh-start rule does not apply to reinsurance agreements entered into or modified after September 27, 1983, and before January 1, 1984. Under a special exception, intended to benefit small companies, an insurance company with less than $100 million in assets may elect not to recompute its life insurance reserves for existing business and may use instead statutory reserves for such business for tax purposes.

The recalculation of tax reserves on this new basis will put a severe strain on the financial and actuarial departments of most life insurance companies. It will require timely administrative guidance from the IRS to answer many specific unanswered questions. The determination of the fresh-start amount and its turnaround in 1984 will require prompt action by most companies since it may impact their 1984 estimated tax payments as well as their financial statements.

Policyholder Dividends—The new law expands the definition of policyholder dividends to include excess interest, premium adjustments and experience-rated refunds. Generally, companies are permitted to deduct policyholder dividends without limitation. However, in the case of a mutual life insurance company, the deduction for policyholder dividends is reduced by a "differential earnings amount." This amount effectively represents that portion of the mutual company's earnings that has been returned to the policyholders in their capacity as owners of the company.

Balance in Policyholders Surplus Account—The balance in the Policyholders Surplus Account (PSA) at December 31, 1983, has been "frozen." No additions are allowed to the account after that date. However, amounts accumulated in the account can be triggered into taxable income under prior law rules. The shareholders' surplus account will continue to be maintained under the new law.

Company's Share-Policyholders' Share—The new law retains the concept of prorating tax-exempt income and the dividends-received deduction between the company and its policyholders based on their respective shares of investment income. However, the method of determining the policyholders' share of net investment income has been changed to include all amounts paid or credited to policyholders plus a portion of policyholder dividends. For purposes of this proration, the new law defines net investment income as 90% of a company's gross investment income. This provision was put into the law to simplify the proration computation and to eliminate the necessity of having to identify and allocate expenses between investment and underwriting activities.

Waiver of Estimated Tax Penalty

—The new law waives any penalty for underpayment of 1984 estimated taxes by an insurance company to the extent that the underpayment resulted from the retroactive application of the new law provisions.

Effective Dates—In general, the provisions of the new law affecting life insurance companies are effective for taxable years beginning after December 31, 1983. However, the law contains certain transition rules and special provisions that apply in specific situations.

Taxation of Life Insurance Products

During the mid-1970s, the design of life insurance products, which had been relatively stable for several decades, began to change. Over a period of several years, numerous new products entered the marketplace. Many of the new products functioned more like short-term investment contracts than vehicles for protection against premature death or accumulation of long-term retirement funds. As a result, these products raised significant questions about the propriety of certain tax benefits that had been provided for traditional life insurance products.

In response to the issues raised by these new products, TEFRA enacted the following tax provisions in 1982:

☐ A definition of life insurance was provided for flexible-premium (universal-life) products.

☐ The taxation of annuity contracts was modified to reduce their use as short-term investment vehicles.

☐ The group-term life insurance rules were modified to reduce the tax benefits of plans that discriminated in favor of key executives.

To a large extent, the new law simply expands and "fine tunes" the provisions enacted in TEFRA.

Definition of Life Insurance

—The new law increases the requirements that must be met if a contract is to qualify as life insurance for income tax purposes. In addition, these requirements are expanded to cover all types of life insurance contracts.

Generally, traditional types of life insurance are unaffected by the new provisions. However, some increasing whole-life and universal-life policies will require modification to meet the new requirements. Those contracts that do not meet the new guidelines will be treated as a combination of term life insurance plus a currently taxable fund. All income under the contract (as defined) that was earned in prior years is taxable to the policyholder in the year the contract fails to qualify as life insurance under the rules.

The new definition of life insurance generally applies to contracts issued after December 31, 1984. However, there are a number of exceptions for certain types of contracts.

Group-Term Insurance

—The new law strengthens the nondiscrimination rules that existed under prior law. Under TEFRA, where a group-term life insurance plan was considered discriminatory, the $50,000 exclusion was lost for all key employees. The new law continues this treatment and also eliminates the use of the favorable "Table I rates" for all key employees covered by a discriminatory plan.

The TEFRA nondiscrimination rules are extended to retired employees under the new law. For purposes of determining whether a plan is discriminatory, insurance coverage for retired employees is tested separately from insurance for active employees.

Under prior law, post-retirement group-term life insurance coverage in any amount was excluded from income of the retired employee. Now, the exclusion for post-retirement coverage is limited to $50,000. Amounts in excess of $50,000 are taxed to the retiree under the favorable "Table I rates" unless the plan is discriminatory.

In general, the new provisions apply to taxable years beginning after December 31, 1983. However, the new rules do not apply to certain individuals covered by group-term life insur-

ance plans that were in existence on January 1, 1984.

Taxation of Annuities—

TEFRA created a 5% penalty on premature distributions from deferred annuities. However, the penalty did not apply where the distribution related to investments made more than 10 years before the distribution. The new law removes this 10-year exception. In addition, the new law modifies the rules regarding required distributions upon the contract holder's death to generally conform with the individual retirement account and qualified pension plan distribution rules. This provision applies to annuity contracts issued six months or more after the date of enactment.

Index

accidental death benefits, 195–96
advertising, 131–33, 146, 147, 148, 149, 150
Aetna Insurance Company, 103, 145, 224, 228
affirmative action, 95–96, 98
Alliance of American Insurers, 101, 211, 219
All Industry legislation, 41–42, 155, 171
All Industry Research Advisory Council (AIRAC), 90
Allstate Insurance Company, 192, 210, 223
Allstate v. Lanier, 42
American Academy of Actuaries, 88
American Association of University Women, 94
American Civil Liberties Union (ACLU), 221
American Column Company v. United States, 165
American Council on Life Insurance (ACLI), 71, 78, 103, 104, 105, 180, 184–85, 189, 190, 211, 212, 217, 229
American Enterprise Institute, 85
American Express Company, 222, 223
American Insurance Association (AIA), 88–89, 90, 91, 116, 162, 211, 217, 224
American International Group, 222
American Medical Association (AMA), 14
American Mutual Insurance Alliance, 117
American Political Science Association, 84
American Society of Plastic and Reconstructive Surgeons, 14
American Telephone and Telegraph Company, 23, 30
American Trial Lawyers Association, 118, 126–27
American University, 218
Anglin v. Blue Shield of Virginia, 199
antitrust, 3, 166, 198–99; Clayton Act,

198; and economy, 176; enforcement, 64; exemption, 46, 50, 54, 55, 57, 175, 177, 199, 209, 216; interstate commerce, 25, 32; legislation, 36–37, 39, 40, 41, 44, 47, 52, 56, 155, 169, 212, 213; seminar on, 162; Sherman Act, 165, 166, 167, 198. *See also* McCarran-Ferguson Act
ARCO, 23
Arizona Governing Committee for Tax Deferred Annuity and Deferred Compensation Plans v. Norris, 186–87, 188, 217–18
assigned-risk plan, 159–60
Association of American Trial Lawyers, 118
Attorney General v. Insurance Commissioner (Massachusetts), 177
Auchter, Thorne, 30
Audit Ratios for Property and Liability Companies, 53
Austero v. Washington National Insurance Company, 202
automobile accidents, 90–91, 124, 183, 193–94, 195, 196; compensation of victims, 117–18, 119, 124, 127; men versus women, 89–90, 93, 94–95; negligence, 114, 115; victims, 107–14, 118–22, 129, 130; young drivers, 88, 89
automobile insurance, 49, 69, 93, 138, 155, 162, 168, 169, 190, 194; fault, 38, 109, 110–11; liability, 28, 159; no-fault, 27, 28, 29, 38, 107–30, 230; rates, 26, 36, 50, 88–89, 90–91, 94, 100–104, 156–58, 160–61, 164, 167, 171, 224; unisex, 29, 218–19, 230
Automobile Insurance Plans, 160, 230
automobile safety standards, 192, 194, 195

Bailey, Patricia, 131
Bailey, Robert A., 176